CONTRIBUTIONS

to

THE ARCHAEOLOGY OF OREGON

1989-1994

edited by

PAUL W. BAXTER

Association of Oregon Archaeologists

Occasional Papers No. 5

1994

Published by Association of Oregon Archaeologists, Inc.
Printed by University Printing Office, University of Oregon

1994

Orders and queries should be addressed to:

Association of Oregon Archaeologists
c/o State Museum of Anthropology
1224 University of Oregon
Eugene, Oregon 97403-1224

ISBN 0-929553-04-7

Editor's Preface

The paper's published in this Fifth volume of the *Association of Oregon Archaeologists Occasional Papers* Series testify to the professional vitality of Archaeology in Oregon. Three were presented in somewhat different form at past *Northwest Anthropological Conferences* (Bergland et al.; Oetting; Endzweig), one appeared in a shorter form in *Current Archaeological Happenings in Oregon* (Skinner and Winkler), three were generated by reports (Connolly and Musil; Baxter and Smith; Zenk), and three were written specifically for this volume (Connolly; Minor; Skinner and Radosevich).

Comparing the papers in this volume with those published in past Occasional Papers shows the continued shift to more complex, technically more demanding and essentially more sophisticated approaches to archaeological questions of past human behavior, approaches representative of a context of much higher professional expectations. For example, the paper by Bergland, McAlister and Stevenson presents a tentative hydration rate for Obsidian Cliffs glass, developed using the induced hydration technique. They also point out a discrepancy in data collection between two hydration labs--a cautionary tale for those of us who routinely accept laboratory generated data. Following that theme, Skinner and Radosevich clear up a mystery surrounding a tephra which seemed to mimic Mazama Volcanic Ash. In the following paper by Skinner and Winkler, much of the Western Oregon obsidian characterization data is synthesized and discussed from a regional perspective. Again at a regional level, Endzweig's study synthesizes descriptive data from pithouses in the John Day and Deschutes River basins and discusses its implications for future behavioral interpretations. And Oetting, also worried about the implications for behavioral interpretation, rebuts the assertion that projectile point form is merely a function of refitting and resharpening rather than the result of a temporally significant style. Underlining that thought, the short paper by Connolly synthesizes our knowledge of Paleo-points in the Willamette Valley, and describes two recent finds. However, style gives way to technology when Connolly and Musil use debitage data from sites in Newberry Crater to decipher the complex human use of that obsidian resource. Sounding a somewhat worrisome note, Minor, being involved in the site evaluation process on a daily basis, explores the changing nature of site significance by revisiting a Columbia River site found not archaeologically significant in 1972. Zenk's paper sifts the very limited ethnographic data from the Tualatin Kalapuya to present a picture of village life, a listing of village names and their speculative locations. Baxter and Smith present the results of a testing project in the Luckiamute Valley, a sub-basin of the Willamette Valley, and consider the problem of determining site function.

These ten papers constitute the *Association of Oregon Archaeologists Occasional Papers No. 5*, the latest *Contributions to Oregon Archaeology* by the AOA in its continued efforts to disseminate the results of research in the state.

Paul W. Baxter
Volume Editor

Contributions to the Archaeology of Oregon, 1990-1994
Association of Oregon Archaeologists Occasional Papers No. 5

Table of Contents   Page

AN INDUCED HYDRATION RATE FOR OBSIDIAN CLIFFS GLASS

Eric O. Bergland
Willamette National Forest

Jeffrey C. McAlister
Willamette National Forest

Christopher Stevenson
ASC, Inc. Diffusion Laboratory

ABSTRACT

Confidently assigning occupation dates to prehistoric lithic sites in the Cascade Mountains of western Oregon has always been difficult primarily due to the poor preservation of datable organic cultural materials. This situation is compounded by the apparent longevity of projectile point styles and by the churning of cultural deposits in the forested environment. The authors present an induced hydration rate for Obsidian Cliffs glass (the dominant source of Western Cascades archaeological obsidian) and compare this experimental rate with hydration rim measurements and radiocarbon dates from several Oregon archaeological sites.

Assigning occupation dates to prehistoric lithic sites is often difficult. In the western Cascades this is largely due to the poor preservation of organic cultural materials suitable for radiocarbon dating. But the problem is compounded by the natural turbation of cultural deposits in a forested environment, which often mixes them with non-cultural forest fire charcoal. Further, the apparent longevity of projectile point styles (Baxter 1986; Minor 1981) provides little help in temporal assessments beyond general millennia-long Paleoindian, Early Archaic, Middle Archaic and Late Archaic periods. Thus, often little can confidently be said about the duration or timing of prehistoric occupation at Cascade archaeological sites.

However, at Cascades sites obsidian artifacts are often well preserved and comprise a dominant proportion of the excavated lithic samples. In the Upper McKenzie drainage, recovered assemblages are typically 95-100% obsidian, the vast majority of which is from the Obsidian Cliffs source. Cascades obsidian use follows a classic distance decay model, in which the proportion of obsidian from a particular source decreases with distance from that source (Lindberg-Muir 1988). Such intense and systematic use of specific obsidian sources suggests that much could be gained by site specific obsidian data. In fact, chemical sourcing and hydration band measurements have been increasingly common ancillary analyses in prehistoric site excavations on the Willamette National Forest, as they have been throughout the western United States, and the accumulating data is beginning to be used in wider applications (cf. Skinner and Winkler this volume). Such data will become invaluable for temporal sequencing of lithic sites when the rate of hydration for the various obsidian sources is known.

This paper presents the results of an induced hydration laboratory experiment, and discusses the application of this rate to the radiocarbon dated South Fork Rockshelter, a mid-elevation archaeological site on the Blue River Ranger District in the McKenzie River Drainage on the Willamette National Forest. Our purposes are to present a tentative hydration rate for dating Obsidian Cliffs obsidian assemblages and to discuss some of the problems affecting this rate.

DEVELOPING AN INDUCED HYDRATION RATE

Jon M. Silvermoon, former McKenzie Ranger District Archaeologist, recognized the dating potential of Obsidian cliffs glass (1989). He initiated a study by Christopher M. Stevenson at Diffusion Laboratory (1990) and provided geological samples from the several square mile Obsidian Cliffs source on the western flanks of the North Sister Volcano.

The hydration rate for the Obsidian Cliffs source was developed in the laboratory using a procedure in which a group of three freshly fractured flakes is subjected to 100% relative humidity at a high temperature. For this study, one of four sets of samples was hydrated at each of four temperatures, 150, 160, 170 and 180° C for up to 24 days (Stevenson et al. 1989). At the end of the reaction periods, thin sections were prepared and the hydration band measured (Stevenson et al. 1987). The induced band measurements (Table 1) were used to calculate a hydration rate at 160° C (Figure 1). Using this induced hydration rate, a specific rate can be appraised for obsidian from a site once the effective hydration temperature of the archaeological context has been estimated.

APPLYING THE INDUCED HYDRATION RATE

The South Fork Rockshelter (35LA907) lies at an elevation of 2040 feet near the South Fork of the McKenzie River. It was discovered, surface collected, and subsurface tested in 1990 by Forest Service personnel. The one-half cubic meter of excavated sediments yielded a dense assemblage of over two thousand artifacts, including obsidian,

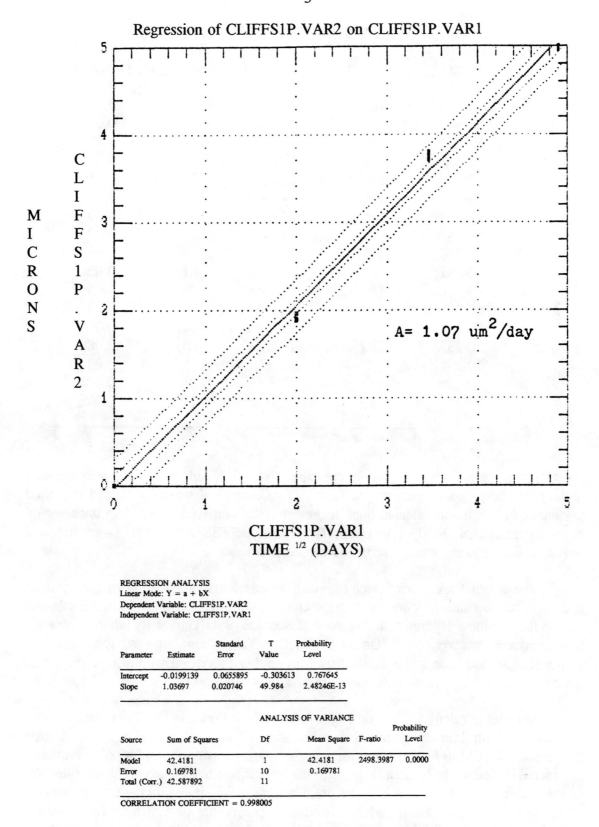

Regression of CLIFFS1P.VAR2 on CLIFFS1P.VAR1

A= 1.07 um²/day

CLIFFS1P.VAR1
TIME ¹ᐟ² (DAYS)

REGRESSION ANALYSIS
Linear Mode: Y = a + bX
Dependent Variable: CLIFFS1P.VAR2
Independent Variable: CLIFFS1P.VAR1

Parameter	Estimate	Standard Error	T Value	Probability Level
Intercept	-0.0199139	0.0655895	-0.303613	0.767645
Slope	1.03697	0.020746	49.984	2.48246E-13

ANALYSIS OF VARIANCE

Source	Sum of Squares	Df	Mean Square	F-ratio	Probability Level
Model	42.4181	1	42.4181	2498.3987	0.0000
Error	0.169781	10	0.169781		
Total (Corr.)	42.587892	11			

CORRELATION COEFFICIENT = 0.998005

Figure 1. Hydration Rate at 160° C for Obsidian Cliffs Obsidian

Table 1. Induced hydration rims for Obsidian Cliffs Glass*

Laboratory Number	Temperature	Duration	Rim Width (um)	Standard Deviation
90-34	160	4 days	1.90	0.05
90-35	160	4 days	1.93	0.05
90-36	160	4 days	1.96	0.08
89-634	160	12 days	3.74	0.07
89-635	160	12 days	3.72	0.07
89-636	160	12 days	3.79	0.05
89-645	160	24 days	5.00	0.08
89-644	160	24 days	4.98	0.09
89-642	160	24 days	4.97	0.07
90-240	150	12 days	2.88	0.09
90-241	150	12 days	2.81	0.05
90-242	150	12 days	2.79	0.05
90-237	170	12 days	4.98	0.07
90-238	170	12 days	4.84	0.05
90-239	170	12 days	4.85	0.08
90-234	180	12 days	6.37	0.08
90-235	180	12 days	6.24	0.09
90-236	180	12 days	6.29	0.09

cryptocrystalline silicate, and basalt debitage. At 18-25 cm below the surface, test probing also exposed a basin-shaped hearth in oxidized soil which contained a limited amount of charcoal and calcined bone fragments. This charcoal yielded an uncorrected radiocarbon age of 2650±170 years (Beta Analytic #38714). The large standard deviation is due to the small size of the charcoal sample.

The South Fork Rockshelter provided an ideal first application of the induced hydration rate because it contained a dense cultural deposit. Obsidian from the site was sent to the Obsidian Hydration Laboratory at Sonoma State University where hydration band measurements were made (Origer 1991). Several of those same artifacts were thin-sectioned a second time and examined by Christopher Stevenson who also re-measured the earlier Sonoma State thin sections.

In order to calculate hydration ages for the South Fork Rockshelter obsidian using the induced hydration rate, the relative humidity of the soil and effective hydration temperature needed to be estimated for the site. Soil temperature and relative humidity cells were buried at the bottom of cultural deposits in the test pit which had yielded the hearth carbon sample. A matching set of cells were staked in a wire cage to the surface at the same location. Each cell consisted of a polycarbonate test tube filled with a desiccant which was placed within a test tube filled with distilled water. The rate of water vapor diffusion through the inner test tube wall is dependent on the temperature of the cell or the relative humidity of the soil. The net increases in cell weights over a one year period (January 1991 to January 1992) were converted to an integrated temperature and a relative humidity, using constants derived from experimentally determined values.

The results indicate that for South Fork Rockshelter, the average annual surface temperature was 11.51° C, with 21% relative humidity. At 50 cm below the surface, the bottom of the cultural deposit, the effective hydration temperature was 10.67° C with a relative humidity of 91%. Applying those data to the induced rate (Figure 2) produces an absolute date using the formula:

$$\text{Years BP} = (((\text{measured microns}^2/1.56) \times 1000) + 42)$$

For example, a rim measurement of 2.8 microns equates to 5068 BP or 3075 BC:

$$(((2.8^2 \text{ microns}/1.56) \times 1000) + 42) = 5068 \text{ BP}$$

A one micron hydration band predicts an age of 683 years, a two micron band an age of 2606 years, a 3 micron band an age of 5811 years and so on. Stevenson observed that Obsidian Cliffs glass is relatively dry and hydrates slowly.

ASSESSING THE SOUTH FORK HYDRATION RATE

Sampling Problems:

At the South Fork Rockshelter, band width measurements generally increase with depth. However, this is neither uniform nor consistent. It is suspected that the use of arbitrary 10 cm excavation levels, tree root penetration, rodent burrowing and hearth excavation by prehistoric people have all contributed to mixing the cultural deposits. The different hydration band widths and proveniences for the South Fork Rockshelter samples as measured by Stevenson (Diffusion Lab) and Origer (Sonoma State) are shown in Tables 3 and 4.

Analytical Problems:

There is a disparity in band measurement between the two laboratories (Table 3 and 4). The Sonoma State measurements are thicker than the Diffusion Lab measurements and that difference increases with band width. However, the variations are consistent suggesting methodological differences may be producing this disparity. The two labs exchanged thin section slides in an effort to resolve the problem. Origer

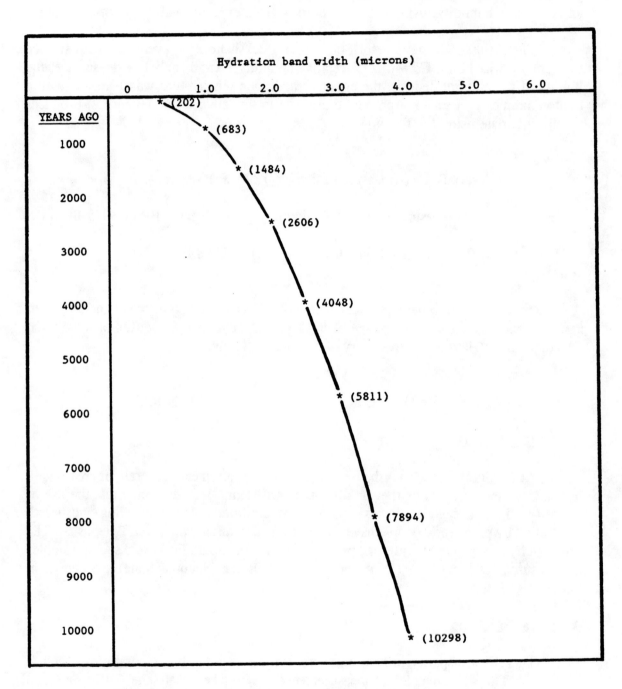

* - Based on rate of $((m^2/1.56 \times 1000 \text{ years}) + 42 \text{ years})$

Figure 2. Induced Hydration Rate Curve for Obsidian cliffs Obsidian at South Fork Rockshelter (35LA907)

Table 2. Obsidian Hydration Study for South Fork Rockshelter (35LA907)[1]

USFS Number	Origer Number	Stevenson Number	Unit/ Level	Origer		Stevenson	
				Rim 11/91	Width 2/92	Rim 1/92	Width 2/92
82C	10		4/3	4.2			2.84
82C		92-54	4/3		3.6/1.8	2.45/1.51	
82C		92-56	4/3		3.7	1.51	
118	2		4/2	2.0			1.64
118		92-55	4/2		1.8	1.53	
118		92-57	4/2		1.9	1.53	
70	24		2/2	3.4			2.59
71	25		2/2	2.8			2.55
78a	4		4/2	5.7/3.2			5.29/2.38
78b	5		4/2	3.6			2.72
78c	6		4/2	3.6			2.81
78d	7		4/2	3.5			2.81
96	22		5/2	3.3			2.56
104	23		5/2	3.7			2.87
75	20		2/3	2.9			2.41
74	21		2/3	3.7			3.40/2.86
82a	8		4/3	3.0			2.29
82b	9		4/3	1.7			1.61
82d	11		4/3	3.8			3.28/1.74
82e	12		4/3	3.6			2.86
111c	17		5/3	4.0[2]			5.00/2.83
111d	18		5/3	3.7			2.90
111e	19		5/3	3.6			2.84
87d	1		4/4	3.7			2.74
87c	3		4/4	4.5			4.06
114c	13		5/4	3.7			2.94
114d	14		5/4	3.7			3.39/2.86[2]
76a	15		2/4	3.2[2]			-[2]
76b	16		2/4	3.5			2.87

1 - Elevation 2040 ft.
2 - Flake Weathered

consistently measures somewhat thinner bands on slides produced by Stevenson than he does on slides produced by the Sonoma lab from the same artifact, while Stevenson consistently measures thicker bands from slides produced by Sonoma than he does from slides he produces from the same artifact. Stevenson noted that the Sonoma State slides

Table 3. South Fork Rockshelter Obsidian Band Clusters.

Laboratory	Cluster	Measurements (microns)	Number Artifacts	Dates BP
Sonoma State	1	1.7-2.0	5	1895-2606
(Origer)	2	2.8-3.0	3	5068-5811
	3	3.2-3.8	19	6606-9298
Diffusion	1	1.51-1.74	7	1504-1983
Laboratory	2	2.29-2.59	7	3404-4342
(Stevenson)	3	2.72-2.94	14	4785-5583
	4	3.28-3.40	3	6938-7452

were physically thicker than his slides, which may affect the light transmitting properties of the obsidian. It may be too, that some equipment differences are contributing to the discrepancies.

APPLICATION OF THE INDUCED RATE

Whatever the case, the two sets of measurements, when seriated, each produce clusters of band measurements (Table 4). A cluster is 'a continuous run of band measurements separated from other clusters by two-tenths of a micron or more. Assuming that all Obsidian Cliffs obsidian in the rockshelter is hydrating at the same rate, and assuming that clusters of rim measurements relate to general periods of rockshelter use, there were three to four periods of occupation. Applying the rate of 1.56 microns^2 /1000 years yields the following sequences, depending on which set of rim measurements one accepts.

Stevenson observed six double band artifacts, suggesting re-use of older materials by later occupants of the shelter. Half of those show bands from the immediately preceding cluster. The induced rate ages of hypothetical occupations seems more realistic in the Stevenson sequences, and yet, the radiocarbon age of the South Fork hearth (2650±170) fits most closely to the Origer's Cluster 1.

Comparisons With Other Sites:

Data for three other Cascades sites, Trio site (07-164) and Dale Beam site (35LA793) on the McKenzie Ranger District and the Posey Site (35CL022) on the Mt. Hood National Forest are contained in Table 5. The Trio and Posey Sites yielded cultural radiocarbon dates, while the Dale Beam Site yielded a non-cultural radiocarbon date. For

Table 4. Hydration Seriation, South Fork Rockshelter.

DIFFUSION LABORATORY

Unit/Level	Rim Widths	Cluster	Induced Rate Age for Cluster
4/3	1.51/2.45[1]	1	1505-1983 BP
4/3	1.51	1	
4/2	1.53	1	
4/2	1.53	1	
4/3	1.61	1	
4/2	1.64	1	
4/3	1.74/3.28	1	
4/3	2.29	2	3404-4342 BP
4/2	2.38/5.29	2	
2/3	2.41	2	
4/3	2.45[2]	2	
2/2	2.55	2	
5/2	2.56	2	
2/2	2.59	2	
4/2	2.72	3	4785-5583 BP
4/4	2.74	3	
4/2	2.81	3	
4/2	2.81	3	
5/3	2.83/5.00	3	
5/3	2.84	3	
4/3	2.84	3	
2/3	2.86/3.40	3	
4/3	2.86	3	
5/4	2.86/3.39	3	
5/2	2.87	3	
2/4	2.87	3	
5/3	2.90	3	
5/4	2.94	3	
4/3	3.28[2]	4	6938-7452 BP
5/4	3.39[2]	4	
2/3	3.40[2]	4	
4/4	4.06	Not Clustered	
5/3	5.00[1]	Not Clustered	
4/2	5.29[1]	Not Clustered	

SONOMA STATE

Unit/Level	Rim Widths	Cluster	Induced Rate Age for Cluster
4/3	1.7	1	1895-2602 BP
4/2	1.8	1	
4/3	1.8/3.6	1	
4/2	1.9	1	
4/2	2.0	1	
2/2	2.8	2	5068-5811 BP
2/3	2.9	2	
4/3	3.0	2	
2/4	3.2	3	6606-9298 BP
4/2	3.2/5.7	3	
5/2	3.3	3	
2/2	3.4	3	
2/4	3.5	3	
4/2	3.5	3	
4/2	3.6	3	
4/2	3.6	3	
4/3	3.6	3	
5/3	3.6	3	
4/3	3.6[2]	3	
5/2	3.7	3	
2/3	3.7	3	
5/3	3.7	3	
5/4	3.7	3	
4/4	3.7	3	
4/3	3.7	3	
4/3	3.8	3	
5/3	4.0	Not Clustered	
4/3	4.2	Not Clustered	
4/4	4.5	Not Clustered	
4/2	5.7[2]	Not Clustered	

1 - 1.51/2/45 = two bands measured on same artifact; 2 - Older of two hydration bands

both the Posey Site (Burchard 1991) and the Dale Beam Site (Spencer 1988) chronological correlations for hydration band measurements were proposed. Predicted hydration ages were compared with radiocarbon dates from the Posey, Trio and Dale Beam sites. All hydration measurements were by the Sonoma State lab.

Table 5. Obsidian Hydration studies of the Posey, Dale Beam and Trio sites.

Site Number Name	Elevation	Unit/Level	Rim Width	Radio Carbon Date
35CO22 Posey	4600 feet	1052N 1030E/5	1.1-1.2	1400±80
		1051N 1028E/5	1.1-1.2	1190±80
35LA793 Dale Beam	3260 feet	C/0	2.9	3130±90
		C/2	1.9	
		D/1	1.2	
		D/3	1.2	
		D/5	2.3	
		D/7	3.1	
		D/9	1.8	
07-164 Trio	3340 feet	180.5N 374.5W/1	4.2	
		180N 374.5W/1&2	1.2	
		180N 374.5W/1&2	2.4	
		180N 374W/3	3.5	
		180N 374W/3	1.2	
		180N 374W/3	1.2	
		180N 374W/3	1.2	
		180N 374W/3	1.2	
		180N 374W/3	1.3	1550±70
		180N 374W/3	1.3	
		180N 374W/3	1.3	
		180N 374W/3	1.4	
		180N 374.5W/4	1.2	
		180N 374.5W/4	1.5	
		180N 374.5W/4	1.7	
		180N 374.5W/4	2.2	
		180N 374W/4	1.3	
		180N 374W/4	1.8	
		180N 374W/4	2.3	

When evaluating the Dale Beam Site, it should be kept in mind that the measured obsidian sample is small, and the dated charcoal was interpreted as non-cultural. Even so, the radiocarbon date of 3130±90 falls within the range of predicted obsidian ages for that site (965-6202 years BP). Spencer advanced "a speculative correlation of the ca 3100 BP date with a rind thickness of 2.1±0.2 microns" and estimated a linear rate of "1500 years per 1.0 micron of hydration (1989:51)". As suggested by the induced rate curve, we would not expect obsidian to hydrate at a constant rate through time. However, the South Fork Rockshelter rate would predict an age of 2869 years for an average rim thickness of 2.1 microns. Considering the 1220 feet difference in elevation between the two sites, the calculated synchronic dates may be close.

The Trio Site shows a tight cluster of eight hydration bands (1.2-1.4 microns) from the level of the hearth, radiocarbon dated to 1550±70 years BP. However, the South Fork Rockshelter induced hydration rate predicts an age of 965-1298 years ago. The Trio site, at 3340 feet, is some 1300 feet higher in elevation than South Fork Rockshelter.

The Posey site yielded a range of band measurements between 1.2 and 1.4 microns in association with radiocarbon dates of 1190±80 and 1400±80 radiocarbon years. The South Fork Rockshelter hydration rate predicted age would be 965-1298 years ago. The Posey site lies at 4500 feet, some 2460 feet higher than South Fork Rockshelter. It is not surprising that the Trio Site and Posey Site predicted ages are younger than the radiocarbon dates since obsidian hydrates more slowly at higher elevations due to lower effective hydration temperatures.

Recently US Forest Service archaeologists excavated a cache of over thirty obsidian bifaces from a mid-elevation site on Sweet Home Ranger District of the Willamette National Forest. Ten of the bifaces were submitted for sourcing and hydration. All ten were made from Obsidian Cliffs obsidian and yielded hydration rim measurements ranging between 2.3 and 2.4 microns (with an error of ±1 micron). With the error factor added, the rims ranged from 2.2 to 2.5 microns. The proposed South Fork hydration rate suggests that the bifaces date to between 3145 and 4048 years ago. A charcoal sample collected from pit fill associated with the cache yielded an uncorrected date of 4075±55 years ago, reasonably close to the predicted age (Rogers 1993).

SUMMARY AND CONCLUSIONS

This paper presents an experimentally induced hydration rate for Obsidian Cliffs glass. The induced rate, combined with climatic data from the South Fork Rockshelter in western Oregon yields a quadratic rate of: Microns squared divided by 1.56 times one thousand years plus 42 years. This is a very slow rate of hydration. It is best applied to archaeological sites where the effective hydration temperature is similar to that recorded for the South Fork Rockshelter. Obsidian at sites with a lower effective hydration temperature will hydrate at a slower rate, while those with a higher temperature will hydrate at a higher rate. Two factors that effect hydration temperature include humidity and elevation.

The data presented here also demonstrates that two different labs can read differing hydration band thicknesses from the same artifact and even the same thin section slide. This situation may relate to the thickness of the thin section itself or to the equipment differences. Clearly this is a problem which requires resolution and both hydration labs involved in this study are presently addressing the issue. This apparent methodological problem may simply be a "growing pain" analogous to those experienced during the early years of radiocarbon dating.

In comparing the two sets of hydration band measurements from the South Fork Rockshelter, the identified clusters of hydration bands probably represent periods of occupation. When the induced quadratic rate is applied to the measurements, the radiocarbon date best relates to the most recent cluster of measurements.

There are a number of factors which can alter the effective hydration temperature, of course, including long and short term climatic changes, changes in depositional environment and possibly controlled or uncontrolled fires. Obsidian hydration rates hold the most promise for approximating the age of cultural deposits in the damp, forested Western Cascades.

Regardless of the applicability of the proposed hydration rate, or of the outcome of the methodological controversy, it will always be necessary to refine rates with more radiocarbon dates, to get good climatic data, to improve laboratory methods, and to conduct additional experiments. The proposed rate is a start.

A version of this paper was presented at the 45th annual Northwest Anthropological Conference held in Burnaby, British Columbia, Canada, 1992.

REFERENCES

Baxter, Paul W.
  1986   *Archaic Upland Adaptations in the Central Oregon Cascades.* Ph.D. dissertation, Department of Anthropology, University of Oregon, Eugene.

Burtchard, Greg C.
  1990   *The Posey Archaeological Project: Upland Use of the Central Cascades: Mt Hood National Forest.* Cultural Resource Investigation Series Number 3. Portland State University, Oregon.

Lindberg-Muir, Catherine
  1988   *Obsidian: Archaeological Implications for the Central Oregon Cascades.* Master's thesis, Department of Anthropology, Oregon State University.

Origer, Thomas
  1991   Letter report on South Fork Rockshelter Obsidian Hydration Measurements.
         Sonoma State University Obsidian Hydration Laboratory, Rohnert Park,
         California. On file Willamette National Forest, Eugene.

Rogers, Ann B.
  1993   Personal Communication between 1992-1993 with Eric Bergland concerning
         Sweet Home obsidian biface cache excavation, dating, sourcing and hydration
         rim measurements.

Sheetz, B. E. and C. M. Stevenson
  1988   The Role of Resolution in Hydration Rim Measurement: Implications for
         Experimentally Determined Hydration Rates. *American Antiquity* 53:110-117.

Silvermoon, Jon M.
  1989   Upper McKenzie River Drainage Prehistory: a view from the J&K Enterprises
         Site. Paper presented at the 42nd Annual Northwest Anthropological
         Conference, Spokane, Washington.

Skinner, Craig and Carol Winkler
  1991   Prehistoric Trans-Cascade Procurement of Obsidian in Western Oregon: The
         Geochemical Evidence. *Current Archaeological Happenings in Oregon*
         16:(2):3-8.

Spencer, Lee
  1989   *Archaeological Testing of the Dale Beam Site (35LA793) on the McKenzie
         Ranger District of the Willamette National Forest, Lane County, Oregon.* Lee
         Spencer Archaeology Paper No. 1989-3, Eugene, Oregon.

Stevenson, Christopher M.
  1990   *Hydration Rate Development for Obsidian Cliffs, Oregon.* Diffusion
         Laboratories, Spring Mills, Pennsylvania. Submitted to Willamette National
         Forest, Eugene, Oregon.

Stevenson, C. M., J. Carpenter and B. E. Sheetz
  1989   Obsidian Dating: Recent Advances in the Experimental Determination and
         Application of Hydration Rates. *Archaeometry* 31:193-206.

Stuiver, Minze and Paula J. Reimer
  1993   Extended 14C data base and revised Calib 3.0 14C age calibration program.
         Radiocarbon 35(1): 215-230.

THE GEOLOGIC SOURCE OF THE MAZAMA "MIMIC" MYSTERY TEPHRA: A GEOCHEMICAL REASSESSMENT OF VOLCANIC TEPHRA FROM VINE ROCKSHELTER (35LA304), CENTRAL WESTERN CASCADES, OREGON

Craig E. Skinner
INFOTEC Research, Inc.

Stefan C. Radosevich
University of Oregon

ABSTRACT

Previous neutron activation analyses of volcanic ash from two Western Cascades archaeological sites, Vine Rockshelter (35LA304) and nearby 35LA51, suggested that the source of the tephra at these sites was not the expected climactic eruptions of Mount Mazama about 6,850 ^{14}C years ago. The tephra was very similar in appearance to the ejecta from the Mazama event, however, and the ash was termed the Mazama Mimic tephra. Archaeological evidence suggested that the eruption that produced this tephra was post-Mazama in age. Because a new tephra horizon would have significant tephrochronological implications in Western and High Cascades archaeological research, instrumental neutron activation studies were initiated to further investigate the tephra and its possible sources. A resampling and reanalysis of the archaeological tephra and potential tephra sources revealed that Mount Mazama was clearly the source of the archaeological tephra, after all. The initial misidentification is attributed to unexpected geochemical variation during the correlation of the samples. The positive identification of Mazama tephra at Vine Rockshelter also indicates that the span of human occupation at this site may be considerably longer than was initially thought.

Vine Rockshelter is located in the central Western Cascades of Oregon immediately south of the Middle Fork of the Willamette River and about 20 km west of the Cascade Divide (Figure 1). During excavations in 1983, a thick primary deposit of silicic volcanic ash and pumice lapilli was found near the bottom of the deposits in front of the rockshelter. Pumice lapilli were also found scattered throughout the lower part of the rockshelter deposits. The tephra was initially thought to have originated from the violent 6,845 B.P. climactic eruptions of Mount Mazama - the resultant caldera, located 65 km south of Vine Rockshelter, later filled with water to form Crater Lake. Surprisingly, neutron activation analysis (INAA) by Dr. Gordon Goles, University of Oregon, of a pumice sample from a test pit in front of the rockshelter suggested that Mount Mazama was not the source of the tephra (Figure 2). When graphically compared

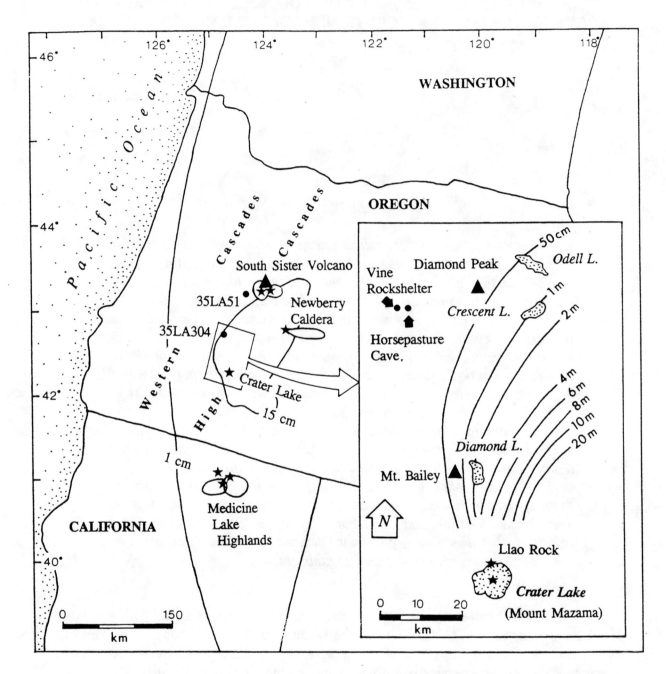

Figure 1. Location of archaeological sites and volcanic tephra sources mentioned in the text. Mazama isopachs are from Sherrod, 1986:101. The solid line surrounding each tephra vent marks the 1 cm isopach for ash deposits originating from that vent. The 15 cm designation refers to the approximate 15 cm isopach of Mazama tephra. Base map is adapted from Sarna-Wojcicki et al. 1983.

with published INAA literature values, the archaeological samples fell outside the range of known Oregon tephra sources. The Vine Rockshelter tephra was very similar in color, lapilli-size, and mineralogical characteristics to Mazama ash, however, and became known as the Mazama Mimic tephra. Tephra from another archaeological site located about 50 km NNE of Vine Rockshelter, 35LA51, was characterized at the same time and was also found to have originated from the same source. Although chronologic evidence from Vine Rockshelter was limited, the cross-dating of projectile point frequencies at this site with nearby Horse Pasture Cave (35LA39) suggested that the Mazama Mimic tephra might be as much as several thousand years younger than the Mazama tephra (Baxter and Connolly 1985:19-21,73-74; Baxter 1986a:67-69).

Materials suitable for radiocarbon dating are relatively uncommon in archaeological sites in the Vine Rockshelter region and archaeological chronologies in the central High and Western Cascades are still poorly-known. The identification of a new tephra horizon in the Oregon central Cascades would provide an important chronostratigraphic horizon for archaeologists working in the region. Additionally, a tephra horizon would prove of considerable value for geological, volcanological, geomorphological, and palynological research in this region. A new source of volcanic tephra would also call into question all previous archaeological (and geological) conclusions that had been based on the unquestioned assumption of the presence of Mount Mazama as the source of any silicic volcanic ash that had been found in the central Western and High Cascades. Any former archaeological studies that had assumed that silicic ash originated from Mount Mazama would have to be reevaluated (see Skinner and Radosevich 1991, for a summary of archaeological research). The resolution of the Mazama Mimic problem, as pointed out by Baxter and Connolly (1985:20), was essential to the development of Western Cascades archaeological chronologies.

The presence of a new source of volcanic ash in the geologically well-known central Cascades, however, would be quite unexpected. Was the Mazama Mimic tephra from a new and previously unidentified source or was it from an already known source? Could the source of the ash be Mount Mazama, after all? Was the problem a real or an analytical one? Only a reinvestigation of the tephra could provide evidence that would answer these questions.

RESEARCH OBJECTIVES

In an attempt to solve these nagging questions, we initiated a new study of the Mazama Mimic tephra in 1989 (Skinner and Radosevich 1989; Skinner and Radosevich 1991). Our research objectives were to resample and recharacterize, once again using neutron activation analysis, both the known geologic sources of tephra in the Cascades and the tephra in question from the Vine Rockshelter and 35LA51 archaeological sites. By including all analyzed samples in one experiment, the effects of laboratory analytical variation could be minimized. If the archaeological pumice could be correlated with a known source, the mystery would be solved. If not, the search for evidence of a new tephra source could begin in earnest.

Pumice lapilli were collected from several different Holocene volcanic vents in the Vine Rockshelter region for comparison to the archaeological tephra: Mount Mazama (Crater Lake), Newberry Volcano, Rock Mesa, and the Devils Hill chain of domes (Figure 2). Tephra samples from several late Holocene eruptions in the Medicine Lake Highlands of Northern California, Glass Mountain, Little Glass Mountain, and the Crater Glass Flow were also included, though these vents were considered unlikely sources of the Mazama Mimic tephra.

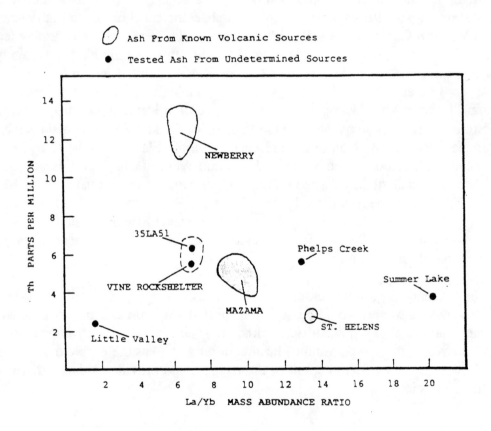

Figure 2.   Scatterplot illustrating the Lanthanum/Ytterbium ratio versus the Thorium content for small pumice lapilli from Vine Rockshelter, 35LA51, and several other Oregon tephra sources. The lack of graphical correlation between the archaeological tephra and published values for other sources led to speculation about the existence of a new Mazama Mimic tephra source somewhere in the Cascades. The diagram is from Baxter and Connolly 1986:21.

GEOCHEMICAL CHARACTERIZATION OF THE TEPHRA

Sources of Volcanic Tephra

Samples of volcanic tephra were gathered from airfall tephra deposits that were clearly associated with the three most likely known source areas of silicic volcanic tephra in the central and southern Cascades region of Oregon (Table 1). For comparative purposes, samples of volcanic ash were also collected from three late Holocene tephra sources located in the Medicine Lake Highlands of Northern California (Heiken 1978; Sarna-Wojcicki et al. 1983).

Table 1. Holocene geologic sources of volcanic tephra that were geochemically characterized in the current investigation.

Tephra Source	[14]C Age	Reference
Medicine Lake Highlands[1]		
Crater Glass Flows	Undated; probably coeval with other eruptions	Donnelly-Nolan, et al.1990;Heiken 1978
Glass Mountain	~1000 yrs BP; overlies Little Glass Mountain	Donnelly-Nolan, et al.1990;Heiken 1978
Little Glass Mountain	~1065 yrs. BP	Donnelly-Nolan, et al.1990;Heiken 1978
Mazama Climatic Eruption[2]	~6850 yrs. BP	Bacon 1983
Newberry[3]	~1350 yrs. BP	Jensen 1988
South Sister Volcano[4]		
Devil's Hill	~2000 yrs. BP	Scott 1987
Rock Mesa	~2100 yrs. BP	Scott 1987

1-Northern California; 2-Oregon Southern High Cascades; 3-Newberry Caldera, Central Oregon; 4-Oregon Central High Cascades

Mazama Eruptions. The most widespread Holocene deposits of volcanic tephra in Oregon originated during several eruptive events that culminated in the construction of the Crater Lake caldera. Two of these events, the Llao Rock eruption of 7015 ± 45 radiocarbon years ago and the much larger climactic eruption of 6845 ± 50 years ago (Table 1), resulted in significant volumes of airfall ash deposits (Figure 1; Bacon 1983). Tephra from the Llao Rock eruption is compositionally very similar to the ash from the climactic eruption and the two ashfall units are geochemically indistinguishable from one another (Bruggman et al. 1987). The airfall ash deposits of the climactic eruptions are widely distributed in the Western United States, particularly to the east and northeast of the vent, and have been identified in Alberta, Canada, more than 1500 km from Crater Lake.

South Sister Volcano. Tephragenic eruptions occurred along the southern and high northern flanks of South Sister Volcano during three related eruptive events that took place about 2,000 radiocarbon years ago (see Table 1). These three events, the Rock Mesa episode, the Devils Hill Dome Chain episode, and the Carver Lake episode, are today marked by groups of obsidian-rhyolite domes that were extruded shortly after the eruption of the volcanic ash. Tephra from the two most widespread and best-dated episodes, Rock Mesa and Devils Hill Dome Chain, were collected for the present investigation. Tephra from all three eruptions has been reported to be virtually geochemically indistinguishable (Scott 1987).

Newberry Volcano. Approximately 1,350 radiocarbon years ago, a Newberry Volcano Caldera vent was the source of a locally extensive deposit of silicic volcanic tephra (Jensen 1988). The Big Obsidian Flow, a prominent caldera obsidian source, was later extruded from this same vent. The main axis of the ashfall lies east-northeast of its source and can be easily identified for several tens of kilometers from the vent (Figure 1).

Medicine Lake Highlands. Late Holocene silicic volcanic tephra is associated with three eruptive episodes at Medicine Lake Volcano, a large shield volcano located in northern California. These eruptions were followed by the extrusion of obsidian flows: Little Glass Mountain, Glass Mountain, and the Crater Glass flows (Heiken 1978; Sarna-Wojcicki et al. 1983; Donnelly-Nolan et al. 1990). All are thought to be about 1000 years old (see Table 1).

Tephra Preparation and INAA Trace Element Analysis

Sample preparation of the volcanic tephra for neutron activation analysis was kept to a minimum. Individual pumice lapillus clearly associated with each eruptive event were used to characterize the geologic sources of volcanic tephra. As recommended by Steen-McIntyre (1977:13), samples of medium-grained (2-64 mm) tephra pyroclasts were chosen for characterization. The weathered exterior of each lapillus was removed and the clean interior used for analysis. The smaller lapilli from the two archaeological sites were ultrasonically cleaned in a water bath to remove contaminants and iron stains. After initial cleaning, each sample was gently crushed and any visible crystals were removed. A magnet was used to remove the magnetic fraction from the tephra. Tephra samples were then crushed to a fine powder with a mullite mortar and pestle and immediately stored in sealed plastic vials.

Following preparation, the samples were characterized ("fingerprinted") with trace element abundances provided by instrumental neutron activation analysis (INAA). Irradiation and subsequent data analysis of all samples was carried out at the Oregon State University Radiation Center in Corvallis, Oregon. The analytical uncertainty for all elements is reported in percent and reflects the relative standard deviation (using one standard deviation) obtained for each element, based on repeated counts of standards containing that element. The analytical uncertainties reported in Table 2 are not related to the sample counting error. The net counts in some photopeaks were relatively high and the resultant counting errors shown for the corresponding analytical results were comparatively small. Used as the only measure of confidence, these counting error values would indicate a misleadingly large degree of accuracy. (The counting error values, not listed in Table 2, are available from the authors). The principles of INAA methods are discussed in more detail elsewhere (Goles 1978).

Correlation, Clustering, and Statistical Methods

The ideal element for characterizing a tephra source is one which exhibits a small degree of intrasource variability, a large degree of intersource variation, a small amount of analytical uncertainty, and relative compositional stability in post-depositional environments. Prior to examining the data set for clusters, we eliminated elements that did not meet these criteria.

The coefficient of variation (CV%; standard deviation/mean x 100) was used to quantitatively ascertain the extent of intraunit compositional variability for the analyzed Mazama samples (Table 1). A small CV% indicates a small degree of intrasource variation. Elements with a CV% of less than 15 were used in the characterization of the tephra sources. The CV% for all tephra samples was also computed so as to provide us with an estimation of those elements that were likely to show adequate inter-source variability for tephra characterization, i.e., those with a large CV%. Elements such as Na, K, and U which are known to be susceptible to mobility through post-depositional weathering processes were also eliminated from consideration (Fisher and Schmincke 1984:327-345). Elements that met the preceding criteria and which exhibited an analytical uncertainty of five percent or less were chosen to characterize the tephra.

Because of the small size of the data set, graphical correlation and clustering methods (scatterplots and ternary diagrams) were initially used to identify geochemical clusters and to correlate the archaeological samples and the geologic source groups. Cluster analysis methods served to independently confirm the results of the graphical analysis of the sample data (Figure 3). All cluster analyses were performed with the MVSP 2.0 multivariate statistical package using the Euclidean distance coefficient and the unweighted pair-group method. When applied to the INAA data set, different clustering algorithms yielded almost identical results.

Results of INAA Analysis

The results of INAA studies of tephra from the six sampled geologic sources and the two archaeological sites are presented in Table 2.

When selected trace element ratios or pairs are plotted on bivariate scatterplots, individual geologic tephra sources are distinguishable as discrete visual clusters. The four tephra samples from the two archaeological sites consistently fall into the cluster defined by the Mazama pumice lapilli. When plotted with the new INAA data, the same trace element ratios that initially suggested the existence of a Mazama Mimic tephra source now point to a different and less surprising conclusion (Figure 4).

Cluster analysis results of the INAA data set (Figure 4) were consistent with the results of the graphical correlation of the data. The volcanic ash samples from Vine Rockshelter and 35LA51 clearly fall within the same groups as those originating from the climactic eruptions of Mount Mazama.

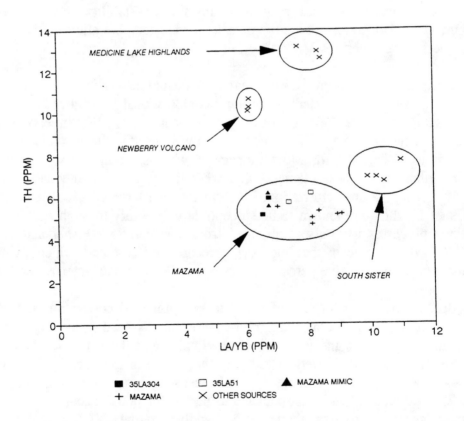

Figure 3. Scatterplot of the Lanthanum/Ytterbium ratio versus Thorium, the same elements and archaeological tephra samples that were illustrated in Figure 2. These results are from the current reanalysis of the samples.

	FEO	NA2O	SC	CO	SB	RB	CS	SR	BA	LA	CE	ND	SM	EU	TB	YB	LU	ZR	HF	TA	TH	U
VINE-1	2.46	3.74	11.7	3.1	0.3	39	2.0	419	510	14.5	35.2	17.8	4.3	1.2	0.6	2.1	0.3	206	7.0	0.5	5.9	2.4
VINE-2	2.27	3.89	10.4	3.1	0.3	26	1.7	440	508	13.4	26.2	16.2	3.9	1.2	0.6	2.1	0.3	200	5.9	0.4	5.2	1.7
LA51-1	2.29	3.99	7.3	2.3	0.5	37	2.3	286	534	15.8	36.0	19.8	4.2	1.0	0.6	2.0	0.3	225	7.3	0.5	6.2	2.6
LA51-2	2.21	3.99	6.9	2.3	0.5	43	2.4	260	549	15.7	34.3	20.4	4.2	0.9	0.6	2.1	0.3	267	7.1	0.5	5.7	2.5
MAZA-2	2.86	4.15	7.7	4.7	0.5	43	2.5	300	566	17.7	42.5	21.4	4.6	0.9	0.6	2.5	0.3	239	6.7	0.5	5.5	2.6
MAZA-4	2.05	3.78	6.0	3.0	0.5	51	3.7	376	676	18.3	40.0	18.6	4.1	0.7	0.6	2.0	0.3	185	5.9	0.5	5.2	2.4
MAZA-5	2.28	4.73	6.4	3.6	0.4	55	3.0	422	699	17.9	40.0	19.3	4.3	0.9	0.6	2.2	0.3	191	5.7	0.4	4.7	1.9
MAZA-7	2.70	4.75	7.0	4.8	0.5	49	3.0	431	678	19.6	46.2	18.6	4.6	1.0	0.7	2.2	0.3	230	5.9	0.4	5.2	2.4
MAZA-8	2.24	4.56	6.8	3.3	0.5	49	2.8	349	692	19.1	45.2	22.1	4.6	1.0	0.6	2.3	0.3	201	6.3	0.4	5.3	2.3
MAZA-9	2.23	4.37	6.6	3.9	0.4	47	2.6	384	646	18.6	44.8	21.1	4.7	1.0	0.7	2.3	0.4	187	6.0	0.4	5.0	2.2
NEWT-1	2.01	4.94	5.8	1.1	0.5	109	4.7	104	728	29.9	58.5	30.4	6.5	0.8	1.1	4.9	0.7	276	8.6	1.5	10.3	4.4
NEWT-2	1.99	4.61	5.8	1.4	0.5	119	4.6	99	741	30.1	60.4	26.8	6.5	0.8	1.1	4.9	0.7	320	8.5	1.4	10.7	4.3
NEWT-3	2.01	4.85	6.0	1.0	0.5	107	4.3	111	748	29.9	60.1	27.4	6.5	0.8	1.3	4.9	0.7	305	8.8	1.4	10.1	4.1
DOME-1	1.92	4.19	4.0	3.2	0.3	70	2.8	224	656	19.0	37.1	14.3	3.3	0.7	0.5	1.9	0.3	213	4.6	0.8	6.9	2.9
DOME-2	1.75	4.05	3.7	2.8	0.4	78	3.0	208	693	19.4	37.6	16.8	3.2	0.6	0.4	1.8	0.3	194	4.6	0.9	7.7	3.3
ROCK-1	1.78	4.32	3.8	2.7	0.3	69	2.7	204	678	18.7	36.1	13.9	3.1	0.7	0.6	1.8	0.3	168	4.3	0.8	6.7	2.8
ROCK-2	1.77	4.05	3.9	3.3	0.3	70	2.6	222	670	18.3	37.3	19.9	3.2	0.7	0.4	1.8	0.3	171	4.6	0.8	6.9	2.9
CRGT-1	1.67	3.89	4.5	2.1	0.7	139	9.5	102	713	21.8	42.0	19.0	4.6	0.6	0.7	2.8	0.4	235	5.5	0.9	13.2	5.7
LGMT-1	1.74	3.96	4.8	2.3	0.7	143	9.4	133	688	22.0	43.1	23.1	4.7	0.6	0.7	2.6	0.4	198	5.4	0.9	13.0	5.6
LBT-1	1.69	3.62	4.8	2.3	0.7	139	9.0	139	700	21.6	42.7	22.9	4.6	0.6	0.7	2.6	0.4	213	5.6	0.9	12.7	5.6
UNCERTAINTY	5%	3%	3%	5%	5%	10%	5%	12%	10%	3%	7%	12%	5%	5%	5%	5%	5%	15%	5%	5%	5%	7%
CV% MAZAMA	12	8	8	18	7	7	13	12	7	3	6	7	4	12	5	7	6	10	5	10	5	9
CV% ALL	15	9	33	36	26	50	61	46	11	23	20	20	22	22	32	39	38	19	21	47	37	39

VINE: VINE ROCKSHELTER (35LA304) TEPHRA

LA51: TEPHRA SAMPLES FROM 35LA51

MAZA: MAZAMA TEPHRA (CRATER LAKE)

NEWT: NEWBERRY TEPHRA

DOME: SOUTH SISTER DOME CHAIN TEPHRA

ROCK: ROCK MESA TEPHRA

CRGT: CRATER GLASS FLOW TEPHRA

LGMT: LITTLE GLASS MOUNTAIN FLOW TEPHRA

LBT: GLASS MOUNTAIN FLOW TEPHRA

UNCERTAINTY = REALATIVE STANDARD DEVIATION FOR ELEMENT BASED ON REPEATED COUNTS OF STANDARDS (UNRELATED TO SAMPLE COUNTING ERROR)

Table 2. Results of instrumental neutron activation analysis of silicic pumice lapilli from Vine Rockshelter (35LA304), 35LA51, and known Oregon and Northern California Holocene tephra sources.

The Solution to the Mystery

The solution to the mystery of the Mazama Mimic tephra is, of course, that the tephra originated from the climactic eruptions of Mount Mazama. There is no Mazama Mimic source. Neutron activation analysis and correlation of tephra from Vine Rockshelter, 35LA51, and the Oregon and Northern California tephra sources indicated that Mount Mazama was clearly the source of the so-called Mazama Mimic tephra. Unexpected analytical variation between published values and those determined by the earlier Vine Rockshelter study was responsible for the initial misidentification of the source of the tephra samples. The problem was, in other words, strictly an analytical one.

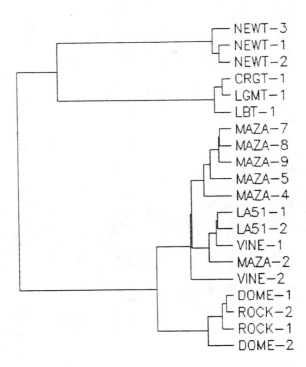

Figure 4. Dendrogram illustrating the results of the trace element cluster analysis classification of the geological and archaeological tephra samples. Sample names are defined in Table 2.

CONCLUSIONS

The identification of Mount Mazama as the source of the Vine Rockshelter and 35LA51 tephra effectively solves the mystery of the Mazama Mimic tephra - the mystery source simply did not exist and was only an analytical fiction. Using INAA characterization methods and minimal sample preparation techniques, the Mazama tephra is easily distinguishable from other Oregon Holocene Cascades sources. It is still safe to assume that silicic tephra deposits found at most southern and central Western and High Cascades archaeological sites, unless they are located in the South Sister vicinity, are almost certainly from Mount Mazama.

The correct identification of the source of the tephra does suggest that the initial occupation of Vine Rockshelter may have begun at an earlier date than was previously thought. The cultural sequence at Vine Rockshelter is potentially considerably longer than was initially hypothesized on the basis of the artifact assemblage and limited radiocarbon dates. The presence of Mazama tephra near the bottom of the rockshelter deposits suggests a possible span of seasonal occupation lasting nearly 7,000 years.

This investigation demonstrates that great care must be taken when published literature values are used for geochemical tephra correlation studies. The tale of the Mazama Mimic mystery tephra clearly illustrates the dangers that may be encountered.

Tephrochronological research such as that carried out at Vine Rockshelter can play a very important role in chronologically and stratigraphically dating and linking archaeological sites within a geographic region. The central Western and High Cascades of Oregon are just such a region and contain deposits from numerous Holocene tephragenic silicic and basaltic volcanic events. The availability of these tephrochronologic possibilities can provide Oregon archaeologists with a chronologic opportunity that should not be overlooked in future regional geoarchaeological research.

ACKNOWLEDGEMENTS

Our thanks to Tom Connolly and Linda Audrain for critical readings of the manuscript. Gordon Goles also provided helpful comments regarding the results of the study. We would especially like to express our appreciation to the Oregon State University Radiation Center for the Reactor-Sharing Grant that made this INAA research a possibility. Our special thanks go to Paul Baxter for his comments on the manuscript and for freely sharing his samples and earlier INAA data for this restudy.

REFERENCES

Bacon, Charles R.
1983 Eruptive History of Mount Mazama and Crater Lake Caldera, Cascade Range, U.S.A. *Journal of Volcanology and Geothermal Research* 18(1-4):57-114.

Baxter, Paul W.
1986 *Archaic Upland Adaptations in the Central Oregon Cascades.* Ph.D. Dissertation, Department of Anthropology, University of Oregon. Eugene.

Baxter, Paul and Thomas J. Connolly
1985 *Vine Rockshelter: A Report of Excavations at An Intermittent Hunting Camp in the Western Cascades.* Report prepared for the Willamette National Forest, Eugene, Oregon. Baxter & Connolly Archaeological Data Consultants, BC/AD Report 6. Eugene, Oregon.

Bruggman, Peggy E., C.R. Bacon, P.J. Aruscavage, R.W. Lerner, L.J. Schwarz, and K.C. Stewart
1987 Chemical Analyses of Crater Lake National Park and Vicinity, Oregon. *U.S. Geological Survey Open-File Report* 87-57.

Donnelly-Nolan, Julie M.; Duane E. Champion; C. Dan Miller; Timothy L. Grove, and Deborah A. Trimble
1990 Post-11,000-Year Volcanism at Medicine Lake Volcano, Cascade Range, Northern California. *Journal of Geophysical Research* 95(B12):19,693-19,704.

Fisher, Richard V. and Hans-Ulrich Schmincke
1984 *Pyroclastic Rocks.* Springer-Verlag. New York.

Goles, Gordon G.
1978 Instrumental Methods of Neutron Activation Analysis. In *Physical Methods in Determinative Mineralogy*, edited by J. Zussman, pp.343-368. Academic Press, New York.

Heiken, Grant H.
1978 Plinian-Type Eruptions in the Medicine Lake Highland, California, and theNature of the Underlying Magmas. *Journal of Volcanology and Geothermal Research* 4(3-4):375-402.

Jensen, Robert A.
1988   *Roadside Guide to the Geology of Newberry Volcano*. CenOreGeoPub,
            Bend, Oregon.

Sarna-Wojcicki, Andrei M.; Duane E. Champion, and Jonathon O. Davis
1983   Holocene Volcanism in the Conterminous United States and the Role of
            Silicic Volcanic Ash Layers in Correlation of Latest-Pleistocene and
            Holocene Deposits. In *Late-Quaternary Environments of the United States,
            Vol.II, The Holocene*, edited by H.E. Wright, Jr., pp.52-77. University
            of Minnesota Press. Minneapolis, Minnesota.

Scott, William E.
1987   Holocene Rhyodacite Eruptions on the Flanks of South Sister Volcano,
            Oregon. In *The Emplacement of Silicic Domes and Lava Flows*, edited by
            Jonathan H. Fink, pp.35-53. Geological Society of America Special Paper
            212. Boulder, Colorado.

Sherrod, David R.
1986   *Geology, Petrology, and Volcanic History of a Portion of the Cascade
            Range Between Latitudes 43-44° N., Central Oregon, USA*. Ph.D.
            dissertation, Department of Geology, University of California. Santa
            Barbara.

Skinner, Craig E. and Stefan C. Radosevich
1989   The Source of the Mazama 'Mimic' Mystery Tephra: Geochemical Studies
            of Volcanic Tephra from Vine Rockshelter (35LA304), Central Western
            Cascades, Oregon (Abstract). *Current Archaeological Happenings in
            Oregon* 14(4):15-16.

Skinner, Craig E. and Stefan C. Radosevich
1991   *Holocene Volcanic Tephra in the Willamette National Forest, Western
            Oregon: Distribution,   Geochemical   Characterization,   and
            Geoarchaeological Evaluation*.   Northwest Research and Trans-World
            Geology. Submitted to the Willamette National Forest. Eugene, Oregon.

Steen-McIntyre, Virginia
1977   *A Manual for Tephrachronology*.   Colorado School of Mines Press,
            Colorado.

PREHISTORIC TRANS-CASCADE PROCUREMENT OF OBSIDIAN IN WESTERN OREGON: A PRELIMINARY LOOK AT THE GEOCHEMICAL EVIDENCE

Craig E. Skinner
INFOTEC Research, Inc.

Carol J. Winkler
Willamette National Forest

ABSTRACT

Recent obsidian characterization data from western Oregon archaeological sites were examined for evidence of trans-Cascade obsidian procurement. Analysis of the spatial distribution and frequency of 1,071 characterized artifacts from major Western Cascades drainages resulted in the identification of several trends of central Oregon obsidian use in the region west of the Cascade Divide. Numerous eastern Oregon obsidian sources, particularly those in the Newberry Volcano, Silver Lake, and Spodue Mountain vicinities, were represented at many western Oregon archaeological sites. While found in varying frequencies in all major Western Cascade drainages, the proportion of glass from eastern Oregon rises dramatically in drainages including and south of the Willamette River Middle Fork. This shift from predominantly western Oregon to eastern Oregon sources may be attributable to the interplay of a variety of different processes including the presence of trans-Cascade travel corridors and procurement systems, the existence of trans-Cascade exchange systems, artifact curation behavior, ethnic or cultural boundaries, and geographic variables such as source distance and ease of access. An analysis of the relationship of artifact sample size and the number of identified obsidian sources (source diversity) indicates that source diversity differs considerably from drainage to drainage. Examination of a subset of characterized artifacts from the Willamette River Middle Fork drainage also suggests that the proportion of characterized artifacts originating from eastern and western sources may vary by artifact category. Several suggestions regarding sampling strategies and future directions in western Oregon obsidian characterization research are made.

For many years, Oregon archaeologists have speculated about the timing and extent of prehistoric contact between western and central Oregon inhabitants across the Cascade Mountains. Ethnographic accounts of post-contact food procurement excursions from central Oregon into the western Cascades are known (Rarick 1962:32; Henn 1975; Murdock 1980; Minor 1987:23-24; Silvermoon 1988:18), as are rather poorly-documented trans-Cascade trail systems (Minto 1903; Vernon 1934; Rarick 1962; Minor and Pecor 1977:154-157; Starr 1983). While limited artifactual evidence suggests the possibility of trans-Cascade interactions (see Tuohy 1986, for an example), little convincing evidence of prehistoric trans-Cascade procurement or exchange has been forthcoming from the archaeological record until recently. In the last few years, trace element studies of obsidian artifacts from western Oregon archaeological sites have begun to provide the hard evidence needed to construct a model of prehistoric trans-Cascade obsidian procurement.

During the past ten years, obsidian trace element characterization studies of archaeological collections in western and central Oregon have come to play an increasingly important role. The relatively low number of major obsidian sources in western Oregon, when combined with a rapidly growing body of characterization data, has helped both to simplify obsidian studies and to provide a large enough database for the preliminary identification and analysis of regional patterns of use and procurement.

These western Oregon characterization studies have revealed the presence of obsidian artifacts not only from western Oregon sources, but from several central Oregon sources. We examine here the spatial distribution of these obsidian artifacts and some of the archaeological implications of their presence in western Oregon. The data summarized in this article provide an initial glimpse of the prehistoric patterns of obsidian procurement and utilization in western Oregon, particularly those in the central Western Cascades.

THE STUDY AREA

The Sources of the Data

We currently have in our database a total of 1,941 reliably characterized obsidian artifacts from 192 Oregon archaeological sites (see Figure 1). Of these artifacts, 1,155 are from 145 archaeological sites located in the major Cascades drainages of western Oregon; the remainder are from scattered sites in central and south-central Oregon, the Oregon coast, and the Willamette Valley. The number of artifacts from each site ranges from one to 109. Almost all of the data originated from x-ray fluorescence (XRF) trace element analyses by Richard E. Hughes; a much smaller proportion of XRF and instrumental neutron activation analyses (INAA) came from Craig E. Skinner. Most of the artifacts (99%) were characterized with XRF methods; the remaining analyses were carried out using INAA techniques at the Oregon State University Radiation Center, Corvallis, Oregon. Eighty-four of the artifacts came from 79 different sites in the Rogue River National Forest and are not considered further in this analysis because of a lack of reported specific geographic information and the small sample size at each site (LaLande 1990). In this analysis, we considered only the characterization research of Hughes and Skinner. Although we have XRF data for 703 artifacts from 17 sites by R. L. Sappington, for reasons of non-comparable data or methodological problems, we have chosen not to include his analytical results here.

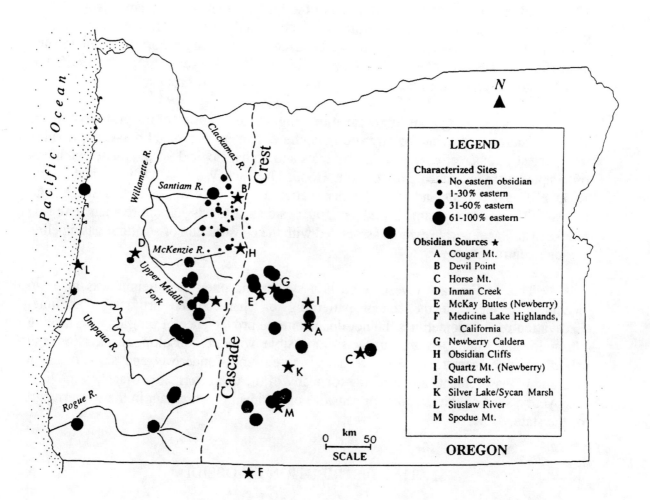

Figure 1.   Distribution of archaeological sites in Oregon for which trace element obsidian characterization data by Hughes and Skinner are available.   The obsidian sources indicated are those which have been correlated with characterized obsidian artifacts from western Oregon sites.

The XRF and INAA data used in the present investigation have been culled from many published and unpublished literature sources. For the sake of brevity, we have not listed all the sources of information used to compile this article, but refer you to Skinner (1991a) for a complete listing of Oregon obsidian-related references. Descriptions of most of the obsidian sources mentioned here can be found in Skinner (1983, 1986, 1991b) and Hughes (1986). Obsidian from the Inman Creek and Siuslaw River alluvial and river gravel sources are geochemically identical and share the same primary source, a probable Miocene obsidian flow near Salt Creek in the Middle Fork Willamette sub-basin (Skinner 1991b). The Inman Creek glass is found in two geochemically-identifiable varieties and is referred to here as the Inman Creek chemical groups.

Thanks to a vigorous test excavation program and a policy of integrating obsidian characterization studies into research designs, the Willamette National Forest has provided the greatest number of characterized samples and archaeological sites. Lesser numbers of samples were examined from the Mt. Hood, Umpqua, Winema, Ochoco, and Rogue River National Forests and several other scattered sites. As we write this article, the available database of characterized Oregon obsidian artifacts has more than doubled, thanks to archaeological research associated with the construction of a natural gas pipeline through central Oregon.

This preliminary investigation is a synchronic one - no attempt was made to document changes in the spatial patterning of characterized artifacts over time. Excavation reports sometimes did not document the provenience of the samples, making chronological studies of the artifacts impossible without consulting excavation and laboratory documentation. Such reanalysis is currently underway and since obsidian hydration measurements are available for many of the characterized artifacts, some light may yet be shed on the temporal dimensions of obsidian procurement in the western part of the state.

SPATIAL DISTRIBUTION OF OBSIDIAN

The Sub-basins

Much of the archaeological research to date in western Oregon has proceeded in the context of settlement and subsistence patterns within the separate basins and sub-basins of major drainages and we follow that pattern in our analysis of the obsidian characterization data. The eastern obsidian source data also include artifacts for which no specific source was known. For the purposes of this preliminary analysis, we are assuming that most unknown sources are located in eastern Oregon.

Overall, from north to south in the Willamette Basin, there is a marked shift in

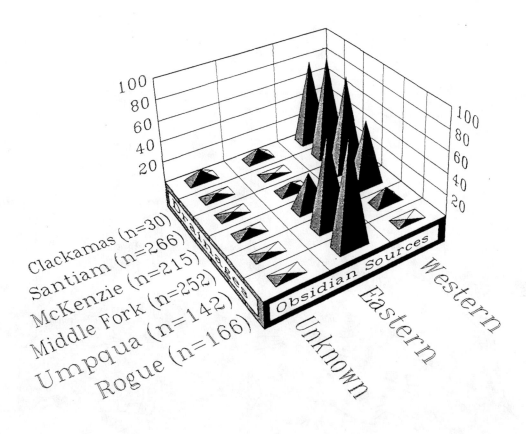

Figure 2.   Percent of obsidian artifacts from major western Oregon drainages that have been assigned to obsidian sources east and west of the Cascade Crest.

reliance from western Oregon to eastern Oregon obsidian sources beginning at the Middle Fork Willamette River drainage and continuing through other Western Cascades drainages to the south of the Middle Fork (Figures 2 and 4). The contour and trend surface maps (Figure 3) clearly illustrate this change though it must be kept in mind that the considerable disparities in sample sizes and the very uneven geographic distribution of sites leaves these maps primarily of heuristic value. The most commonly represented eastern obsidian sources at western Oregon archaeological sites were in the Newberry Volcano area (Newberry Caldera, Big Obsidian Flow, McKay Butte, and Quartz Mountain), the Silver Lake and Sycan Marsh area, and the Spodue Mountain area along the northeastern periphery of the Klamath Lake Basin (Figure 4). Data used in our analysis of the characterized artifacts are summarized in Tables 1 and 2.

Clackamas and Santiam Sub-Basins. The data for the Clackamas and Santiam sub-basins indicate a heavy reliance on Obsidian Cliffs material (about 72%) with a

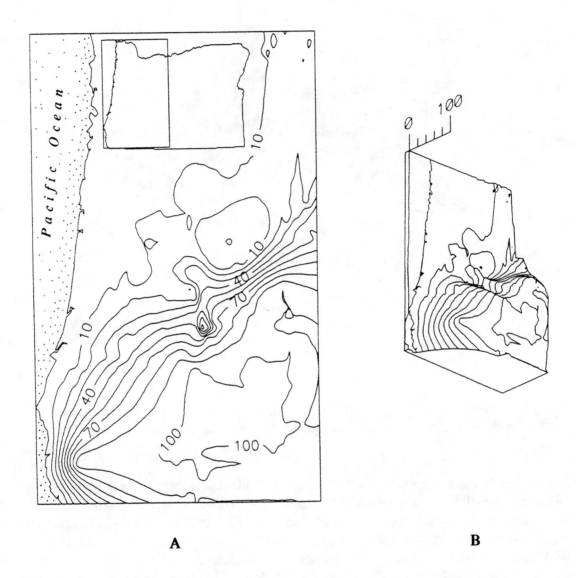

A   **B**

Figure 3.   Contour map (A) of western Oregon illustrating the percentage of eastern
Oregon (and northern California) obsidian found in characterized
archaeological sites.   The trend surface map (B) (note coastline for
orientation) provides a slightly different perspective of the same data and
geographic area.   The rapid shift from western to eastern Oregon sources in
the Middle Fork Willamette sub-basin is clearly illustrated.

significant component of a minor source, Devil Point (about 22%), less than 1% from Inman Creek, and the remainder from eastern Oregon sources. The utilization of the Devil Point obsidian appears to diminish rapidly within ten to twenty kilometers of the source. It appears that procurement of natural glass from the Devil Point source was very locally restricted, due perhaps to the marginal quality and small nodule size of the obsidian, the relative inaccessibility of the source, and the existence of glass of much higher quality at Obsidian Cliffs to the south.

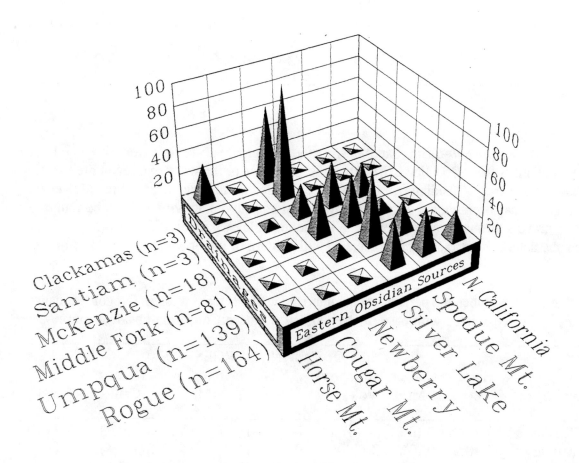

Figure 4.   Percent of artifacts from western Oregon drainages correlated with eastern Oregon and northern California obsidian sources.

Table 1. Number and percent of characterized obsidian artifacts from western Oregon drainages which correlate with sources east and west of the Cascade Crest.

| | OBSIDIAN SOURCES | | | |
Drainage	Western	Eastern	Unknown	Total
Clackamas	24 (80%)	3 (10%)	3 (10%)	30 (3%)
Santiam	255 (96%)	3 (1%)	8 (3%)	266 (25%)
McKenzie	193 (90%)	18 (8%)	4 (2%)	215 (20%)
Middle Fork	155 (62%)	83 (33%)	14 (5%)	252 (24%)
Umpqua	20 (14%)	121 (85%)	1 (1%)	142 (13%)
Rogue	0 (0%)	164 (99%)	2 (1%)	166 (15%)
Total	647 (60%)	392 (37%)	32 (3%)	1071

* - See Figure 2 for a graphical representation of the data.

McKenzie Sub-Basin. Samples from the McKenzie sub-basin are dominated (about 85%) by glass from Obsidian Cliffs, the most extensive of the western Oregon prehistoric obsidian quarries. Obsidian from this source, located at the headwaters of the McKenzie sub-basin, has been widely distributed by glacial and fluvial activity and can be found in river gravels throughout much of the Willamette Valley (Skinner 1986). About 10% of the characterized artifacts were correlated with eastern or unknown sources. Most of the

Table 2. Number and percent of characterized artifacts from western Oregon drainages correlated with eastern Oregon and northern California obsidian sources.

| | EASTERN OBSIDIAN SOURCES | | | | | | |
Drainage	Horse Mt.	Cougar Mt.	Newberry Volcano	Silver Lake	Spodue Mt.	Northern Calif.	Total
Clackamas	1 (33%)	0 (0%)	2 (67%)	0 (0%)	0 (0%)	0 (0%)	3 (1%)
Santiam	0 (0%)	0 (0%)	3 (100%)	0 (0%)	0 (0%)	0 (0%)	3 (1%)
McKenzie	0 (0%)	1 (6%)	5 (28%)	7 (39%)	5 (28%)	0 (0%)	18 (4%)
Middle Fork	0 (0%)	3 (4%)	34 (42%)	35 (43%)	9 (11%)	0 (0%)	81 (20%)
Umpqua	0 (0%)	3 (2%)	14 (10%)	86 (62%)	36 (26%)	1 (1%)	140 (34%)
Rogue	0 (0%)	0 (0%)	0 (0%)	62 (38%)	61 (37%)	40 (24%)	163 (40%)
Total	1 (0%)	7 (2%)	58 (14%)	190 (47%)	111 (27%)	41 (10%)	408

* - See figure 4 for a graphical representation of the data.

remaining 5% were linked to the Inman Creek sources. The two geochemically-distinguishable groups of natural glass that make up the Inman Creek chemical groups have been geochemically correlated with several primary and secondary outcrops in the Salt Creek drainage of the Western Cascades, in the southwestern Willamette Valley, and at the mouth of the Siuslaw River at the Oregon Coast.

Middle Fork Willamette Sub-Basin. The Middle Fork Willamette sub-basin data, however, are strikingly different. Although the basin is geographically closer to Obsidian Cliffs than the eastern Oregon sources, only 34% of the samples are from the Obsidian Cliffs source. Inman Creek obsidian comprises 28% of the characterized artifacts, while central Oregon sources including Newberry Volcano, McKay Butte, and Cougar Mountain make up 15% and the Silver Lake, Sycan Marsh, and Spodue Mountain sources make up 17% of the obsidian. The two closest obsidian sources, Obsidian Cliffs and Salt Creek (Inman Creek chemical group) together make up only 62% of the artifacts. It is clear that factors other than distance to source have influenced the distribution of obsidian in this sub-basin.

Umpqua Sub-Basin. The Umpqua sub-basin pattern indicates an increasing reliance on eastern Oregon sources, particularly those in the Silver Lake, Sycan Marsh, and Spodue Mountain areas (78%). Although Obsidian Cliffs is nearly equidistant from these sources, it comprises only 8% of the samples. A single sample was correlated with the Medicine Lake Highlands area in northern California, the source area that dominates the characterized samples from the southern Cascades and Siskiyou Mountains.

Rogue Sub-Basin. In the Rogue sub-basin, a shift begins towards the procurement and use of obsidian from the Medicine Lake Highlands region of northern California with 23% of the obsidian reported from those sources. Most of the remainder of the characterized glass (74%) originated from the Silver Lake, Sycan Marsh, and Spodue Mountain sources.

Sub-Basins and Source Diversity

The obsidian source diversity (the relationship of the number of identified sources to artifact sample size) was markedly different for many of the western Oregon drainages (Figure 5). The greatest source diversity was noted in the Middle Fork of the Willamette where multiple sources are often found represented at single sites, even those with few characterized artifacts. The lowest diversity was found in the Santiam and McKenzie drainages where the Obsidian Cliffs and locally-utilized Devil Point sources dominated the assemblages. These differences in source diversity among the different basins and sub-basins may prove especially significant when it comes to allotting limited obsidian characterization resources in future archaeological research.

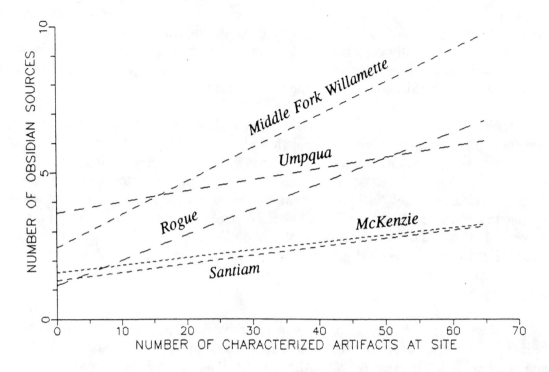

Figure 5.   Obsidian source diversity (number of identified sources) plotted versus sample size for archaeological sites in western Oregon drainages. Linear regression lines with steeper slopes indicate greater diversity. Data points have been omitted. The Clackamas drainage was excluded because of the small sample size (n=2 sites).

Differential Source Use and Formal Artifact Categories

We also examined the source frequencies of different categories of characterized artifacts from sites in the Middle Fork drainage of the Willamette River. We speculated, following the reasoning of Hughes and Bettinger (1984) in their investigation of northern California and southern Oregon utilitarian and non-utilitarian obsidian, that different classes of artifacts might reflect different procurement systems. Obsidian projectile points, for example, might be more subject to curation, long distance procurement, or exchange, and might be expected to originate from more distant sources than obsidian debitage. However, when we examined the relative frequencies of debitage and projectile points, the proportion of western obsidian to eastern obsidian was about two to one in both artifact categories. Our "other tool" category (bifaces, utilized flakes, preforms) showed a different pattern, with both eastern and western sources being used in equal frequencies (figure 6). While the low sample sizes provide us with a less than complete picture of differential source use for different artifact classes, the data suggest that this is an area worth exploring in future western Oregon obsidian characterization studies.

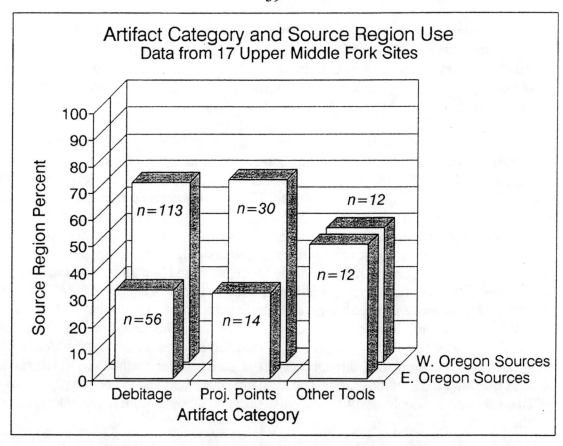

Figure 6.   Comparison of the relative frequencies of types of artifacts from sites in the Middle Fork of the Willamette that have been correlated with eastern and western Oregon sources.

CONCLUSIONS AND SPECULATIONS

What might the spatial patterning of the central Oregon obsidian found in western Oregon archaeological sites mean in behavioral terms? It is the reconstruction of prehistoric patterns of behavior, after all, that is the ultimate objective of all this geochemical data gathering. While it is too soon for us to make any definitive judgements about the cultural or environmental processes responsible for the distribution of obsidian in western Oregon sites, we can engage here in a little speculation.

It is clear from trace element obsidian studies of western Oregon artifacts that obsidian from several central Oregon sources is finding its way into the western part of the state. A number of different environmental and sociocultural processes, however, may influence the spatial distribution and patterning of the obsidian. Whether the occurrence of eastern Oregon obsidian in western Oregon sites is due to the presence of long-distance direct procurement strategies or to the existence of trans-Cascade exchange systems is not yet clear. There also exist the possibilities of embedded obsidian procurement strategies and the curation of obsidian as part of any long-distance direct procurement system. Direct and indirect procurement systems leave many of the same archaeological traces and some other independent artifactual means may be eventually required to pinpoint the specific processes responsible for the trans-Cascade distribution of the glass.

The north-south shift from predominantly western Oregon to eastern Oregon sources illustrated in Figure 4 may be attributable to the interplay of a variety of different processes. Cultural variables could include the presence of travel corridors through the major Cascades passes (Winkler 1990 and 1991), the existence of established trans-Cascade exchange systems, the presence of ethnic or cultural boundaries, the functions of the sites that are sampled for characterization studies, and preferences for certain sources of glass. It is tempting, for instance, to associate the abrupt rise in eastern obsidian sources (particularly those from the Medicine Lake Highlands) with the northern boundaries of the historic and late prehistoric period southern Oregon-northern California culture area that was examined in the characterization studies of Hughes and Bettinger (1984). Geographic variables such as source distance, the proximity of competing sources, and physiographic ease of access to obsidian sources are also important factors that may influence the spatial distribution of the glass. Other methodological variables such as the sample size of the characterized artifact collections and the uneven distribution of characterized archaeological sites may also prove to be significant in our interpretation of the data.

But it is a big jump from the identification of spatial patterns to the confident reconstruction of prehistoric human behavior. As more obsidian characterization data becomes available and as techniques for the interpretation of the spatial patterning of characterized obsidian become more sophisticated, we may be able to better sort out and identify the behavioral systems responsible for the distribution of the obsidian.

RECOMMENDATIONS FOR FUTURE
OBSIDIAN CHARACTERIZATION STUDIES

After reviewing much of the available Oregon obsidian characterization research, we would like to advance several comments and recommendations:

1. The selection of obsidian artifacts for characterization should be made with explicit research objectives in mind, particularly when only small sample sizes are available. Are the research objectives to explore local procurement systems, to examine long-distance procurement systems (exchange or long-distance direct access), to make inter- or intra-site comparisons, to survey a site as a synchronic unit, or to document changes over time? The selection of categories of artifacts, sample sizes, and sample provenience will all certainly depend on the choice of these research objectives.

2. Considering the limited total resources available for most characterization studies, the known obsidian source diversity should play a role in future obsidian research designs. Future excavation contracts should call for larger samples in areas such as the Middle Fork of the Willamette River sub-basin where obsidian source use has been demonstrated to be more diverse. The small number of artifacts (typically 10 to 20) that is often prescribed in archaeological excavations may often prove inadequate to pick up a representative sample in areas of demonstrated high source diversity.

3. The provenance of characterized obsidian artifacts should be thoroughly documented in reports of excavations. This should include the intrasite provenience of the samples and the relationship of artifacts to other features of chronologic significance.

4. A physical description of the characterized artifacts should be included with the analytical results. This may include the type of artifact, the metric dimensions of the artifact, and the visual characteristics of the glass (color, luster, inclusions, and so on). Artifact sizes may provide clues about the original geologic and geomorphic contexts of some source material while a record of megascopic attributes will help in defining the visual range of variation in glass from specific sources.

5. We are still lacking the basic geoarchaeological background information for most Oregon obsidian sources. Ongoing geoarchaeological and geochemical studies of western Oregon obsidian sources must be carried out to document the visual, petrographic, and chemical ranges of variation, to ascertain the secondary distribution of available obsidian, and to identify any remaining western Oregon obsidian sources. Are the numerous western Oregon artifacts identified as being from "unknown sources" from central Oregon or do they come from as yet unidentified minor sources of obsidian in western Oregon?

6. An effort should be made to provide further obsidian characterization data for areas in western Oregon in which coverage is still sparse to non-existent. At this time, only the central Western Cascades have begun to provide enough data to allow for the examination and analysis of regional procurement and exchange problems.

7. If the full value of future obsidian characterization research is to be realized, the data must be made easily accessible to the archaeological community. Most of our time in this investigation, for example, went not into the analysis of the data, but into its collection from widely scattered sources in the "gray" literature. We recommend that an effort be made to make data such as these more widely available to interested archaeologists.

ACKNOWLEDGEMENTS

Our thanks go to Felicia Beardsley, Tom Connolly, Cathy Lindberg, Rick Minor, Ann Rogers, Kathryn Winthrop, and the many others who helped us to locate the characterization and site data used in this analysis. Our thanks also go to the Oregon State University Radiation Center and Bob Walker for providing the Reactor-Sharing Grant that made the INAA artifact analyses possible. An earlier version of this article appeared in <u>Current Archaeological Happenings in Oregon</u> (Skinner and Winkler 1991).

REFERENCES

Henn, Winfield
  1975   The Indian Ridge Site, Lane County, Oregon. In *Archaeological Studies in the Willamette Valley, Oregon*, edited by C.M. Aikens, pp. 455-468. University of Oregon Anthropological Papers 8. Eugene.

Hughes, Richard E.
  1986 *Diachronic Variability in Obsidian Procurement Patterns in Northeastern California in Southcentral Oregon.* University of California Publications in Anthropology 17. Berkeley.

Hughes, Richard E. and Robert L. Bettinger
  1984   Obsidian and Prehistoric Sociocultural Boundaries in California. In *Exploring the Limits: Frontiers and Boundaries in Prehistory*, edited by Suzanne P. DeAtley and Frank J. Findlow, pp. 153-172. British Archaeological Reports, International Series 223. Oxford.

LaLande, Jeff
  1990   Summary Report on the 1989 Obsidian-Sourcing Project. Report prepared for the Rogue River National Forest. Medford, Oregon.

Minor, Rick
  1987 *Cultural Resources Overview of the Willamette National Forest: A 10-Year Update.* Heritage Research Associates Report 60. Eugene.

Minor, Rick and Audrey F. Pecor
  1977 *Cultural Resource Overview of the Willamette National Forest, Western Oregon.* University of Oregon Anthropological Papers 12. Eugene.

Minto, John
  1903   Minto Pass: Its History, and An Indian Tradition. *Oregon Historical Quarterly* 4(3):241-250.

Murdock, George P.
1980   The Tenino Indians. *Ethnology* 19(2):129-149.

Rarick, Theodore M.
1962   *Changing Landscapes in the McKenzie Valley, Oregon.*   Master's thesis, Department of Geography, University of Oregon. Eugene.

Silvermoon, Jon
1988   Research Design for the Scott Mountain Plateau Study Unit, Upper McKenzie River Study Area, McKenzie Ranger District, Willamette National Forest, Western Oregon. Ms. on file, Willamette National Forest, Eugene.

Skinner, Craig E.
1983   *Obsidian Studies in Oregon: An Introduction to Obsidian and An Investigation of Selected Methods of Obsidian Characterization Utilizing Obsidian Collected at Prehistoric Quarry Sites in Oregon.*   Master's Terminal Project, Interdisciplinary Studies, University of Oregon. Eugene.

Skinner, Craig E.
1986   The Occurrence, Characterization, and Prehistoric Utilization of Geologic Sources of Obsidian in Central Western Oregon: Preliminary Research Results. Ms. on file, Oregon State Museum of Anthropology, University of Oregon. Eugene.

Skinner, Craig E.
1991a *Obsidian in Oregon: An Interdisciplinary Bibliography.*   Northwest Research. Corvallis.

Skinner, Craig
1991b Obsidian at Inman Creek: Geoarchaeological Investigations of an Unexpected Geologic Source of Obsidian in the Southwestern Willamette Valley, Oregon. Ms. in possession of the author.

Skinner, Craig E. and Carol J. Winkler
1991   Prehistoric Trans-Cascade Procurement of Obsidian in Western Oregon: The Geochemical Evidence. *Current Archaeological Happenings in Oregon* 16(2): 3-9.

Starr, Karen J.
1983   The Cultural Significance of Mountain Regions: Implications for the Cascade Divide, Oregon.   Master's thesis, Interdisciplinary Studies, Oregon State University. Corvallis.

Tuohy, Donald R.
  1986   A Maidu Coiled Basket from the North Fork of the Willamette River, Oregon. *Journal California and Great Basin Anthropology* 8(2):260-263.

Vernon, Stivers
  1934   Sage of the Skyline Trail Recited: Nomadic Indians First Traveled Over the 200-Mile Route on the Roof of the Cascades. *Oregonian*, Magazine Section, pp. 5:2-6.

Winkler, Carol J.
  1990   Recent Archaeological Investigations in the Fall Creek and Middle Fork Willamette Watersheds, Lowell Ranger District. *Current Archaeological Happenings in Oregon* 15(4):12-14.

Winkler, Carol J.
  1991   The Middle Fork Willamette River Corridor as Trans-Cascade Travel Route: The Evidence from Obsidian Sourcing. Paper presented at the 44th Annual Northwest Anthropological Conference, Missoula, Montana.

HOUSEPITS ON THE JOHN DAY AND DESCHUTES RIVERS: A SUMMARY OF THE EVIDENCE

Pamela Endzweig
Department of Anthropology, University of Oregon

ABSTRACT

Surface information from 85 pithouse sites along the lower John Day and Deschutes rivers is summarized to provide a descriptive baseline for pithouse sites in this area. The distribution, location, and dimensions of archaeo-logical pithouse sites, together with data on house size, are examined and compared with the ethnographic record. It is concluded that the ethnographic picture of the 19th century may not be representative of prior centuries or millennia, a fact that must be borne in mind when pithouses are used as diagnostic criteria to infer particular subsistence strategies.

Pithouses have long served as pivotal elements in discussions of cultural process on the Columbia Plateau and elsewhere in North America. Pithouse sites have served to document changes in settlement patterns and subsistence, and as evidence for population size and movement. On the Columbia Plateau, the appearance of pithouses has traditionally been linked to the inception of the "Ethnographic" or "Winter Village Pattern" (Nelson 1969, 1973). This inference has recently come under considerable scrutiny as it becomes apparent that presence of pithouses alone does not necessarily connote the kind of logistical adaptive strategy practiced by native peoples of the region during historic times (Ames and Marshall 1980; Ames 1988; Chatters 1989). This conclusion is reinforced when the nature and distribution of habitation sites are examined. In this paper I will focus on pithouse sites along the lower reaches of the Deschutes and John Day rivers, i.e. from Township 10S to the Columbia River[1]. My objective is to provide a descriptive baseline for the area, and to identify and discuss patterns that emerge from the evidence. At the least, I hope to have made a contribution by liberating some very interesting data from some not very widely distributed "grey literature."

I have relied primarily on two cultural resource inventories conducted by the Prineville BLM in the mid 1970s. These represent the only large-scale surface reconnaissance surveys undertaken to date along the lower Deschutes and John Day rivers. Initial information on site types, locations, and dimensions was derived from the computerized site database prepared by INFOTEC Research, Inc. for the Prineville District BLM. Specific information on house depressions (including numbers and dimensions) was assembled from archaeological site records filed at the State Museum of Anthropology at the University of Oregon.

SITE DISTRIBUTION

The lower reaches of both the Deschutes and John Day rivers are entrenched into the Deschutes-Umatilla Plateau, a broad expanse of gently northward-sloping Miocene flood basalts (Baldwin 1976). Climate is semi-arid, with vegetation characterized by typical high desert Shrub-Steppe communities (Franklin and Dyrness 1973). The John Day River, 364 km long (Fulton 1968), is fed primarily by snow pack from the Blue Mountains, causing an extremely variable seasonal flow which peaks in April and reaches its yearly low between August and October (Willamette Kayak and Canoe Club 1986). The Deschutes River, at a comparable length of 392 km (Fulton 1968), drains the east slope of the Cascades and exhibits a particularly constant flow because of the region's porous volcanic aquifers (Loy et al. 1976).

During ethnographic times, most of the study area was used by four sub-divisions of Tenino, although there has been some question of an earlier Molala presence along part of the lower Deschutes (Ray et al. 1938). To the south were several Northern Paiute bands. The exact location of the cultural boundary between peoples of the northern Great Basin and the southern Plateau, while situated at the southern edge of the area covered here, is not clear and probably fluctuated during both historic and prehistoric times (for ethnographic overview and sources, see Suphan 1974).

According to ethnologist George Peter Murdock (1938:397), the Tenino were

... divided into four subtribes or rather pairs of villages - one, with flimsy and temporary buildings, located on the river and used during the fishing season in the warmer months; the other, with substantial permanent buildings, located several miles distant, usually away from the river, at a spot which provided water, fuel, and shelter from the winds during the colder half of the year.

Murdock later (1980:129) added that "in several instances ... a portion of a subtribe occupied a smaller secondary site during either the winter or the summer season." For three of the subtribes, summer villages were located on the south shore of the Columbia River, with winter villages situated just upstream along adjacent tributaries. Only members of the Tygh subtribe were based inland away from the Columbia River, wintering at Tygh Valley and fishing within the vicinity of Sherar's Bridge on the Deschutes River. Interior areas were visited during the spring and fall for game, roots, nuts, and berries.

Figure 1 represents the distribution of villages, camps, and fishing sites recorded by Verne Ray (Suphan 1974:Petitioner's Exhibits 403, 404c) and George Peter Murdock (1980:132-136). It shows a total of twelve camps and villages along the Deschutes and nine along the John Day (Murdock 1980:33; Ray in Suphan 1974:Petitioner's Exhibit #403). Archaeological surface evidence, although without the benefit of temporal control, suggests a considerably more intensive use of the two lower river courses (Table 1). The 1976 survey of BLM lands along the Deschutes River between Macks Canyon and Warm Springs Bridge by Hibbs, Gannon and Willard, reported 135 archaeological sites, 27 of which exhibited definite housepits (Hibbs, Gannon and Willard 1976). While the total area covered during this reconnaissance is not given in their report, a tally of BLM lands by river length suggests that ca. 50% of land between Macks Canyon and Warm Springs Bridge was surveyed, or about 40% of the lower Deschutes as a whole[2]. As of spring of 1992, the count for the 95 lower river miles stands at 160 sites, 40 or 25% of which exhibit depressions identified as housepits.

A systematic survey of the John Day River canyon was undertaken by Michael and Ann Polk in 1976. Here, 16 one-mile-long segments were examined, one randomly chosen for each stretch of ten river miles, regardless of land ownership, if I understand correctly. Sites recorded during this project (Polk 1976), together with those reported by Wilde et al. for the lower ten miles of the river (Wilde et al. 1983), and by INFOTEC Research, Inc. in the vicinity of Thirtymile Creek (Moratto et al. 1990, 1991), make up the bulk of the 113 sites known for this region. Housepits have been noted at forty-five of these, or 40%.

Because of the disparate survey strategies and attendant gaps in the record, inferences on site distribution must remain highly tentative. But some generalizations are possible. Along the lower Deschutes, firm evidence of pithouses ends south of Trout Creek. No housepits were observed at the 31 sites reported by Ross from his survey for Round Butte Dam, some 20 miles farther upstream (Ross 1963). The archaeological distribution of pithouse sites matches the general distribution of ethnographic sites recorded along this river. The large number of prehistoric *habitation sites* in contrast to the historic preponderance of "hunting camps" and "fishing sites," however, may suggest changes in the way the area was used, eg. a shift towards more specialized resource exploitation, with shorter, and seasonally more restricted stays. Without chronological controls, of course, it is impossible to ascertain how many of the sites were occupied simultaneously.

A question remains regarding the northern limits of housepit sites along the Deschutes. Unfortunately, the unsurveyed portion of the river between Macks Canyon and the Columbia River is coextensive with what appears to be a gap in ethnographic sites, leaving the question of prehistoric occupation open. The absence of pithouse sites along the lower 33 miles of the John Day River, on the other hand, does appear to reflect a cultural reality, as thirty-five sites of various other kinds, primarily lithic scatters, have been recorded along this stretch. As along the Deschutes River, the currently held

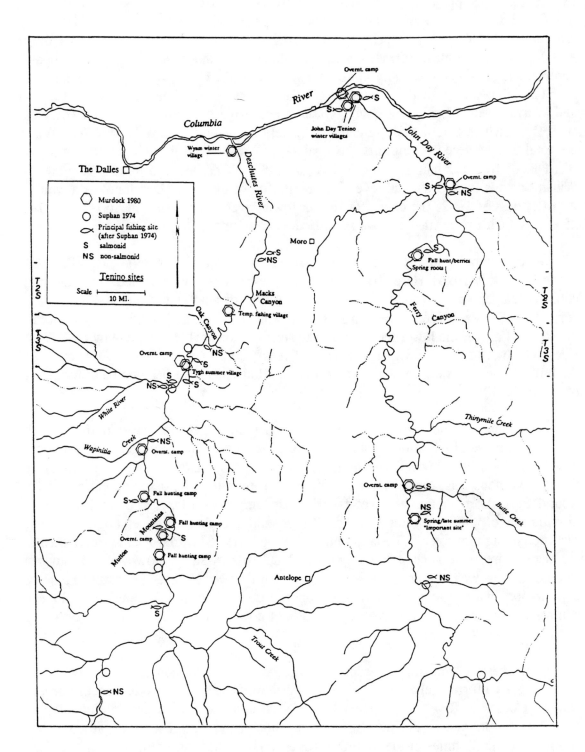

Figure 1. Tenino sites along the Lower John Day and Deschutes Rivers, according to published ethnographic sources (after Murdock 1980, Suphan 1974).

Table 1. Distribution of Archaeological Pithouse Sites by Township and River.

Township	1N	1S	2S	3S	4S	5S	6S	7S	8S	9S	Total
Deschutes R.	0	0	10	13	2	5	1	4	3	2	40
John Day R.	1	2	11	9	4	13	2	2	0	1	45
										Total	85

southern limit of pithouses along the mainstem of the John Day is at Township 9S, except for three sites near Spray, 40 miles upstream and outside of the area of present concern. The spatial distribution of prehistoric pithouse sites along the lower John Day River bears less resemblance to the ethnographic picture than that along the Deschutes. All lie within traditional Tenino big game-hunting territory (Suphan 1974:Petitioner's Exhibit No. 404A) (Figure 2). The high density of prehistoric habitation sites south of Thirtymile Creek and south of Ferry Canyon is particularly striking, in light of the historic void along this stretch. Equally impressive is the high density of archaeological pithouse sites in Townships 2S and 3S along both the Deschutes and John Day rivers. A clue to this puzzling distributional parallel may be found in the ethnographic resource areas documented by Verne Ray for the Tenino. Not only are the two riverine site clusters located where the Deschutes and the John Day are closest to one another (separated by a mere 20 miles), but they also coincide with the northern limits of the root and landfowl-hunting areas situated on the divide between the two drainages (Suphan 1974:Petitioner's Exhibits No. 404b,c) (Figure 3). Habitation sites placed along this stretch of river thus have access not only to fish (and game along the John Day), but also to the broader resource catchment of their "sustaining hinterland" (Burghardt 1959, cited in Flannery 1976:174), the nearby uplands. The social proximity between John Day and Deschutes communities provided by this arrangement may have presented an additional incentive.

SITE SIZE

There is a clear hierarchy of distribution with regard to numbers of housepits per site that holds true for both the Deschutes and the John Day rivers. First a word on the derivation of the counts. In looking at site record forms, one is faced with the difficulty of distinguishing between features identified as "housepits," "possible housepits," and "pits." Dimensions recorded by field personnel, in addition, encompass depressions ranging in size from storage pits to potential multifamily structures. Rather than imposing a classification upon this varied data, I have calculated two sets of numbers for each site, HPMIN (minimum housepits) and HPMAX (maximum number of housepits).

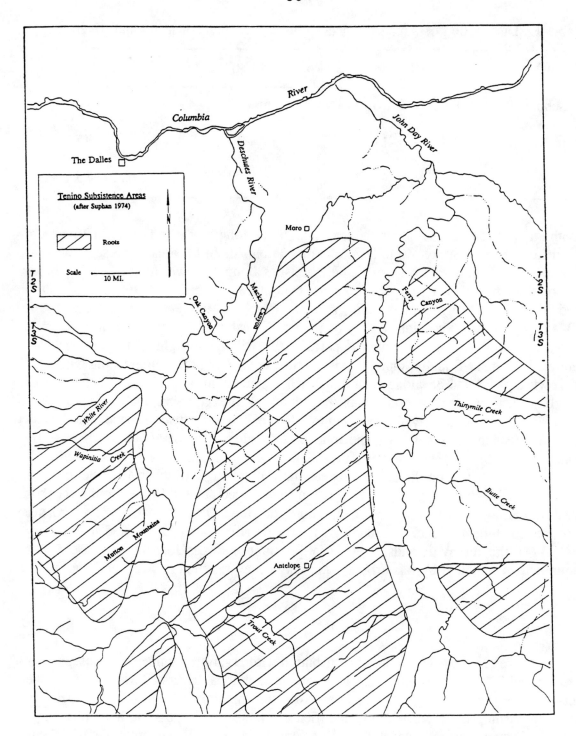

Figure 2. Traditional Tenino large game hunting areas (after Suphan 1974).

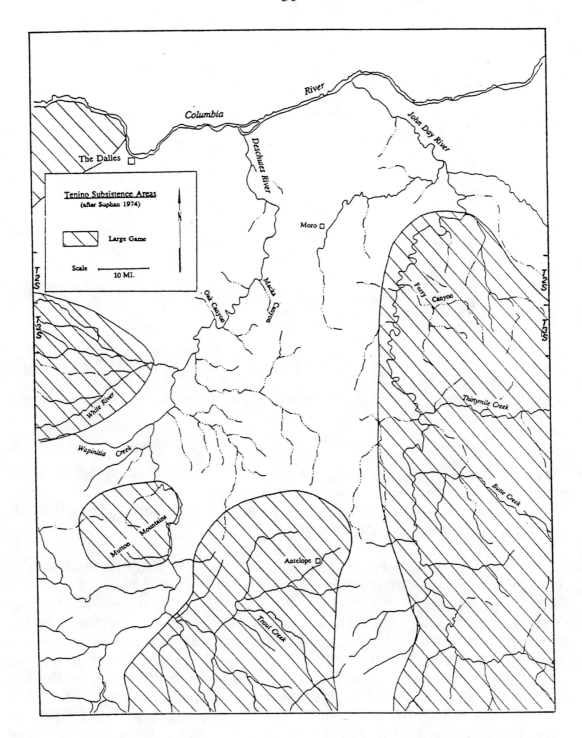

Figure 3. Traditional Tenino root-gathering areas (after Suphan 1974).

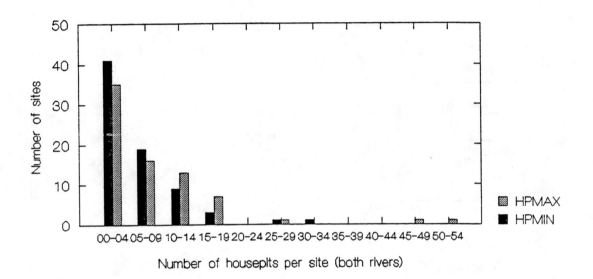

Figure 4. Frequency distribution of housepits by site, Deschutes and John Day Rivers combined.

The latter is a total for *all* depressions observed at a site, the former only includes those features definitively identified as house depressions in the field. A correlation coefficient of 0.91 between HPMIN and HPMAX suggests that, as far as patterns in the data are concerned, either data set should be useable.

On both the lower John Day and the lower Deschutes, sites with few housepits outweigh by far the few larger concentrations (Figure 4). This pattern has also been observed by Hackenberger et al. (n.d.) for the Middle Snake, Salmon and Middle Fork rivers in western Idaho. The thirty-one sites for which counts are available on the Deschutes River exhibit from 1 to 33 or 51 depressions, depending on whether the most conservative or the most liberal count, i.e. HPMIN or HPMAX, is used (Figures 5 and 6). Fifty-two percent of these sites are characterized by 1 to 3 depressions for HPMIN or 1 to 4 depressions for HPMAX. The largest proportion of sites (7, or 23%) exhibits only one housepit (HPMIN and HPMAX). A small secondary peak at 5-7 pits for HPMIN or 10-13 for HPMAX accounts for 19-26% of all pithouse sites on the lower Deschutes.

Sites along the John Day are characterized by fewer housepits overall, with counts ranging from 1 to 17 depressions. Here too, small sites predominate (Figures 5 and 6). Of 43 sites, 24 or 56% are represented by 1-4 depressions, if the conservative count,

HPMIN, is used. Eight (19%) exhibit only one, and another eight have two depressions. As along the Deschutes, there may also be a secondary peak, here between 8 and 10 pits. This distribution becomes blurred if HPMAX is used, but sites with 1-5 housepits continue to dominate, making up 61% of the total.

While a discussion of individual sites is beyond the present scope, some comments are in order. The placement of habitation sites in relation to diverse resources has already been mentioned and is supported by the location of the largest pithouse sites along the lower Deschutes, 35WS42, 35WS43, 35SH23, 35WS66, and 35WS91.

35WS42 and -43, with a minimum of 27 and 11 housepits each (and a maximum of 45 and 18), are situated in Oak Canyon, within a half-mile of the Deschutes. Based on environmental setting and surface artifacts, Hibbs et al. (1976) suggest that WS42 and -43 functioned as specialized acorn processing sites. The Mack Canyon Site, 35SH23, with between 33 and 55 depressions, is one of two pithouse sites along the lower Deschutes and John Day rivers at which some archaeological excavation has taken place. On the basis of artifacts and faunal remains, investigator David Cole concluded that mountain sheep and freshwater mussels were the most important food resources used. This site is, in addition, situated adjacent to a chert source from which much of the raw material recovered in the excavations was thought to have been derived (Cole 1967, 1969).

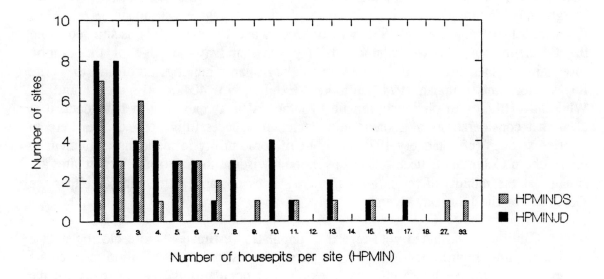

Figure 5. Frequency distribution of housepits by site, HPMIN.
(HPMIN being the most conservative count of purported housepit depressions.)

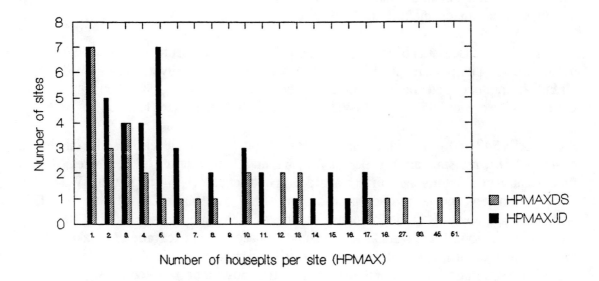

Figure 6. Frequency distribution of housepits by site, HPMAX.
(HPMAX being the most liberal count of purported house pit depressions.)

Site 35WS66, with 13 housepits, is at the mouth of Wapinitia Creek, in an area historically used for non-salmonid-fishing (Figure 1), at the northeastern edge of rootgrounds (Figure 3) and within 10 miles of major oak groves (Suphan 1974). The final larger habitation site, 35WS91, with between 6 and 13 depressions, is situated along the Deschutes in a known salmonid fishing area, and at the edge of the Mutton Mountains, visited historically by Tenino for large game hunting, according to Verne Ray's informants (Suphan 1974:Petitioner's Exhibits No. 404a,c) (Figures 1 and 2). While all of this must obviously remain hypothetical in the absence of hard data, it is clear that considerations of ecotone and catchment, successfully applied elsewhere in riverine settings (cf. Flannery 1976), may be of some utility in modeling settlement in the southern Columbia Plateau. The conventional wisdom that all of the largest sites are situated at the mouths of the largest tributaries does not appear to hold for either the Deschutes or the John Day rivers.

Caution is warranted with regard to population estimates before closing with a brief look at housepit dimensions. I have purposely resisted the temptation to calculate numbers of people per house in order to extrapolate population size and density for the region. Such an undertaking can, at present, simply not be supported by the available data. Major obstacles include the already-mentioned problems of sampling and contemporaneity. The latter, in particular, cannot be resolved without extensive excavation

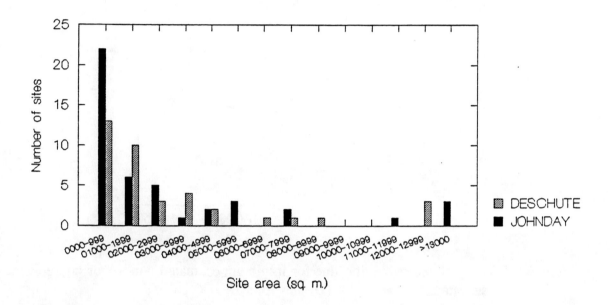

Figure 7. Site area of housepit sites, Deschutes and John Day rivers.

particularly in light of the often sparse complement of surface materials reported for many of these sites.

The use of site area to calculate population densities is similarly risky. Habitation sites which are small in area, like sites with few housepits, predominate along both rivers (Figure 7), but the relationship between site area and number of housepits is by no means linear, even if two extremely large sites (over 70,000 square meters) are excluded (Figures 8a and 8b). It is likely that a variety of physical and social factors, not just population, are involved in determining site area.

HOUSE SIZE

Ethnographic Tenino dwellings involving some degree of excavation appear to have consisted of rectangular mat-covered lodges and circular, semi-subterranean houses covered with mats and earth (Ray 1942:173-182). General dimensions for rectangular lodges are given as 16-30 feet (4.9-9.1 m) in length by 16 feet (4.9 m) in width, with an excavated depth of 1 foot (0.31 m) (Ray 1942:174). Circular, semi-subterranean houses

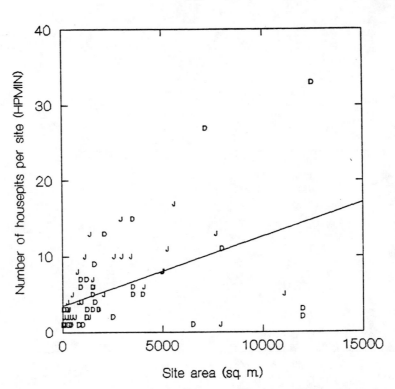

Figure 8a. Scatterplot and regression line for minimum estimated number of housepits versus site area, Deschutes (D) and John Day (J) rivers.

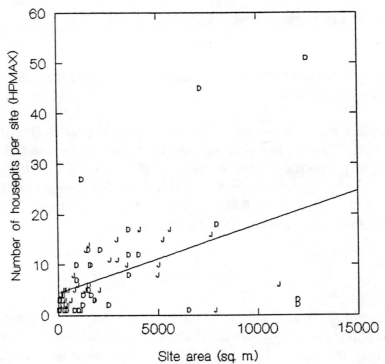

Figure 8b. Scatterplot and regression line for maximum estimated number of housepits versus site area, Deschutes (D) and John Day (J) rivers.

are said to have measured 16 feet (4.9 m) in diameter, with an excavated depth of 8 feet (2.4 m) (though a question mark in Ray's text expresses his uncertainty regarding this last dimension) (Ray 1942:177). According to Murdock, these were winter dwellings, abandoned in spring in favor of flat-roofed rectangular structures and "mat-covered tipis" (Murdock 1958:300-301). Temporary conical structures, presumably built on level ground, and covered with mats, served for storage as did excavated pits (Ray 1942:173-182).

Northern Paiute wintering along the upper reaches of the John Day lived in tule- or grass-covered domed or conical structures, which generally measured 8-14 feet (2.4-4.3 m) in diameter and 6-10 feet (1.8-3.0 m) in height and were sunk in the ground 4-6 inches (0.1-0.15 m) (Stewart 1941). Cooler brush windbreaks or shades were inhabited by Northern Paiute during the warm months of the year (Fowler and Liljeblad 1986:443).

Archaeological housepits recorded along the lower reaches of the Deschutes and John Day rivers are generally circular to oval in shape. For the lower Deschutes, data on surface area are available for 162 depressions, from 30 sites (Figure 9). These range in area from 0.8 to almost 104 square meters, with a mean of 18.4 square meters. This average is equivalent to a 4.8 m diameter circle, with the full range encompassing diameters of 1.0 to 11.5 m. Surface area is known for 180 depressions at 33 sites along the lower John Day (Figure 9). Ranging in area from 1.6 to 95 square meters (equivalent to circles measuring 1.8 to 11m in diameter), pits average 24.6 square meters, approximating a circle with a diameter of 5.6 m. Depths range from 10 cm to 1 m and average 26 cm on the Deschutes. For the John Day, they span 10 cm to 1.5 m, with a mean of 49 cm (Figure 10).

On average, thus, housepits and other depressions along the John Day are 25% larger and 47% deeper than along the lower Deschutes. The significance of this difference is not clear, if, in fact, it is real and not some odd sampling bias. Both Tenino and Northern Paiute ethnographic structures are, in any case, accommodated within the wide size range represented by the archaeological record, though the observed *means* fall closer to Tenino house dimensions.

Housepits in the 10-20 square meter range (3.5-5 m diameter), which account for almost 42% of all housepits on the lower Deschutes, and 37.3% of all housepits on the lower John Day, make up the largest size category along both rivers. The function of the substantial proportion of pits measuring less than 10 square meters in area or less than 3.5 m in diameter (30.3% on the Deschutes and 17.2% along the John Day) is not clear. If Cook's and Heizer's minimum requirement of 9.5 square meters of floor area for a single-family dwelling is accepted (Cook and Heizer 1965), the smaller depressions may have served as storage pits or other features. However, house depressions as small as 1.5-1.6 m in diameter (1.8-2 square meters) have been recorded from archaeological sites in western Nevada (cf. summary in Oetting 1989:Table 31), and the lower limit for Northern Paiute wickiups is given at 2.4 m (see above), so the question remains open.

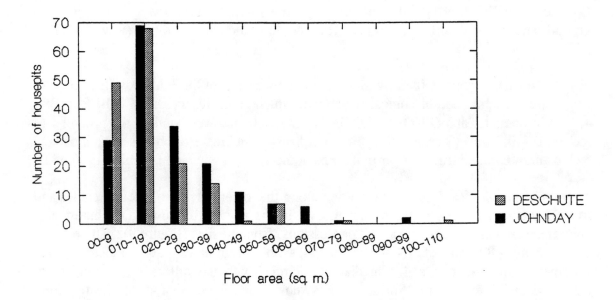

Figure 9. Surface area of housepits, Deschutes and John Day rivers.

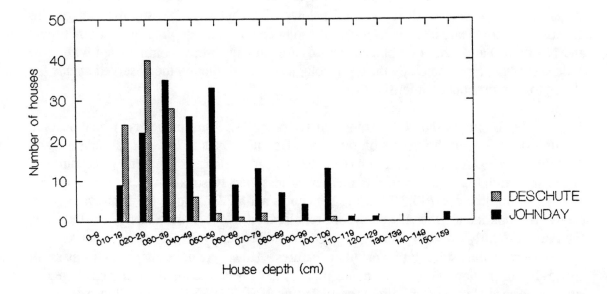

Figure 10. Depth measurements for housepits, Deschutes and John Day rivers.

SUMMARY AND CONCLUSIONS

Looking beyond all the numbers (the curse of access to statistical software), I hope to have communicated some more general points with regard to the archaeological potential of the lower Deschutes and John Day rivers, the critical need for probabilistic survey in these regions, and the necessity to test as hypotheses the data provided by the ethnographic record. It has been shown that pithouse sites in this area are numerous and that they are situated within reach of diverse food resources, including fish, roots, and game. Sites with one to two depressions are most common, and those with the most housepits are not necessarily located at the mouths of the largest tributaries. Pits in the 10-20 square meter range predominate along both rivers, but, on average, housepits and other depressions are larger and deeper along the lower John Day. It has further been shown that either Tenino or Northern Paiute ethnographic habitation structures could be represented by the archaeological record, but that housepit means approximate more closely the dimensions of Tenino houses.

It is clear that the ethnographic picture of the 19th century may not be representative of prior centuries or millennia. The distribution of pithouse sites along the lower Deschutes and John Day rivers, together with recent evidence from adjacent uplands (Endzweig 1992), indicates a major reorganization of settlement some time in the past leading to increased population aggregation along the Columbia River. The nature of this reorganization, its timing and causes, are as yet unknown, and answers will not be forthcoming without systematic excavation and analysis. As always, much work remains to be done. The need is, however, particularly urgent in this area in which vandalism and natural erosion are taking an increasing toll on the archaeological record.

NOTES

1. I use the term "pithouse" loosely in this context to refer to any dwelling involving an excavated floor, without attempting to distinguish between structures erected in pits and those built over them (houses within excavations vs. excavated houses as defined by Rice 1985:91). A more precise distinction is not possible on the basis of surface data alone.

2. Extrapolated from <u>Lower Deschutes Public Lands</u>, map edited and published by Bureau of Land Management, 1989.

ACKNOWLEDGEMENTS

I am indebted to Suzanne Crowley Thomas and John Zancanella, past and present Prineville BLM archaeologists, for access to the District's computerized site database. I owe additional thanks to Thomas J. Connolly, Don E. Dumond, and A. C. Oetting for commenting on an earlier draft of this paper. The present version has benefitted considerably from their suggestions and insights. An earlier version of this paper was presented at the 45th Northwest Anthropological Conference in Burnaby, B.C., 1992.

REFERENCES

Ames, Kenneth M.
>1988   Instability in Prehistoric Residential Patterns on the Intermontane Plateau. Paper presented at the 41st Annual Northwest Anthropological Conference, Tacoma, Washington.

Ames, Kenneth M. and Alan G. Marshall
>1980   Villages, Demography and Subsistence Intensification on the Southern Columbia Plateau. *North American Archaeologist* 2(1):25-52.

Baldwin, Ewart M.
>1976   *Geology of Oregon.* Kendall/Hunt Publishing Company, Dubuque, Iowa.

Burghardt, A.F.
>1959   The Location of River Towns in the Central Lowland of the United States. *Annals of the Association of American Geographers* 49:305-323.

Chatters, James C.
>1989   Resource Intensification and Sedentism on the Southern Plateau. *Archaeology in Washington* 1:3-19.

Cole, David L.
>1967   *Archaeological Research of Site 35SH23, the Mack Canyon Site. Interim Report 1965-1966.* Museum of Natural History, University of Oregon. Submitted to the Bureau of Land Management, Oregon-Washington State Office, Portland.

>1969   *1967 and 1968 Archaeological Excavations of the Mack Canyon Site. Interim Report 1968.* Museum of Natural History, University of Oregon. Submitted to the Bureau of Land Management , Oregon-Washington State Office, Portland.

Cook, S. F. and Robert F. Heizer
   1965   *The Quantitative Approach to the Relation Between Populations and Settlement Size.*   University of California Archaeological Survey, Report No. 64. Berkeley.

Endzweig, Pamela
   1992   *Canyons and Crests: An Archaeological Survey of the Pine Creek Basin, North-Central Oregon.* Oregon State Museum of Anthropology Report 92-2. Eugene.

Flannery, Kent V.
   1976   Linear Stream Patterns and Riverside Settlement Rules.   In *The Early Mesoamerican Village*, ed. by K. V. Flannery, pp. 173-180. Academic Press, New York.

Fowler, Catherine S. and Sven Liljeblad
   1986   Northern Paiute. In *Great Basin*, edited by W. L. D'Azevedo. Handbook of North American Indians 11:435-465.   Smithsonian Institution, Washington, D.C.

Franklin, Jerry F. and C. T. Dyrness
   1973   *Natural Vegetation of Oregon and Washington.* USDA Forest Service General Technical Report PNW-8. Portland, Oregon.

Fulton, Leonard A.
   1968   *Spawning Areas and Abundance of Chinook Salmon (Oncorhynchus tshawytscha) in the Columbia River Basin - Past and Present.*   Special Scientific Report - Fisheries No. 571, United States Fish and Wildlife Service, Washington, D. C.

Hackenberger, Steven, David Sisson, and Bruce Womack
   n.d.   Middle and Late Prehistoric Period Residential Strategies: House Size and Frequency on the Middle Snake, Salmon, and Middle Fork Rivers. Draft Manuscript on file with authors.

Hibbs, Charles H., Brian L. Gannon, and Cynthia H. Willard
   1976   Lower Deschutes River Cultural Resources Survey: Warm Springs Bridge to Macks Canyon Sherman, Wasco, and Jefferson Counties. Report on file with the Bureau of Land Management, Prineville District, Prineville.

Moratto, Michael J. et al., eds
   1990   *Final Cultural Resources Assessment Report PGT-PG&E Pipeline Expansion Project, Idaho, Washington, Oregon, and California. Phase 1: Survey, Inventory, and Preliminary Evaluation of Cultural Resources.* Infotec, Inc. Submitted to Pacific Gas Transmission Co., San Francisco, California.

1991   *Archaeological Testing and Evaluation Report, 1990 Field Season, and Historic Properties Treatment Plan for 1991 Field Season, PGT-PG&E Pipeline Expansion Project, Idaho, Washington, Oregon, and California.* Infotec, Inc. Submitted to Pacific Gas Transmission Co., San Francisco, California.

Loy, William G., et al.
1976   *Atlas of Oregon.* University of Oregon Books, Eugene.

Murdock, George Peter
1938   Notes on the Tenino, Molala, and Paiute of Oregon. *American Anthropologist* 40:395-402.

1980   The Tenino Indians. *Ethnology* 19(2):129-149.

Oetting, Albert C.
1989   *Villages and Wetlands Adaptations in the Northern Great Basin: Chronology and Land Use in the Lake Abert-Chewaucan Marsh Basin, Lake County, Oregon.* University of Oregon Anthropological Papers 41. Eugene.

Polk, Michael R.
1976   Cultural Resource Inventory of the John Day River Canyon. Report on file with the Bureau of Land Management, Prineville District, Prineville.

Ray, Verne F.
1942   *Culture Element Distributions: XXII, Plateau.* University of California Anthropological Records 8(2). Berkeley.

Ray, Verne F. and Others
1938   Tribal Distribution in Eastern Oregon and Adjacent Regions. *American Anthropologist* 40:384-415.

Rice, Harvey S.
1985   *Native American Dwellings and Attendant Structures of the Southern Plateau.* Eastern Washington University Reports in Archaeology and History 100-44, Cheney.

Ross, Richard E.
1963   *Prehistory of the Round Butte Area, Jefferson County, Oregon.* Master's thesis, Department of Anthropology, University of Oregon, Eugene.

Stewart, Omer C.
1941   *Culture Element Distributions: XIV, Northern Paiute.* University of California Anthropological Records 2(3):361-446. Berkeley.

Suphan, Robert J.
  1974   *Oregon Indians II.*   Garland Series in American Indian Ethnohistory, New York.

Wilde, James D., Rinita Dalan, Steve Wilke, Ralph Keuler, and John Foss
  1983   *Cultural Resource Survey and Evaluations of Select Parcels in the John Day Reservoir, Oregon.*   Geo-Recon International, Seattle.   Submitted to the U. S. Army Corps of Engineers, Portland District.

Willamette Kayak and Canoe Club
  1986   *Soggy Sneakers Guide to Oregon Rivers.*   Corvallis.

ANOTHER LOOK AT PROJECTILE POINTS AS TEMPORAL INDICATORS

Albert C. Oetting
Heritage Research Associates, Inc.

ABSTRACT

The morphological stability of projectile point types and their use as temporal indicators has been debated in a series of recent papers. Replicative technological studies suggest that Great Basin dart points may pass through a variety of morphological forms as a result of use and rejuvenation, making their form a by-product of breakage and reworking, not an indicator of age. These arguments are reviewed and are found wanting, since they fail to account for the phenomena that originally suggested that point types might have temporal significance: discernible patterns in artifact assemblages and type correlations with radiocarbon ages.

The recognition that certain types of objects might be chronologically significant and that similar objects found elsewhere should be of similar age is based on the *index fossil* concept first identified in geology. Archaeologists have adopted and refined this concept by developing "temporal types," artifact classifications which focus on morphological differences that vary with their age, and "typological cross-dating," assigning age spans to similar artifact types found in other parts of a region (Thomas 1979, 1981). The distribution of a temporally sensitive artifact type through time reflects its evolution--the style is introduced, flourishes for a period of time, and then declines in popularity, forming a distinctive lenticular, or "battleship-shaped" distribution curve when such types are seriated (Ford 1962). Temporal types and their associated age spans have been developed by trial and error, through observing and recognizing shifting patterns in stratigraphically, or radiometrically, controlled contexts, delineating types and ages based on these patterns, and testing the resulting types against independent stratigraphic and radiometric evidence at other locations.

In the Great Basin, analysis of recurring artifact patterns and the application of these principles over many years has suggested that particular projectile point types are chronologically significant (summarized in Heizer and Hester 1978; Hester 1973; Holmer 1986; Thomas 1981; Wilde 1985). Coarse-grained temporal spans of point types have been developed, with general chronological periods spanning 2,000 years or more (Table 1, Figure 1). It was realized that the method and results could be skewed or obscured in individual applications through a variety of factors, including misclassification,

Table 1. Temporal spans of Great Basin point types[1]

Projectile Point Type	Estimated Age Span
Desert Side-notched (DSN)	750 BP -- historic
Cottonwood Triangular (CT)	1,000 BP -- historic
Rosegate Series (RGS)	2,000 BP -- historic
Elko Series (ES)[2]	4,500 BP -- 1,000 BP[3]
Gatecliff Contracting Stem (GCS)	3,800 BP -- 2,200 BP
Gatecliff Split Stem (GSS)	5,000 BP -- 2,700 BP
Humboldt Concave Base (HCB)	6,000 BP -- 1,300 BP
Willow Leaf/Cascade (WL)	10,000 BP -- 1,000 BP
Northern Side-notched (NSN)	7,000 BP -- 4,000 BP
Great Basin Stemmed (GBS)	11,000 BP -- 8,000 BP

1 based on Thomas 1981, Wilde 1985, Oetting 1989
2 varieties combined
3 does not include Wilde's early ELK2 (7,200 BP -- 5,800 BP)

stratigraphic mixing, "heirloom" reuse, and alteration through reworking (Thomas 1986a). In addition, the effectiveness of and confidence in temporal types and cross-dating diminishes as distance to firmly dated typological sequences increases (Beck 1984, 1988). Nevertheless, the general usefulness of temporal markers has been accepted by most Great Basin archaeologists.

REPLICATION AND THE "INSTABILITY" OF TYPES

However, the "typological stability" and, hence, temporal sensitivity of projectile point forms, has been questioned on the basis of recent replicative technological studies conducted by Jeffrey Flenniken and his co-workers. In their initial presentations these researchers argued that projectile points may pass through a variety of morphological forms during the course of their use-life, the various forms resulting from repeated cycles of use, breakage, and rejuvenation (Flenniken and Raymond 1986; Flenniken and Wilke 1986). Thus, rather than representing different "types" of points, forms which might have been used by particular groups or during distinct chronological periods, the morphological forms of projectile points were, in large, simply the by-products of breakage and reworking.

Subsequent papers by Flenniken and Wilke have continued this line of reasoning, but have restricted their arguments to broad-necked point forms, those thought to have been used to tip atlatl darts (Flenniken and Wilke 1989; Wilke and Flenniken 1990,

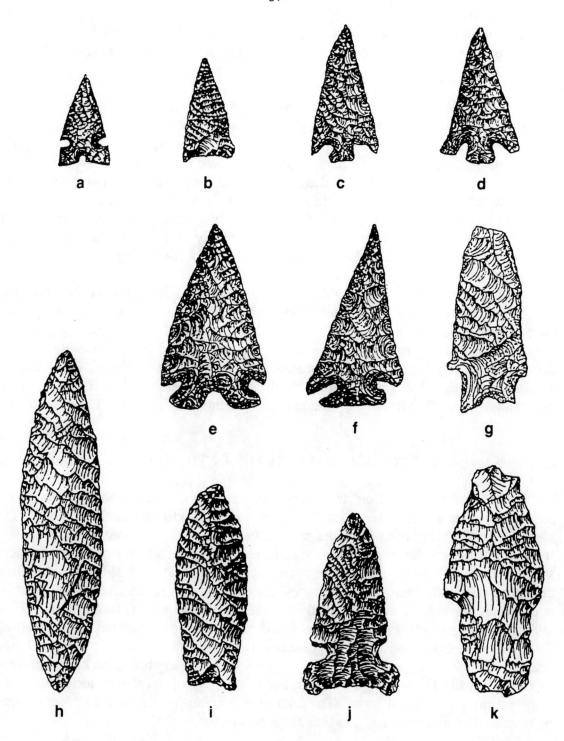

Figure 1. Examples of Great Basin point types: a, Desert Side-notched; b, Cottonwood Triangular; c-d, Rosegate series; e-f, Elko series; g, Gatecliff series; h, Willow Leaf/Cascade; i, Humboldt Concave Base; j, Northern Side-notched; k, Great Basin Stemmed.

arrowpoints and Early Holocene stemmed points) can indeed function as viable temporal types reflects the effectiveness of rebuttals to the original rejuvenation argument (Thomas 1986a, 1986b).

They base their current conclusions on the replicative manufacture, use, and rejuvenation of broad-necked points. Replicative experiments found that dart points were often damaged in use, but were designed to minimize this damage by breaking in certain ways. Damaged tips, barbs, and bases could be reflaked to render the point serviceable again. These fracture patterns facilitated reuse but often resulted in morphological changes to the hafting element, which, of course, could alter the point's "type" (Figure 2). The morphological form of discarded worn-out or broken points, then, might bear no resemblance to the specimen's original form, or to any of its intermediate rejuvenated forms, making typologies based on morphological attributes meaningless.

These studies have been useful in exploring the design and function of dart points, but conclusions regarding the efficacy of point types do not seem fully justified. They have demonstrated that the use-life of broad-necked points *could* be long and morphologically variable, but they have not demonstrated that this morphological variability, in fact, *did* occur with any regularity during prehistoric times (Thomas 1986a). This, then, is the basic question-- does rejuvenation actually account for enough broad-necked forms to invalidate their effectiveness as time markers (Bettinger et al. 1991; Thomas 1986a)?

TYPOLOGICAL PATTERNS IN THE DATA

The replication position, that morphological "types" are essentially random by-products of maintenance and rejuvenation technologies, fails to adequately account for the observations that suggested point types might have temporal significance in the first place. If the morphological forms of points are incidental by-products of reworking, then there should be no discernible patterns to their occurrence in stratified deposits, in their distribution across the landscape, or in their associations with radiocarbon ages. That is, if points are repaired to most efficiently use the remaining mass (Flenniken and Wilke 1989:152) without regard to form, there should be little or no consistency to the resulting forms. As Flenniken and Wilke's rejuvenation flow diagrams illustrate (Figure 2, see also Flenniken and Wilke 1989:154-155, Figures 1 and 2), any broad-necked point form should be equally likely to co-occur with any other-- except in cases of identical breaks being repaired in identical ways. That such stratigraphic, spatial, and age patterns *can* be discerned at sites seriously weakens these arguments.

The seriated stratigraphic patterning of Gatecliff points underlying Elko points underlying Rosegate points at Gatecliff Shelter in Nevada (Thomas 1983:177) is an exceptionally well-delineated example of stratigraphic relationships between types, but such relationships are seen at sites across the Great Basin, including in the northern Great

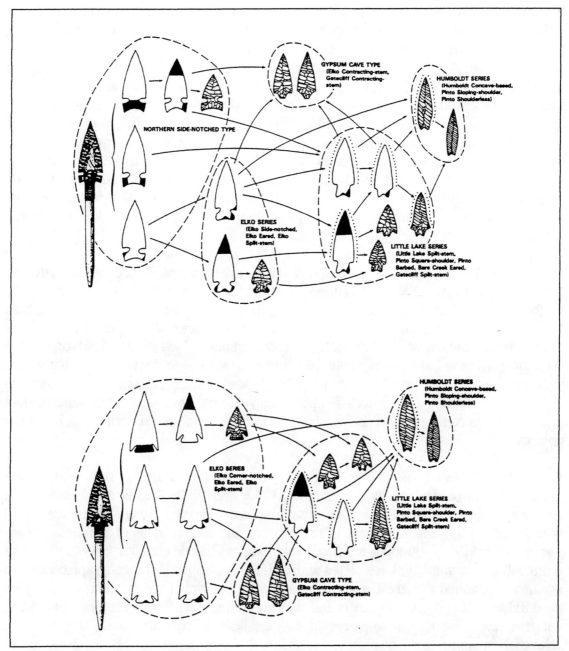

Figure 2. Rejuvenation flow charts as presented in arguments by Flenniken and Wilke (after Flenniken and Wilke 1989:154-155). *(Flenniken and Wilke's notes for flow chart: "Morphological and typological evolution in use-life of Elko Corner notched dart points. Black indicates use-damage, except for basal concavities or bifurcations, which commonly occur in fitting the point to the foreshaft. Arrows indicate rejuvenation options. Dots indicate resharpening and thinning to regain acceptable width/thickness ratio. Complete but functionally exhausted points likely to have been discarded intact are detailed.")*

Basin the Rodriguez and Silent Snake Springs sites in northwestern Nevada, the Surprise Valley sites in northeastern California, and Dirty Shame Rockshelter or Skull Creek Dunes in southern Oregon (summarized and illustrated in Beck 1984). Seriations with distinctive lenticular, or "battleship-shaped," clusters should not occur if morphological form is completely variable (Figure 3). Likewise, assemblages that are dominated by single broad-necked point types, such as Gatecliff points at Hidden Cave (Thomas 1985) or Elko points at James Creek Shelter (Elston and Budy 1990), *should not occur* according to the rejuvenation approach-- unless 1) all the points were lost prior to rejuvenation, 2) all the points broke in the same way and could thus be repaired in the same manner, or 3) the points broke in different ways but were repaired in ways which resulted in a common shape. The first two alternatives are unlikely, while the third would suggest that a particular morphological form *was* sought, which would reinforce the usefulness of the typological approach.

Spatial distributions of point styles across large regions should not be patterned if types are random. Yet the Northern Side-notched point style is rare outside of the northern Great Basin (and Columbia Plateau) while the Gatecliff/ Pinto bifurcate base style is common in the southern and central Great Basin, but is less so in the north (Beck 1984; Heizer and Hester 1978; Holmer 1986; Thomas 1981). Analysis of surface assemblages in the Lake Abert region of south-central Oregon demonstrates that spatial patterns of types are observable within smaller regions as well (Oetting 1989). Northern Side-notched points and Gatecliff Split Stem points have restricted and distinct distributions in comparison to one another and to other broad-necked forms such as Elko points.

Robert Heizer and James Hester began compiling a list of radiocarbon ages associated with particular point styles in the 1960s and 1970s (Hester and Heizer 1973; Heizer and Hester 1978). They found that certain point types did tend to be correlated with particular age spans, at least in the western and central areas of the Great Basin. James Wilde (1985), building on these compilations, has tabulated a larger number of radiocarbon determinations associated with point types from a wider geographic area and again demonstrated that these ages do cluster with individual types. Some point types have tighter age clusters than others and thus are more discriminating temporal markers, but that *any* clustering is apparent in this analysis is contrary to the logic of the rejuvenation approach.

DISTRIBUTION AND AGE OF ELKO POINTS
IN THE FORT ROCK VALLEY CAVES

Typological patterning and age-span can be explored using projectile points in the caves of Fort Rock Valley in Oregon. These points were among the collections examined by Flenniken and Wilke (1989), who found that the broad-necked point assemblages here paralleled their replicated assemblages of worn out and discarded points-- implying that

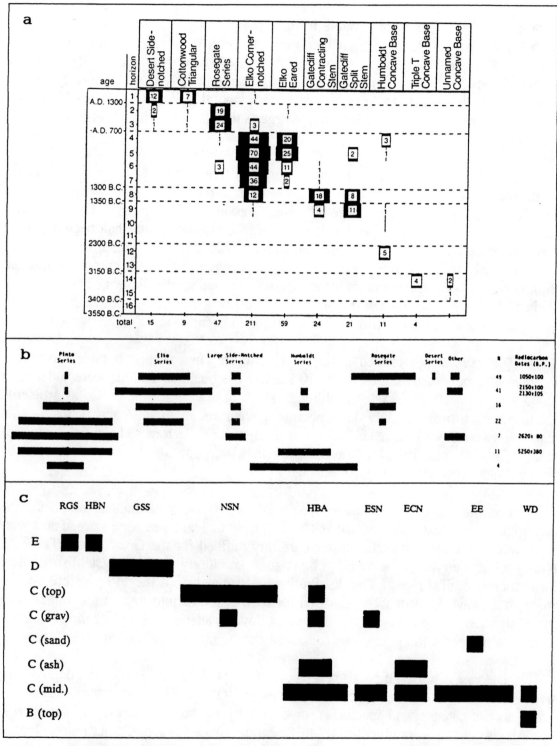

Figure 3. Seriations of projectile point types at selected sites in the Great Basin; a, Gatecliff Shelter, Nevada (from Thomas 1983); b, Rodriguez and Silent Snake Springs sites, Nevada (from Beck 1984); c, Skull Creek Dunes, Oregon (after Wilde 1985).

the broad-necked points were variable in their morphology and therefore not useful as chronological indicators. The original reports on the Fort Rock research documented that Elko series points had been found in 7,000 year old, pre-Mazama, contexts in the Connley Caves (Bedwell 1969) and subsequent researchers have cited these early ages as evidence that Elko points are not very discrete temporal indicators (Aikens 1982). A brief re-examination of the data, however, suggests that these interpretations are not fully warranted.

Nine caves or shelters, including a cluster of five small caves known as Connley Caves, were tested by Stephen Bedwell and crews from the University of Oregon in 1966 and 1967, under the general guidance of Luther Cressman (Bedwell 1969, 1973; Bedwell and Cressman 1971). The upper levels of all of these sheltered sites had been damaged to some degree by relic collectors, but the damage was primarily limited to the interior areas of the shelters. Therefore, excavations were conducted at cave entrances near the dripline and in some interior units below presumably undisturbed layers of Mazama ash (Bedwell 1973:14-19). In these interior units the disturbed sediments above the ash were mechanically stripped away with a backhoe prior to excavation.

The excavations yielded a variety of cultural, faunal, and botanical remains. Twenty-eight radiocarbon ages, from 10 sites, were obtained and all were older than 3,000 BP (Bedwell 1973:35-36). Although Bedwell used a sample of 1,500 projectile points for classification, only 116 specimens were found in the cave deposits-- the remainder were from surface collections made by relic collectors. The entire sample of 1,500 points was classified into a typology with 43 morphological types, developed by Bedwell and Cressman for this collection.

For the current study these specimens were not re-examined. Instead, the descriptions and illustrations of Bedwell's 43 morphological types were studied and these types were re-assigned into the classes currently defined for the Great Basin (Table 2). Nearly all of the types were found to be cognate or closely similar to established Great Basin morphological types. The distribution and frequency of the 116 projectile points found in the cave deposits were tabulated for each of the various excavation units (Table 3). Only these 116 points were used in the following analysis. Eight of the excavation units yielding projectile points also contained one or more radiocarbon ages (Table 4).

The vast majority of broad-necked projectile points found in the cave deposits can be classified as Elko series specimens (Table 3). Of the 53 specimens classified in a broad-necked category, 45 specimens, or 84.9% of the dart points, can be identified as Elko series points. As outlined above, this clear dominance of a particular morphological shape contradicts the Flenniken and Wilke notion of variable dart point morphology. Rather than resulting in a random assortment of morphological styles, nearly all of the broad-necked points are corner-notched with expanding bases. A counter-argument could

Table 2. Bedwell's point types and corresponding Great Basin types

Bedwell Type[1]	Great Basin Type
1, 4	Willow Leaf
2, 9, 10, 16, 17, 18, 19, 22, 23	Great Basin Stemmed
3, 6, 12	biface knives/formed bifaces
5	preform
7, 13	contracting base points[2]
8	Humboldt Basal Notched
11, 14	Fluted (?)
15	Black Rock Concave Base[3]
20, 21	Gatecliff Contracting Base
24, 37	miscellaneous broad-necked
25, 26, 27	Rosegate series
28	Desert Side-notched
29, 32, 34, 35, 36, 39	Elko Corner-notched
30, 31, 33	Elko Eared
38	Gatecliff Split Stem
40, 42, 43	miscellaneous side-notched
41	Northern Side-notched

1-described and illustrated in Bedwell 1969 and 1973; 2-no Great Basin cognates, see Columbia River CB classes (Dumond and Minor 1983); 3-defined in Clewlow 1968:13-15

be made that the points discarded in caves went through several morphological changes in their use-life and all ended up corner-notched, simply by chance. This seems unlikely. It is also immaterial if this morphological style, no matter how it came about, can be usefully associated with a particular age span.

The effectiveness of Elko series points as temporal indicators has been questioned since individual specimens have been found in contexts predating the Mount Mazama eruption, broadening the temporal span and thus decreasing the temporal discrimination of the type (Aikens 1982; Hanes 1988; Holmer 1986; Wilde 1985). Without closer inspection this seems warranted since *individual* Elko points were associated with radiocarbon ages older than 7,000 BP. However, if the *population* of Elko series specimens is considered, a somewhat different interpretation can be made.

The Fort Rock area investigations produced 34 Elko series points in cave deposits that also yielded radiocarbon ages (Table 4). The stratigraphic positioning of the points revealed that 27 of the 34 points (79.4%) occurred in levels associated with or above ages of 4,450 BP or less (Table 4), while only six (17.6%) were in levels below Mazama ash.

Table 3. Projectile point assemblages from caves in the Fort Rock area[1]

Site /Unit	DSN	RGS	EE[2]	ECN[2]	GSS	GCS	HBN	WL	NSN	GBS	FLU[3]	Other[4]	Total
Fort Rock Cave													
#4	-	2	-	1	-	-	-	-	-	1	-	-	4
#5	-	1	-	1	-	-	-	-	1	2	-	-	5
#6	-	1	-	-	-	-	-	-	-	2	-	-	3
#7	-	-	1	-	-	-	-	-	-	-	-	-	1
#9	-	-	1	-	-	-	-	-	-	1	-	-	2
#10[5]	-	2	1	1	-	-	-	2	1	3	-	-	10
#11	-	1	-	-	1	-	-	-	-	1	1	-	4
Cougar Mtn. Cave													
#2	-	-	-	-	-	-	-	1	-	-	-	1	2
Connley Cave													
#1	-	1	3	4	1	1	1	-	-	-	-	1	12
#3[5]	-	3	-	-	-	-	-	-	-	-	-	-	3
#3 ext.	-	-	-	-	-	-	-	-	-	1	-	-	1
#4A[5]	-	-	1	1	-	-	1	2	-	-	-	1	6
#4B[5]	-	-	-	1	-	-	-	-	-	5	-	-	6
#5A[5]	-	1	1	4	-	1	-	-	-	-	-	-	7
#5B[5]	-	-	2	3	-	-	-	-	-	3	3	1	12
#6[5]	1	1	2	5	2	-	-	1	-	1	1	2	16
Table Rock													
#2[5]	-	9	9	3	-	-	-	-	-	-	-	-	22
Total	1	22	21	24	4	2	3	6	2	20	5	6	116

1-data compiled from Bedwell 1969:Appendix V;
2-varieties combined to form Elko series;
3-FLU = Fluted (?);
4-Other includes contracting base, miscellaneous side-notched, miscellaneous broad-necked, and Black Rock Concave Base specimens;
5-radiocarbon ages obtained in these units.

One point (2.9%) was recovered from a level below an age of 4,450 BP and above an age of 8,550 BP. Thus, nearly 80% of the population of Elko points in this sample are less than 4,500 years old.

Curiously, and perhaps significantly, all six of the specimens associated with pre-Mazama ages were found in units that had disturbed upper levels. None of the units near cave driplines, units that were fully excavated through undisturbed sediments, produced

Table 4. Elko points and stratigraphically associated radiocarbon ages

| Site and Unit | ¹⁴C Age (RCYBP) | Level of Elko points | | | Total |
		Same	Above	Below	
Table Rock #2	3,060 ± 420	1	11	-	12
Connley Cave #5A	3,330 ± 110	2	2	-	4
Connley Cave #6	3,720 ± 270	1	5	1[1]	7
Connley Cave #4A	3,730 ± 90	1	1	-	2
Connley Cave #5A	4,320 ± 100	1	-	-	1
Fort Rock #10	4,450 ± 100	1	-	1[2]	2
Connley Cave #4B	7,240 ± 150	1	-	-	1
Connley Cave #5B	7,430 ± 140	2	2[3]	1	5
Total		10			34

1 - above age of 4,350±100 BP; 2 - above age of 8,550±150 BP; 3 below Mazama ash

any Elko series points in pre-Mazama contexts (Bedwell 1969: Appendix V). The only units yielding these points in early contexts were Connley Caves 4B and 5B-both of which were interior units where fill disturbed by pothunters had been mechanically stripped away down to the level of Mazama ash (Bedwell 1969: Appendix V). Rather than indicating an early age for Elko points in the Fort Rock Basin, the presence of Elko points in the uppermost levels of these units may, in fact, indicate that the pothunter disturbance was deeper than thought or the disturbed fill was not fully removed.

However, things are not quite that simple. The Fort Rock caves produced *no* radiocarbon ages between approximately 7,000 BP and 5,000 BP (Bedwell 1973:39). This lack has been interpreted as a hiatus in cave occupation, although it may only be a hiatus in dateable charcoal. However, we cannot *directly* compare the proportions and, hence, the popularity of Elko series points occurring before and after 5,000 BP in these caves. We will need to look to other sites in the region. Fortunately ongoing research by Cannon and Mehringer (Cannon 1992) and by the University of Oregon Fort Rock Prehistory Project (Jenkins 1992) are beginning to locate and document sites from this period. Thus far, it appears that points of the Northern Side-notched type are most common in the few cases where points are directly associated with radiocarbon ages. However, these data are still emerging, so this interpretation can only be tentative.

CONCLUSIONS

Still, it seems that the stratigraphic positioning and radiocarbon associations support a temporal span of about 5,000 BP to less than 3,000 BP for *most* Elko points in the Fort Rock area caves. Although a few points *may* be associated with older deposits these point styles do not seem to have become popular or common until the later period. This distribution, in fact, is exactly the kind expected for a temporal type--it is introduced, after a period of time it becomes popular, and then it fades away. It is important, then, to examine and use the populations and proportional frequencies of point types in assemblages and components, not just the presence, or absence, of individual specimens.

The two patterns represented in this Fort Rock Basin example--stratigraphic association of particular styles and association of particular styles with restricted age spans--are the hallmarks of temporal types that the rejuvenation approach and its assertion of typological randomness has failed to refute. Flenniken and his co-workers are certainly right that there are problems with point typologies and that, in some places, typological cross-dating is not very effective in dealing with time, but these difficulties are no reason to reject *all* typologies and cross-dating out-of-hand. Rather, archaeologists need to be cognizant of the various problems while attempting to classify potential time markers, we must assess the distribution of artifacts to determine if their use in a chronological framework appears warranted, and we must make judicious, rather than indiscriminate, use of these temporal types.

REFERENCES

Aikens, C. Melvin
    1982   Archaeology of the Northern Great Basin: An Overview. In *Man and Environment in the Great Basin*, edited by David B. Madsen and James F. O'Connell, pp. 139-155. SAA Papers No. 2. Society for American Archaeology, Washington, D.C.

Beck, Charlotte
    1984   *Steens Mountain Surface Archaeology: The Sites.* Ph.D. Dissertation, Department of Anthropology, University of Washington. Seattle.

    1988   Diffusion and Great Basin Chronology. Paper presented at the 21st Great Basin Anthropological Conference, Park City, Utah.

Bedwell, Stephen F.
    1969   *Prehistory and Environment of the Pluvial Fort Rock Lake Area of South Central Oregon.* Ph.D. Dissertation, Department of Anthropology, University of Oregon. Eugene.

    1973   *Fort Rock Basin: Prehistory and Environment.* University of Oregon Books, Eugene.

Bedwell, Stephen F. and Luther S. Cressman
1971 Fort Rock Report: Prehistory and Environment of the Pluvial Fort Rock Lake Area of South-Central Oregon. In *Great Basin Anthropological Conference 1970, Selected Papers*, edited by C. Melvin Aikens. University of Oregon Anthropological Papers 1:1-25. Eugene.

Bettinger, Robert L., James F. O'Connell, and David H. Thomas
1991 Projectile Points as Time Markers in the Great Basin. *American Anthropologist* 93(1):166-172.

Cannon, William J.
1992 Establishing a Stratigraphic Chronology for the Fort Rock Basin. Paper presented at the 45th Northwest Anthropological Conference, Burnaby, British Columbia.

Clewlow, C. William
1968 Surface Archaeology of the Black Rock Desert. In *Papers on the Archaeology of Western Great Basin*, pp. 1-93. Reports of the University of California Archaeological Survey 73.

Dumond, Don E. and Rick Minor
1983 *Archaeology in the John Day Reservoir: The Wildcat Canyon Site, 35-GM-9*. University of Oregon Anthropological Papers 30. Eugene.

Elston, Robert G., and Elizabeth E. Budy (editors)
1990 *The Archaeology of James Creek Shelter*. University of Utah Anthropological Papers 115. Salt Lake City.

Flenniken, J. Jeffrey and Anan W. Raymond
1986 Morphological Projectile Point Typology: Replication Experimentation and Technological Analysis. *American Antiquity* 51(3):603- 614.

Flenniken, J. Jeffrey and Philip J. Wilke
1986 The Flaked Stone Assemblage from Hogup Cave, Utah: Implications for Prehistoric Lithic Technology and Culture History in the Great Basin. Paper presented at the 20th Great Basin Anthropological Conference, Las Vegas, Nevada.

1989 Typology, Technology, and Chronology of Great Basin Dart Points. *American Anthropologist* 91(1):149-158.

Ford, James A.
1962 *A Quantitative Method for Deriving Cultural Chronology.* Pan American Union, Technical Manual 1. Reprinted 1972, Museum of Anthropology, University of Missouri-Columbia, Museum Brief 9.

Hanes, Richard C.
1988 *Lithic Assemblages of Dirty Shame Rockshelter: Changing Traditions in the Northern Intermontane.* University of Oregon Anthropological Papers 40. Eugene.

Heizer, Robert F. and Thomas R. Hester
1978 *Great Basin Projectile Points: Forms and Chronology.* Ballena Press Publications in Archaeology, Ethnology and History 10.

Hester, Thomas R.
1973 *Chronological Ordering in Great Basin Prehistory.* University of California Archaeological Research Facility Contributions 17.

Hester, Thomas R. and Robert F. Heizer
1973 *Review and Discussion of Great Basin Projectile Points: Forms and Chronology.* University of California Archaeological Research Facility, nonserial publication.

Holmer, Richard N.
1986 Common Projectile Points of the Intermountain West. In *Anthropology of the Desert West: Essays in Honor of Jesse D. Jennings*, edited by C.J. Condie and D.D. Fowler. University of Utah Anthropological Papers 110:89-115. Salt Lake City.

Jenkins, Dennis L.
1992 Early Neopluvial Marsh Side Occupations at the Big M Site. Paper presented at the 45th Northwest Anthropological Conference, Burnaby, British Columbia.

Oetting, Albert C.
1989 *Villages and Wetlands Adaptations in the Northern Great Basin: Chronology and Land Use in the Lake Abert-Chewaucan Marsh Basin, Lake County, Oregon.* University of Oregon Anthropological Papers 41. Eugene.

Thomas, David H.
1979 *Archaeology.* Holt, Rinehart, and Winston, New York.

1981 How to Classify Projectile Points from Monitor Valley, Nevada. *Journal of California and Great Basin Anthropology* 3(1):7-43.

1983   *The Archaeology of Monitor Valley: 2. Gatecliff Shelter.* Anthropological Papers of the American Museum of Natural History 59(1). New York.

1985   *The Archaeology of Hidden Cave, Nevada.* Anthropological Papers of the American Museum of Natural History 61(1). New York.

1986a   Points on Points: A Reply to Flenniken and Raymond. *American Antiquity* 51(3):619-627.

1986b   Contemporary Hunter-Gatherer Archaeology in America. In *Amercian Archaeology Past and Future: A Celebration of the Society for American Archaeology*, edited by David J. Meltzer, Don D. Fowler, and Jeremy A. Sabloff, pp. 237-276. Smithsonian Institution Press, Washington, D.C.

Wilde, James D.
  1985   *Prehistoric Settlements in the Northern Great Basin: Excavations and Collections Analysis in the Steens Mountain Area, Southeastern Oregon.* Ph.D. dissertation, Department of Anthropology, University of Oregon. Eugene.

Wilke, Philip J., and J. Jeffrey Flenniken
  1990   The Long and Short of Great Basin Archaic Chronology. Paper presented at the 22nd Great Basin Anthropological Conference, Reno, Nevada.

  1991   Missing the Point: Rebuttal to Bettinger, O'Connell, and Thomas. *American Anthropologist* 93(1):172-173.

PALEO POINT OCCURRENCES
IN THE WILLAMETTE VALLEY, OREGON

Thomas J. Connolly
State Museum of Anthropology, University of Oregon

ABSTRACT

Two projectile points are described from the Willamette Valley of Oregon which are consistent with terminal Pleistocene/Early Holocene types. Both artifacts were found in erosional contexts by recreationists, and subsequently reported to the State Museum of Anthropology at the University of Oregon. A Clovis point was found on the west side of the Fern Ridge Reservoir in the Long Tom River drainage. A Western Stemmed point was found in an erosional slump bordering the Lookout Point Reservoir within the Middle Fork Willamette River drainage. The context of these finds and the implications for locating cultural remains of comparable age are briefly discussed.

The earliest evidence of human occupation in western North America that is accepted without controversy is associated with fluted (Clovis and Folsom) and stemmed (known by a variety of names including Western Stemmed and Windust) projectile point complexes. Previously unreported examples of each of these types--one Clovis point and one Western Stemmed point--are presented here. Both were surface occurrences found in the upper Willamette Valley (Figure 1) several decades ago, and recently brought to the attention of the author.

BACKGROUND

From sites on the Great Plains and American Southwest, a chronological relationship between Clovis and stemmed point assemblages has been well documented as a gradual development from early fluted points to later stemmed forms (e.g., Frison 1978; Frison and Stanford 1982). In the Far West, however, such a relationship is generally assumed, but has not been unquestionably demonstrated. Bryan (1980, 1988) argues that stemmed points are at least as old as fluted points in the Far West.

The term Paleo-Indian, though familiar to North American prehistorians, has an

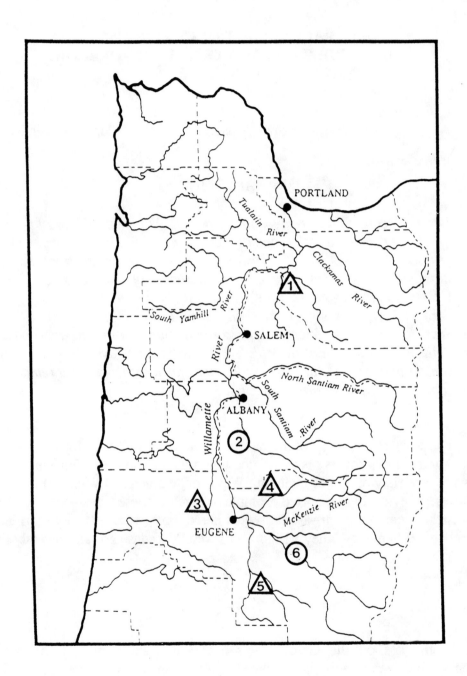

Figure 1. Distribution of reported Clovis (△) and Western Stemmed (○) projectile points in the Willamette Valley.

1. *Canby Clovis (Heinz 1971)*
2. *Tangent stemmed point (Cressman 1947)*
3. *Fern Ridge Clovis*
4. *Mohawk Valley Clovis (Allely 1975)*
5. *Cottage Grove Clovis (Minor 1985)*
6. *Lookout Point Reservoir stemmed point*

imprecise meaning. Some have used the term to refer to cultural assemblages older than about 7000 years, while others restrict the term to fluted point assemblages with extinct megafauna such as mammoth and mastodon. For some, the term identifies a big game hunting tradition that contrasts with later Archaic Period broad-spectrum hunter-gatherers. While associations of extinct megafauna and Clovis artifacts have been frequently reported in some areas of the continent, such associations are rare in the Far West. Effective arguments have been presented that the earliest occupants of this area differed from their descendants more in their tools than in their lifeways, prompting the use of such terms as Paleo-Archaic to identify the Western Clovis complex (Willig 1989).

Clovis and Folsom fluted projectile points recovered from dated contexts elsewhere on the continent fall within the range of 11,500 to about 10,500 radiocarbon years ago. Recent stratigraphic dating of the East Wenatchee Clovis site in central Washington state suggests an occupation soon after the deposition of volcanic pumice from the 11,250 BP eruption of Glacier Peak (Mehringer and Foit 1990).

To date, six fluted points have been reported from western Oregon outside of the Willamette Valley, two from the upper Rogue River basin (Deich 1976; Lalande and Fagan 1982), one on the lower Winchuck River a few miles inland from the coast in extreme southwestern Oregon (Hemphill 1990), two from the Umpqua River basin (Hanes 1976; Minor 1985), and one from the central Oregon coast (Minor 1985). Three previous Clovis point occurrences have been reported from the Willamette Valley (Figure 2), including one near Canby (Heinz 1971), one from the Mohawk River gravels north of Springfield (Allely 1975), and one from the Cottage Grove vicinity (Minor 1985).

Western Stemmed projectile points have a much longer range of occurrence than fluted points, having been found with associated radiocarbon dates ranging from prior to 11,000 years ago to about 7000 years ago. Few occurrences of Western Stemmed points have been reported from western Oregon. Cressman (1947) described a stemmed point found in a drainage slough near the town of Tangent (Figure 2). Remains of a mammoth, including vertebrae, a tooth, and part of a tusk, were also reportedly found in the same locality, but the association between the mammoth remains and the artifact could not be firmly established.

THE FERN RIDGE CLOVIS POINT

Like the others known from western Oregon, the Fern Ridge Clovis specimen was a surface discovery, found in the Long Tom River basin west of Eugene. It was recovered in about 1970 from shallow water at the edge of the low pool range of Fern Ridge Reservoir, by Ron Norton, a resident of the nearby community of Veneta. The find locality was visited in the fall of 1989 by a small party that included Mr. Norton, Dr. Patricia McDowell of the University of Oregon Geography Department, and the author. Fire-cracked rock and chipped stone debris, including cherts of similar colors to the Clovis artifact, were observed. Occasional tree stumps in the find area were suspended above the existing ground surface by a minimum of 20 cm, indicating that erosion within the reservoir pool had stripped the former ground surface. Dr. McDowell excavated a small core (to about 30 cm) into the fine clay of the reservoir floor and observed no soil characteristics. It was concluded that the artifact was transported to the find area or deflated from an eroded soil unit.

The Fern Ridge Clovis point (Figure 3) is made from a caramel to red-brown chert. Its overall length is 82.9 mm, while the medial length (tip to basal indentation) is 78.1 mm. The extreme distal tip exhibits an impact fracture, but the effect on the overall length measurement can be no more than a few millimeters. The maximum thickness is 8.2 mm, maximum width is 31.9 mm, and the specimen weighs 25.85 g.

The first flute flake removal scar measures 20.3 mm long and 14.8 mm wide, and terminates in a hinge fracture. The opposing flute flake scar has a feather termination. It is 29.4 mm long and 11.7 mm wide. Both lateral margins have been ground, one from the proximal tip for about 38 mm, the other for 34 mm.

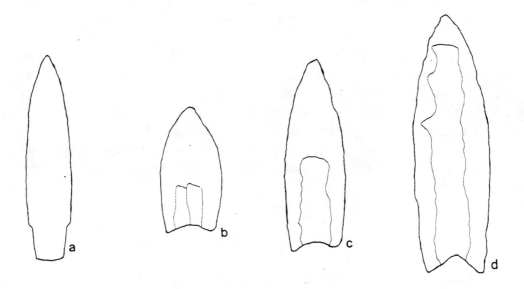

Figure 2. Outline drawings of previously reported fluted and Western Stemmed projectile points from the Willamette Valley, all 50% actual size.

a. *Tangent stemmed point*   b. *Canby Clovis*
c. *Mohawk Valley Clovis*   d. *Cottage Grove Clovis*

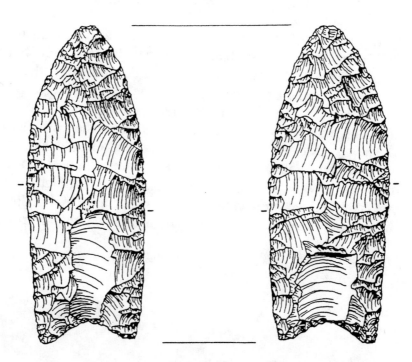

Figure 3. The Fern Ridge Reservoir Clovis point (actual size). Dashes mark extent of basal grinding.

THE LOOKOUT RESERVOIR STEMMED POINT

Harold Young, an amateur geologist from Eugene, reports finding a stemmed point near the high pool level of Lookout Point Reservoir in the mid 1970s. Mr. Young observed that the artifact and its soil matrix had recently slumped from a severely eroded cutbank at the reservoir edge. The precise location of the find has not been field checked by the author, but the situation suggests the possibility that the artifact may have been in a buried and potentially datable context.

The Lookout Reservoir stemmed point is made of a reddish-brown chert. Its overall length is 73.7 mm, and maximum width is 29.9 mm. The neck width, measured at the base of the shoulders, is 23.5 mm, and the maximum base width measured at the proximal end of the stem is 25.3 mm. The stem length, from the proximal end to the base of the shoulders, is 12.8 mm. Maximum thickness is 8.5 mm and the point weighs 20.30 g.

The lateral edges of the base have been blunted by grinding. In addition, the proximal end of the blade forward from the shoulders has been lightly ground (Figure 4).

FURTHER CONSIDERATIONS

Two factors have worked to limit our view of the ancient human occupations of the Willamette Valley. First is a probable small population which would have left a minimal impression on the landscape in terms of discarded tools and other cultural debris. More importantly has been the landscape history of the valley. Geomorphic study of the Long Tom River basin has shown that floodplain development has been dominated by vertical accretion of sediments, punctuated by episodes of erosion (Freidel 1989; Freidel et al. 1989). The processes of sediment deposition and erosion have been operating throughout the Willamette Valley for some 10,000 years subsequent to the occupations of the first Oregonians. While this review shows that ancient artifacts are present in the valley, they are likely buried on ancient surfaces under tons of floodplain sediments. Those which have been recovered and reported are invariably found in erosional contexts.

Figure 4. The Lookout Point Reservoir stemmed point (actual size). Dashes mark extent of basal grinding.

In light of this, my final sentiment is a grateful acknowledgment of Ron Norton and Harold Young for recognizing the significance of their chance discoveries, and for bringing them to light. It is perhaps with the enlightened assistance of a public knowledgeable and respectful of this area's cultural past that we will eventually come to know the human details of those cultures in the intimate manner that eludes us today.

ACKNOWLEDGEMENTS

The Fern Ridge Clovis point is in the possession of Mr. Norton; the Lookout Reservoir Stemmed Point was donated to the State Museum of Anthropology at the University of Oregon. I would like to especially thank John Stamp for his role in bringing the Fern Ridge Clovis point to my attention. The Clovis point (Figure 3) was drawn by Kevin McCornack, the stemmed point (Figure 4) was illustrated by Lance Peterson.

REFERENCES

Allely, Steven
1975   A Clovis Point from the Mohawk River Valley, Western Oregon. In *Archaeological Studies in the Willamette Valley, Oregon*, edited by C. Melvin Aikens, pp. 549-552. University of Oregon Anthropological Papers 8. Eugene.

Bryan, Alan L.
1980   The Stemmed Point Tradition: An Early Technological Tradition in Western North America. In *Anthropological Papers in Honor of Earl H. Swanson, Jr.*, edited by C. N. Warren and D. R. Tuohy, pp. 77-107. Special Publication of the Idaho State Museum of Natural History. Pocatello.

1988   The Relationship of the Stemmed Point and Fluted Point Traditions in the Great Basin. In *Early Human Occupation in Far Western North America: The Clovis-Archaic Interface*, edited by J. A. Willig, C. M. Aikens, and J. L. Fagan, pp. 53-74. Nevada State Museum Anthropological Papers 21. Carson City.

Cressman, Luther S.
1947   Further Information on Projectile Points from Oregon. *American Antiquity* 13:177-179.

Deich, Lyman
1976   Fluted Point Base from Western Oregon. Manuscript on file at the Bureau of Land Management, Medford District.

Freidel, Dorothy E.
1989   *Alluvial Stratigraphy in Relation to Archaeological Features on the Long Tom River Floodplain, Veneta, Oregon*. Master's thesis, Department of Geography, University of Oregon, Eugene.

Freidel, Dorothy E., Lynn Peterson, Patricia F. McDowell, and Thomas J. Connolly
 1989   *Alluvial Stratigraphy and Human Prehistory of the Veneta Area, Long Tom River Valley, Oregon.* Oregon State Museum of Anthropology. Submitted to the National Park Service and the Oregon State Historic Preservation Office, Salem, Oregon.

Frison, George C.
 1978   *Prehistoric Hunters of the High Plains.* Academic Press, New York.

Frison, George C. and Dennis J. Stanford
 1982   *The Agate Basin Site: A Record of the Paleo-Indian Occupation of the Northwestern High Plains.* Academic Press, New York.

Hanes, Richard C.
 1976   Umpqua Valley Prehistory: A First Step Toward Understanding Aboriginal Adaptations to the Southwest Oregon Interior Region. Manuscript on file at the Bureau of Land Management, Roseburg District.

Heinz, Fred
 1971   Another Clovis Point. *Screenings* 20(7).

Hemphill, Claudia B.
 1990   Test Excavations at the Winchuck Site (35CU176), 1989. Report on file at the Chetco Ranger District, Siskiyou National Forest, Brookings.

Lalande, Jeff and John Fagan
 1982   Possible Clovis Point Find--Butte Falls. *Current Archaeological Happenings in Oregon* 7(1):10.

Mehringer, Peter J., Jr., and Franklin F. Foit, Jr.
 1990   Volcanic Ash Dating of the Clovis Cache at East Wenatchee, Washington. *National Geographic Research,* 6(4):495-503.

Minor, Rick
 1985   Paleo-Indians in Western Oregon: A Description of Two Fluted Projectile Points. *Northwest Anthropological Research Notes* 19(1):33-40.

Willig, Judith A.
 1989   *Paleo-Archaic Broad-Spectrum Adaptations at the Pleistocene-Holocene Boundary in Far Western North America.* Ph.D. dissertation, Department of Anthropology, University of Oregon, Eugene.

PATTERNS OF LITHIC PROCUREMENT AND REDUCTION AT THE NEWBERRY CRATER OBSIDIAN QUARRIES

Thomas J. Connolly
State Museum of Anthropology, University of Oregon

Robert R. Musil
State Museum of Anthropology, University of Oregon

ABSTRACT

The distribution of lithic reduction activities over time and across the landscape forms a pattern that is a function of the user group's mobility with respect to various resource needs. Identifying patterns in reduction debris at specific activity sites is a first step in modeling broader prehistoric cultural systems. The goals of this paper are 1) to undertake a technological analysis of lithic debitage employing <u>quantifiable</u> and <u>replicable</u> categories, 2) to evaluate attributes of the lithic debitage in the context of other assemblage attributes (including lithic reduction products), and 3) to use these data to document how lithic procurement strategies were employed across the landscape by mobile cultural groups. The analysis is based on fieldwork conducted in 1990 at a series of sites within the Newberry Volcano caldera in central Oregon, a locality known for its flows of high quality obsidian glass. Sites in the study included a quarry at the edge of an obsidian flow (35DS485), near-quarry lithic reduction workshops (35DS219, 35DS220, and 35DS486), and an apparent base camp (35DS34) located several kilometers from the nearest obsidian flow. The study demonstrates that the metric variables recorded vary as a function of distance from the material source. For the debitage variables of platform thickness and mean flake size, this function takes the form of a logarithm curve, with most dramatic differences seen with close proximity to the material source (in this case, within about 1000 m), then leveling out as distance to source increases.

One of the products of volcanic eruptions in the caldera of Newberry Volcano is high quality obsidian glass that served as an attractive source of tool stone for prehistoric inhabitants of the region. Previous archaeological work in the crater (Scott 1985; Flenniken 1987; Flenniken and Ozbun 1988; Ozbun 1991; Connolly 1991) suggests that cultural activities centered on quarrying this obsidian and the production of bifacial quarry blanks for transport out of the crater.

The present analysis is based on fieldwork conducted in 1990 at a series of sites in the crater that include a quarry at the edge of an obsidian flow (35DS485), near-quarry lithic reduction workshops (35DS219, 35DS220, and 35DS486) and a probable base camp (35DS34). The goals of the work are to 1) undertake a technological analysis of lithic debitage employing quantifiable and replicable categories, 2) evaluate attributes of the lithic debitage in the context of other assemblage attributes (i.e., lithic reduction *products*) and 3) use those data to document how strategies of lithic procurement and use were employed within larger land use systems of mobile cultural groups.

Obsidian Resources in Newberry Crater

Newberry Volcano is a broad, gently sloping volcanic cone covering over 600 square miles, centered about 20 miles southeast of the community of Bend in central Oregon. The caldera of the volcano is about 5 miles across, and holds scenic Paulina and East Lakes. The caldera also contains a number of vents that have been active throughout the Holocene; at least six significant volcanic events have been identified within the last 10,000 years (MacLeod et al. 1982; MacLeod and Sherrod 1988), most of which have produced new obsidian flows.

A number of Pleistocene-age obsidian deposits are exposed in the caldera (Figure 1), including the Northeast Flow, which oozed from the northeast rim and spilled into East Lake, and scattered occurrences of obsidian on the south rim south of the Big Obsidian Flow. The large Buried Obsidian Flow, probably of terminal Pleistocene age, may have been the most important obsidian quarry in the caldera prior to 6000 years ago, before it was deeply buried by Mazama ash and other Holocene tephras from within the crater. The Interlake, Game Hut and Central Pumice Cone flows probably date to just several hundred years after the Mazama eruption. The East Lake Flows are thought to be about 3500 years old. The most recent volcanic activity in the crater, about 1300 years ago, produced the Big Obsidian Flow. All of the Holocene obsidian flows were extensively quarried.

LITHIC REDUCTION ANALYSIS

Background

The manufacture of chipped stone tools is a reductive technology, dependant principally on the mechanics of conchoidal fracture (Speth 1972; Crabtree 1974; Cotterell and Kamminga 1987). The nature of reductive systems in specific cultural contexts is, additionally, a function of the nature and occurrence of suitable rocks across the landscape, and the capacities of knappers to exert and control the forces of fracture on the available raw material (Collins 1975).

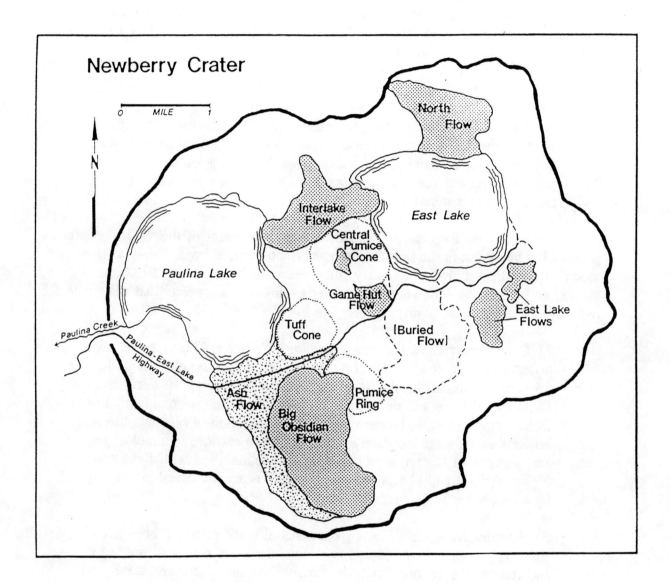

Figure 1. Major obsidian deposits within the Newberry caldera.

While lithic reduction may be considered a linear process, sequent technological stages have been noted by a number of researchers (e.g., Bradley 1975; Callahan 1979, 1991; Collins 1975; Frison and Bradley 1980; Muto 1971; Raymond 1986, 1989, Flenniken 1987). Bradley (1975) suggests that delineating stages in the reduction continuum permits the researcher to approach the original knapper's intent (see also Muto 1971). The following reduction stages, with reference to the Newberry Crater reduction sequence, may be identified (after Bradley 1975; Collins 1975; Callahan 1979, 1991; Flenniken 1987; Flenniken and Ozbun 1988):

1) *Selection of Raw Material at the Quarry.* This stage includes quarrying the raw stone, and preliminary testing of the material. At the Newberry Crater obsidian quarries (Flenniken 1987; Flenniken and Ozbun 1988), large flakes were apparently removed from *in situ* or free-standing boulders; lithic material with inclusions, weathering cracks, froth, or other imperfections was removed or discarded. Most cortex was also removed from selected material at the quarry.

Depending on the nature of the flakes, and the intent of the toolmaker, flakes produced at any point in the reduction sequence can be used immediately as minimally modified expedient tools. Alternately, they can be further modified to bifacial core, blanks, or tools. The following stages refer exclusively to objects that remain in the reductive system as bifacial artifacts.

2) *Core Preparation and Initial Trimming.* Collins (1975) notes that two primary options are available at this stage; one is shaping the parent piece (or core) and discarding the flakes as waste, or optimizing the detachment of desirable flakes and discarding the core as waste. A combination of these options may also be pursued. In the production of bifacial objects, artifacts at this stage frequently have thick cross sections, sinuous edges, and portions of the artifact surface may be unmodified with flake scars highly variable and widely spaced. Shaping is accomplished principally by direct freehand percussion flaking.

3) *Primary Trimming.* Shaping the material is the principal objective at this stage. Objects are reduced to a lenticular cross section, resulting in the removal of all original flake surfaces. Flake scars are closely to variably spaced. Objects at this stage may be reduced further to bifacial preforms and tools (see Stage 4, below), or stored or transported to be used as bifacial blanks and cores.

4) *Secondary Trimming and Thinning.* Cross sections are reduced to a flattened lenticular shape. Flake scars tend to be closely and regularly spaced. Opposing flake scars cross the implement midline. While most

reduction stage classifications assume bifacial symmetry, Skinner and Ainsworth (1990, 1991) have noted cases in which advanced reduction proceeded on a single (usually dorsal) face of an artifact, before the opposing (usually ventral) side was modified. They identify this production trajectory as the Unifacial-Biface Technique.

5) *Shaping*. This stage involves the final shaping of bifacial tools. The form is regularized, unmodified portions of the surface are absent, cross-sections are relatively thin and flat, and edges are straightened. The biface produced at this stage exhibits controlled regularly spaced flake scars and lacks irregular bumps or hinges on the surfaces. This is accomplished by soft hammer percussion or pressure flaking.

6) *Tool Use*.

7) *Optional Maintenance and Modification*. Used and broken tools may be rejuvenated by resharpening, or tools may be reworked into other desired tool forms.

Typically, the range of activities -- from lithic material procurement through tool production, use, and rejuvenation -- is distributed over time and across the landscape. The distribution of these activities forms a pattern that is a function of the user group's mobility with respect to various resource needs. Identifying and quantifying patterning in reduction debris at specific activity sites is a first step in modeling broader prehistoric cultural systems. Flenniken and Ozbun (1988:107-110; Ozbun 1991) observed that raw material selection, initial reduction, and primary thinning are well represented in Newberry crater, especially in material they recovered from excavations at the Big Obsidian Flow quarry site. Later stages of reduction and tool use are represented at other sites in the crater removed from quarries, but early stage reduction and primary thinning remain predominant activities. Quantifying such characterizations, however, is an essential element in documenting how lithic procurement and use strategies were employed within larger land use systems of mobile cultural groups. Our approach will be to examine formed artifact and lithic debitage assemblages to identify characteristics of each assemblage that will permit its relative positioning along a reductive continuum which can, in turn, be related to specific behaviors of lithic procurement and use. This will be accomplished by a statistical analysis of the recorded variables discussed below. Our second objective is to begin relating these patterns to local and larger regional patterns of logistic positioning and mobility (cf. Binford 1980). We will do this by a consideration of other variables, including distance to material sources, and evidence for other subsistence activities not directly related to quarrying, including artifact diversity and the presence of features associated with domestic activities.

LITHIC DEBITAGE

The Data Set

Debitage samples representing ten archaeological components from five different archaeological sites were selected for analysis (Table 1). In all sites with multiple components, the component assemblages were associated with recognizable stratigraphic markers such as distinct paleosol surfaces. The discreteness of each represented component was further demonstrated by decreases in debitage densities between superimposed living surfaces.

The most uncontrolled variable in the present study is age. While five components (35DS486, 485 Upper, 485 Lower, 219 Lower, 220 Lower) may be roughly contemporaneous (1500-2000 years ago), ages ranging from relatively recent (<1300 years ago) to ancient (>7000 years) are represented. On the other hand, if it is assumed that the principal use of the crater throughout the Holocene was reasonably constant (i.e., primarily obsidian procurement), the chronological discrepancies should not seriously

Table 1. Debitage samples selected for each component.

Site/Component	Age	Distance to Contemporary Obsidian Source
35DS485 (Game Hut Obsidian Quarry)		
Upper Component	1590 ± 60	5 meters
Lower Component	1600-4000 BP	5 meters
35DS219 (Hot Springs Boat Ramp Site)		
Upper Component	<1300 BP	150 meters
Lower Component	1840 ± 50	150 meters
35DS220		
Upper Component	<1300 BP	300 meters
Lower Component	1500-2000 BP	300 meters
35DS486	1690 ± 60; 1860 ± 70	850 meters
35DS34 (Paulina Lake Campground Site)		
Upper Component	<6500 BP	>2500 meters
Lower Component-A	7080 ± 80	>2500 meters
Lower Component-B	8210 ± 60	>2500 meters

impair the study's objectives. However, the proximity of obsidian sources to sites has changed over time. For the assemblages older than 1500 years, the Big Obsidian Flow (ca. 1300 years old) was not considered in calculating site distance to nearest source. Likewise, many of the sources available to Middle and Late Holocene visitors to the crater would not have been available to pre-Mazama occupants. The Buried Obsidian Flow, which would have had very limited availability following the Mazama ashfall, was likely an important source prior to this event.

Because of the small scale of test excavations, our approach was to select at least 1500 flakes per component. Thus, even if only 20% of the flakes within a component were sufficiently diagnostic to perform the analysis, this would provide a minimum sample of 300 flakes to characterize an assemblage. Three components had insufficient samples to achieve this target.

A total of 12,026 pieces of flaked stone debitage was selected from the target components. Of that total, all but three of the flakes were obsidian. The three chert flakes were not included in the analysis, but a cursory analysis indicated that they were small (<20 mm) interior flakes, with faceted platforms and single or multiple preparation removals. These attributes identify these flakes as by-products of the later stages of biface reduction, such as artifact manufacture and rejuvenation.

The debitage was initially sorted by flakes exhibiting either a single interior surface or those which exhibited more than one interior surface (cf. Sullivan and Rozen 1985). Flakes with more than one interior surface were classified as angular debris, counted and removed from further analysis. Angular debris accounted for only 68 (<1%) pieces of the total debitage sampled, which is common for obsidian debitage. The small amount of angular debris recovered in debitage assemblages--even in assemblages dominated by core and early stage biface reduction--is most likely a product of the way in which obsidian fractures rather than a significant indicator of lithic reduction behavior.

The second "filter" employed with the remaining flakes (i.e., those which exhibited a single interior surface) was the presence or absence of a striking platform and a bulb of force. Flakes not exhibiting these attributes were designated flake fragments, counted, and as with the angular debris, removed from further analysis. Flake fragments accounted for the majority of debitage (84%) recovered from the assemblage. A high percentage of flake fragments is also common in obsidian-dominated debitage assemblages.

The remaining 1871 (16%) flakes retained the striking platform and were subjected to further analysis (Table 2). This analysis was based on the seven metric, technological, and descriptive debitage classes which are described below.

DEFINITIONS AND ANALYSIS

Prior investigations within Newberry Crater by Flenniken (1987; Flenniken and Ozbun 1988) have included attempts to identify reduction sequences by debitage analysis. Flenniken (1987; Flenniken and Ozbun 1988) attempted to identify "early biface reduction flakes," "late biface reduction flakes," "early pressure flakes," and "late pressure flakes." Unfortunately, his classification system appears to be too esoteric and subjective for general application or replicability. Early biface reduction flakes, for example, are distinguished by "few" dorsal flake scars, and are "usually" the largest of the bifacial thinning flakes. Late biface thinning flakes exhibit "numerous" dorsal flake scars, and "usually" have feather terminations; early pressure flakes are "small" and have "multiple" dorsal flake scars.

Table 2. Summary of the debitage analysis by component for each site.

Analytical Category	35DS34 Upper n	(%)	Lower A n	(%)	Lower B n	(%)	35DS219 Upper n	(%)	Lower n	(%)	35DS220 Upper n	(%)	Lower n	(%)	35DS485 Upper n	(%)	Lower n	(%)	35DS486 n	(%)
FLAKE SIZE																				
0-5 mm	36	(18)	55	(14)	42	(25)	9	(6)	21	(11)	-	-	9	(5)	10	(4)	3	(3)	22	(13)
5-10 mm	75	(38)	183	(46)	86	(50)	40	(25)	53	(29)	1	(4)	48	(28)	68	(25)	22	(18)	58	(33)
10-20 mm	53	(27)	100	(25)	28	(16)	63	(39)	46	(25)	13	(46)	50	(29)	91	(34)	32	(27)	61	(35)
20-30 mm	20	(10)	34	(9)	7	(4)	33	(21)	29	(16)	6	(21)	27	(16)	52	(19)	29	(24)	20	(12)
30-40 mm	8	(4)	16	(4)	6	(3)	7	(4)	18	(10)	1	(4)	21	(12)	18	(7)	8	(7)	6	(3)
40-50 mm	3	(2)	7	(2)	1	(1)	7	(4)	8	(4)	4	(14)	12	(7)	5	(2)	5	(4)	3	(2)
>50 mm	2	(1)	2	(<1)	1	(1)	1	(1)	8	(4)	3	(11)	5	(3)	27	(9)	20	(17)	3	(2)
CORTEX																				
Primary	-		-		-		-		-		-		-		-		-		-	
Secondary	2	(1)	4	(1)	-		-		-		-		1	(1)	6	(2)	2	(2)	1	(1)
Interior	195	(99)	393	(99)	171	(100)	160	(100)	183	(100)	28	(100)	171	(99)	265	(98)	117	(98)	172	(99)
PLATFORM TYPE																				
Crushed	6	(5)	2	(1)	8	(5)	-	-	1	(1)	-	-	9	(5)	3	(1)	-	-	2	(1)
Cortex	-	-	-	-	-	-	2	(1)	-	-	-	-	-	-	11	(4)	3	(3)	-	-
Unfaceted	9	(3)	23	(6)	1	(1)	19	(12)	26	(14)	8	(29)	28	(16)	116	(43)	73	(61)	36	(21)
Faceted	182	(92)	372	(93)	162	(94)	139	(87)	156	(85)	20	(71)	135	(79)	141	(52)	43	(36)	135	(78)
PLATFORM PREP.																				
Unprepared	154	(78)	309	(79)	136	(79)	114	(71)	128	(70)	24	(85)	112	(65)	195	(72)	94	(79)	135	(78)
Reduced	4	(2)	10	(2)	-	-	11	(7)	18	(10)	2	(7)	14	(8)	11	(4)	11	(9)	9	(5)
Single	30	(15)	49	(12)	17	(10)	24	(15)	26	(14)	1	(4)	38	(22)	55	(20)	13	(11)	22	(13)
Multiple	9	(5)	29	(7)	18	(11)	11	(7)	11	(6)	1	(4)	8	(5)	10	(4)	1	(1)	7	(4)
GRINDING																				
Yes	2	(1)	28	(7)	6	(4)	42	(26)	36	(20)	3	(11)	16	(9)	4	(1)	4	(3)	12	(7)
No	195	(99)	369	(96)	165	(96)	118	(74)	147	(39)	25	(89)	156	(91)	267	(99)	115	(97)	161	(93)
LIPPING																				
Yes	10	(5)	6	(2)	1	(1)	7	(4)	4	(2)	-	-	8	(5)	2	(1)	1	(1)	4	(2)
No	187	(95)	391	(98)	170	(99)	153	(96)	179	(98)	28	(100)	164	(95)	269	(99)	118	(99)	169	(98)
FLAKE TYPE																				
Alternate	-	-	1	(<1)	-	-	1	(1)	-	-	-	-	4	(2)	7	(3)	1	(1)	4	(2)
Bulb Removal	-	-	1	(<1)	-	-	-	-	-	-	-	-	-	-	-	-	-	-	-	-
Multiple	2	(1)	15	(4)	3	(2)	9	(5)	11	(6)	-	-	16	(10)	34	(13)	9	(7)	17	(10)
Normal	188	(95)	379	(95)	167	(97)	144	(90)	164	(90)	28	(100)	148	(86)	229	(84)	109	(92)	148	(86)
Biface Edge	7	(4)	1	(<1)	1	(1)	6	(4)	8	(4)	-	-	4	(2)	1	(<1)	-	-	4	(2)
Total	197	(100)	397	(100)	171	(100)	160	(100)	183	(100)	28	(100)	172	(100)	271	(100)	119	(100)	173	(100)

While he does not objectify nor quantify the diagnostic correlates to various reduction stages, Flenniken has observed important systematic patterns throughout the reduction sequence. Many attributes which may be relatable to reduction stage--such as absolute flake size, number of dorsal flake scars, or degree of cortex on dorsal and platform surfaces -- can be objectified and quantified. A discussion of specific flake attributes that may be linked to a staged reduction system is presented below.

Flake Size

Definitions. Stahle and Dunn (1982:85 cf. Newcomer 1971; Neumann and Johnson 1979; Ahler 1989:89) note that:

> the size of waste flakes from the manufacture of bifacial projectile points, knives, or large handaxes will systematically decrease from the initial to final stages of manufacture as the emerging tools is reduced, thinned, and shaped. This underlying regularity suggests that the size distribution of waste flakes may be used to distinguish sequential stages of biface manufacture.

Regarding later stages of reduction, Patterson and Sollberger (1978) have argued that it is not possible to establish clear and reliable dimensional boundaries to isolate pressure flaking from other methods. However, Henry et al. (1975), in line with the logical expectations outlined above (Neumann and Johnson 1979; Stahle and Dunn 1982), argue that pressure flakes are thinner and weigh less, on average, than percussion flakes. Likewise, Ahler (1989:91) argues that "it is widely accepted, based on experimental data, that percussion flaking, on the whole, is capable of producing flakes much larger in size than any produced by pressure flaking. . . . Thus size grade distribution data should provide a fairly direct measure of load application variation."

For the present analysis flakes were assigned to seven size categories as follows: 0-5 mm maximum diameter, 5-10 mm, 10-20 mm, 20-30 mm, 30-40 mm, 40-50 mm, and >50 mm. Flake sizing was accomplished by placing each flake on a template of concentric circles divided as above. This method allowed the measurement of maximum specimen diameter.

While flake size is a useful variable in reduction stage analysis, Patterson (1990:557) states that "flake-size-distribution characteristics alone do not appear to be very useful, however, as a general analytical method for determining which stages of biface manufacture occurred at specific locations." He suggests that analysis of technological attributes of waste flakes, as well as data on the nature of the non-debitage assemblage, are necessary to identify biface-manufacturing trajectories. The attributes discussed below will address these concerns.

Assemblage Patterns. The maximum diameter of each flake retaining a striking platform was recorded (Table 2). Each site included flakes from all size ranges, but a general pattern emerged of larger mean flake sizes close to obsidian flows and increasingly smaller flakes as distance from the flow increased (Figure 2). Site 35DS485, located immediately adjacent to the Game Hut obsidian flow, produced the highest mean flake size value (28.10 mm), and also contained the largest flakes recovered. By contrast, the Paulina Campground site (35DS34), located over 2500 m from the nearest flow, had the smallest mean flake size value (14.35 mm). Mean flake size values from other sites were intermediate between these two extremes.

Dorsal Surface Morphology

Definitions. Initial stages of reduction--involving procurement of tool stone, testing the material, and initially shaping desirable pieces--will result in flaking debris with cortex on dorsal flake surfaces (Fish 1981). Cortex is the naturally weathered outer rind of the parent stone. Ahler (1989: 90) notes that "[a]s tool reduction progresses, cortex is gradually removed from the outer surface of the core/tool and cortex should

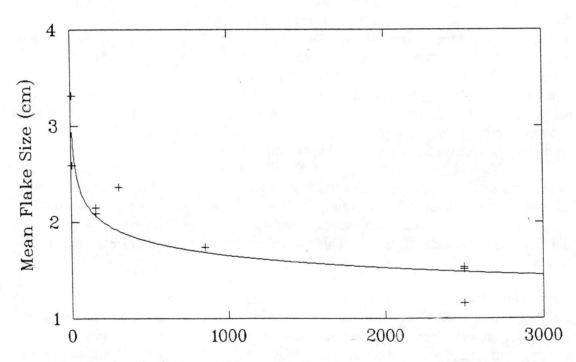

Figure 2. Mean flake size, by distance from the nearest contemporary obsidian quarry. The relationship appears to be best expressed by a logarithm curve.

become less and less frequently represented on the dorsal face of flake byproducts." Similarly, Flenniken and Ozbun (1988:98; Ozbun 1991) logically suggest that assemblages with flakes exhibiting cortex are strongly associated with quarrying and tool stone selection.

As reduction continues and cortex is removed, dorsal flake surfaces will exhibit the scars of prior flake removals. As the reduction process continues, the number of flake scars on the dorsal surfaces of flakes may tend to increase (Frison and Bradley 1980:24; Jones and Beck 1990).

For the present analysis two types of information were systematically recorded for dorsal surface morphology. Each flake was first assigned to one of three cortex classes, Primary (cortex on 100% of the dorsal surface), Secondary (cortex present but on <100% of the dorsal surface), and Interior (no cortex). The number of dorsal flake scars was also recorded for each flake.

Assemblage Patterns. Each flake was examined for the presence of cortex on both the dorsal surface and the striking platform, and although cortex on the striking platform is an attribute reported in conjunction with attributes of striking platform morphology it is also recorded here in the secondary cortex category. Very few flakes from any site exhibited secondary cortex and no primary flakes were recorded. Flakes from the Game Hut Obsidian Flow site (35DS485) exhibited the largest percentage of secondary flakes, but that totaled only 2%, while the remaining sites had less than 1% secondary cortex flakes (Table 2).

The almost complete lack of cortex on even the larger flakes from these sites is undoubtedly a product of the large size of the boulders and large masses of glassy rock from which the flake blanks were produced. The utilization of cores much larger than the bifacial reduction products allowed the removal of the weathered exterior surface while considerable interior mass remained to be removed. This results in flake blanks with little cortex (flakes with cortex were almost exclusively classified as secondary, or with cortex present only on the striking platform). The fact that none of the recovered flake blank or biface blank fragments exhibited any cortex also indicates that very large flakes, lacking cortex, were being removed from large cores, which were also virtually cortex free after initial flaking.

The second attribute recorded on the dorsal surface of each flake was the number of negative flake scars. The inclusion of this category of analysis was based on the assumption that as the biface reduction sequence progressed the number of flake scars would also increase. Although the physical size of the flakes would place some restraints on the number of scars possible it was thought that a correlation between the later stages of biface reduction and the number of flake scars would be observable. This was not the case. There was no correlation between the mean dorsal scar count for each site and mean flake size ($r^2 = .026$), mean dorsal scar count and mean platform thickness ($r^2 = .10$), or mean dorsal scar count and the distance of individual sites from the obsidian flow ($r^2 = .15$). Dorsal scar count provides little, if any, insight into this analysis, although it might if linked with flake size; large, early reduction flakes have few dorsal flake scars, as do small, very late stage flakes. Highest dorsal flake counts were recorded on mid-sized, middle stage flake debris.

Striking Platform Morphology

Definitions. As the reduction sequence progresses, the surfaces available for striking platforms should change concurrently with changes observed in dorsal surface morphology. Flakes removed early in the reduction sequence will more likely employ cortex surfaces as striking platforms (Fish 1981). Later in the sequence striking platforms will more likely be prior flake scars (unfaceted platforms), or previously worked surfaces (faceted platforms).

It has been observed (Speth 1972; Newcomer 1971:88-89; Neumann and Johnson 1979; Ahler 1989:91) that as an object progresses through a reduction sequence, the size of the striking platform will decrease. Ahler (1989:91) explains that "non-marginal" flaking, where the percussion load is applied at a point on the tool/core slightly in from the edge, is generally associated with freehand core reduction and shaping where trimming of larger masses of material is desired. "Marginal" flaking, meaning force is applied directly to the tool/core edge, is often associated with bifacial thinning. Non-marginal flaking, typical of early stage reduction, will result in relatively thicker platforms, while marginal flaking, more frequently associated with later stages of reduction, will produce thinner striking platforms.

Neumann and Johnson (1979) note that as an object progresses through a reduction sequence, the incidence of lipped bulbs--a projection on the proximal ventral surface of the flake (see Crabtree 1972:74)--should also increase. They associate the incidence of lipped platforms with probable use of soft hammer (e.g., antler baton) percussion, as opposed to hard hammer (hammerstone) percussion. Crabtree (1970:150, also 1972:74) suggests that lipping is caused, in part, by the diffusion of force back into the hammer when using an antler baton. Henry et al. (1975) have shown that while lipping is not a diagnostic attribute of soft hammer percussion (cf. Patterson and Sollberger 1978), it produces significantly more lipped platforms than hard hammer percussion.

As discussed above, a flake's thickness (and thickness of the striking platform), is determined by where force is applied on the platform. Too much force applied to a tool/core margin will cause the platform to fail, resulting in a crushed, or collapsed, platform. A flake with a crushed platform retains the bulb of force, but the point of impact is gone. Crushed platforms may be associated with bifacial thinning, where removing large masses of material from the tool/core margin is not desired.

A number of attributes on the striking platform of each flake was recorded, including the presence of cortex, unfaceted or plain (Frison and Bradley 1980:27), faceted, or crushed platforms, the presence of lipping on the ventral surface, and the thickness in millimeters of each platform. The cortex, unfaceted, faceted and crushed platforms were mutually exclusive of one another, but lipping occurred in conjunction with the above attributes.

Assemblage Patterns. The majority of flakes recovered from all sites exhibited either faceted or unfaceted platforms, with fewer flakes exhibiting crushed platforms or platforms with cortex. Most of the flakes analyzed did not exhibit lipping, with the Game Hut quarry site (35DS485) exhibiting the least and the other sites exhibiting slightly higher numbers of lipped platforms (Table 2).

Except for a single flake with cortex on the striking platform at site 35DS219, the remaining flakes with cortex on the striking platform were all recovered from site 35DS485, the Game Hut Obsidian Quarry. Only at site 35DS485 do flakes with unfaceted platforms make up the majority of flakes recovered (Table 2). The high number of unfaceted flakes and platforms with cortex from 35DS485 is interpreted as being a product of the removal of flakes from a core with a flat or cortex-covered platform, or the squared edge of a flake blank during "initial edging" (cf. Callahan 1979). The other sites have considerably fewer flakes with unfaceted platforms. Site 35DS34 (farthest from an obsidian flow) exhibits the most faceted platforms. The presence of unfaceted platforms in sites other than 35DS485 is most likely due to the removal of flakes from the square edges on flake blanks, indicating the presence of the earliest stages of biface reduction to some degree at all sites.

Flakes with crushed platforms were recovered from all sites in small numbers, but the highest proportions were recorded at sites 35DS219 and 35DS220. The tools recovered from these two sites are indicative of the early stages of biface reduction, and the presence of crushed platforms may indicate the use of hard hammer percussion during early stage biface reduction at these sites.

The measurements of platform thickness on each of the flakes that retained a striking platform resulted in a range of <1 mm to 35.2 mm. Mean platform thickness values from each site ranged from a high of 2.955 mm at the Game Hut quarry site (35DS485) and a low of 1.339 mm at the site farthest from a natural obsidian deposit (35DS34). There is a relationship between mean platform thickness and the distance a site was from the flow, which is similar to that shown for mean flake size (Figure 3). Mean flake size and mean platform thickness are strongly correlated ($r=.95$, $r^2=.90$) with the coefficient of determination (r^2) indicating that 90% of the variation in platform thickness is related to the size of the flake. In sum, sites closest to an obsidian flow have flakes with thicker unfaceted platforms that are generally larger than those from sites farther from the flow.

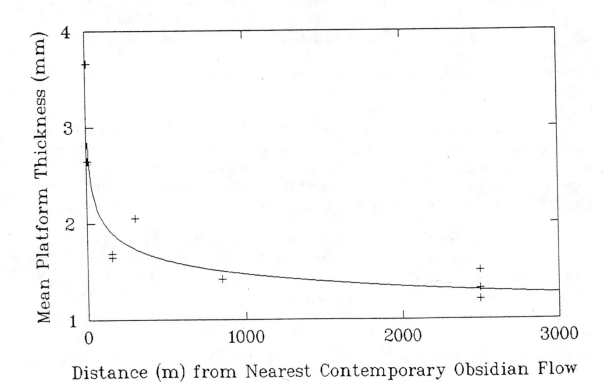

Figure 3. Mean platform thickness, by distance from the nearest contemporary obsidian quarry. The relationship appears to be best expressed by a logarithm curve.

Platform Preparation

Definitions. In conjunction with the recording of the striking platform morphology, the presence of attributes on the platform that indicate purposeful preparation to better control the removal of a flake were noted. Platform preparation was applied if the configuration of the unprepared striking platform might not result in the desired flake removal.

Platform preparation techniques include grinding; the dulling of a core or biface edge to strengthen the striking surface (Crabtree 1972:12). Frison and Bradley (1980:29) also illustrate platforms which they identify as reduced. Reduced platforms have been severely abraded, leaving step fractures on the dorsal margin of the platform. Reducing the platform may serve a similar function to grinding, but results in a more severely abraded and attrited platform.

Preparing a platform by altering its shape may also be done by the removal of short single or multiple flakes from the dorsal face on the proximal end of the flake

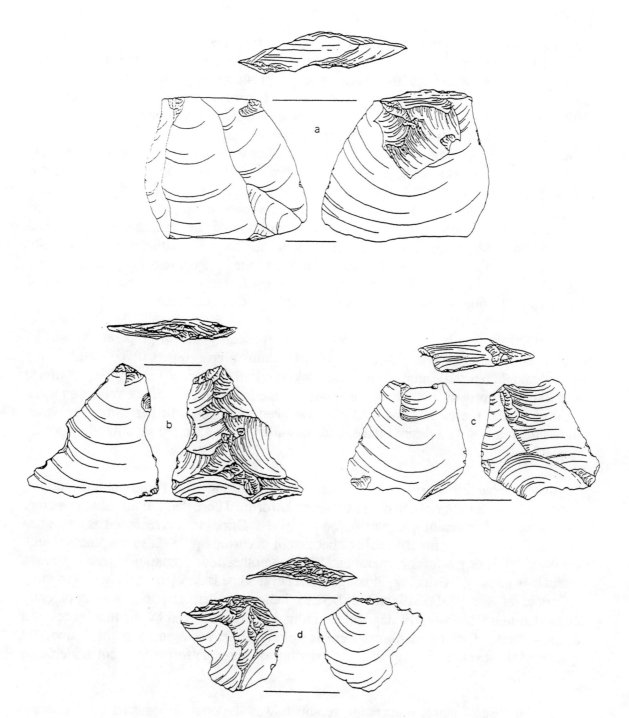

Figure 4. Flakes with diagnostic platform types (platform, dorsal, and ventral views).

     a. Non-cortex unfaceted (485-T4-P0m-5/2a)

     b. Multifaceted (219-T2-P3m-2/2-b)

     c. Crushed (or collapsed platform (219-T2-P3m-2/2-c)

     d. Reduced platform (219-T2-P3m-2/2-a)

adjacent to the striking surface (Callahan 1979:34; Frison and Bradley 1980:27; Patterson 1983: 302; Schneider 1972: 94-95). The technique of single and multiple flaking of the flake's dorsal surface from the platform edge produces flake scars that have been identified as faceted platforms by some analysts (Frison and Bradley 1980; Patterson 1983; Schneider 1972). In order to distinguish faceted platforms that result from previous flake removals during the reduction process, and those platforms that exhibit "facets" from the intentional removal of small flakes to prepare a striking platform, the latter will be designated here as single or multiple platform setup flakes. In extreme cases, platform setup flakes will result in isolating the platform on the edge of a biface. Preparation of isolated platforms will predetermine the point at which the flake will be struck, and permit better control of the configuration of the resulting flake removal (Frison and Bradley 1980:30; for example, note that isolated platforms are commonly associated with the preparation of channel flakes on fluted projectile points, where precise control of the flake removal is critical). Isolated platforms are considered diagnostic of late stage reduction for the lateral removal of biface thinning flakes.

Platforms which show no evidence of purposeful platform preparation will be designated as unprepared. Platforms which exhibit preparation will be divided into ground, single removal, multiple removal, and reduced classes of preparation. Platform preparation is normally thought to correspond to the later stages of biface reduction when platform angle, placement, and configuration need to be controlled in a manner which allows the removal of a desired flake, and thus allow the controlled shaping of a specific biface form.

Assemblage Patterns. The majority of the flakes analyzed from all sites did not exhibit purposeful preparation of the striking platform. Those that did included grinding, reduction, single and multiple preparation removals. Grinding was recorded as a separate analytical category during the analysis because it occurred on flakes in conjunction with the other types of platform preparation, while the other four preparation techniques are mutually exclusive. Grinding, although present on some flakes from all sites, was more prevalent at sites 35DS219 and 35DS220 indicating that grinding was apparently employed more during early stage biface reduction, as evidenced by the tools recovered at those sites. Ground platforms were relatively under-represented at the Game Hut quarry (35DS485), indicating that the grinding of core platforms was not undertaken (Table 2).

The use of single preparation removals was the platform preparation technique most represented at all sites (except for grinding at 35DS219). By definition, multiple secondary flakes have a single flake removal from the dorsal surface of the striking platform; at all sites, except for 35DS34, the single preparation removal category is correlated to the presence of large numbers of multiple secondary flakes (see definition below). At site 35DS34 very few multiple secondary flakes are represented and both the single and multiple preparation removal categories represent the purposeful preparation

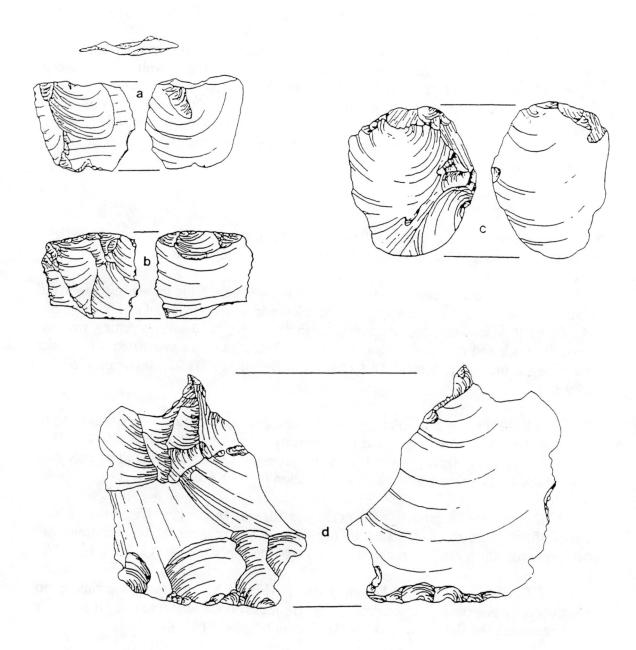

Figure 5. Diagnostic flake types.

 a. Multiple secondary flake   c. Bulb removal flake
   (485-T4-P0m-5/2-b)   (34-P10m-9/2)
 b. Edge removal   d. Overshot flake
   (220-P4-3/2)   (219-P4-4/2)

of the striking platform for flake types other than secondary multiple flakes. Flakes with reduced platforms were more abundant at sites 35DS219 and 35DS220. Both reduced and ground platforms tend to cluster at sites interpreted as early stage biface reduction localities. Site 35DS34, which is farther from obsidian sources and thought to be represented by the later stages of biface reduction, has fewer flakes with either reduced or ground platforms, but proportionally larger numbers of small flakes with single and multiple preparation removals interpreted as being indicative of the later stages of biface reduction. The majority of small flakes from the other sites do not exhibit platform preparation and are most likely the inevitable accumulation of small sized flakes produced during core reduction and early stage biface reduction.

Distinctive Flake Types

In addition to the above classifications, we have also made note of distinctive flake types that may be associated with particular stages of lithic reduction.

Alternate flakes result from removal of a squared edge from the margin of a flake blank in an attempt to produce an acute beveled edge. Alternate flakes are generally wider than they are long, and are triangular in cross-section, a form resulting from an unusually thick and massive striking platform. These flakes are associated with initial reduction and primary trimming of bifacial cores (Flenniken 1987:21; Raymond 1986:16, 1989:93).

Bulb Removal Flakes (Figure 5c) are also associated with primary trimming of bifacial cores. A bulb removal flake is defined by Flenniken and Ozbun (1988:232) as "percussion thinning flake removed from the proximal end of the ventral surface of a flake blank." As a result, it exhibits a percussion bulb on both faces.

Overshot (or Outrepasse') Flakes (Figure 5d) are a product of biface manufacture. The platform of an overshot flake is on one edge of a biface, but the flake continues all the way across the biface and removes a portion of the opposite edge (Crabtree 1972:80).

Edge Removal (Margin Removal) Flakes (Figure 5b) are manufacturing errors which occur when the biface is struck too far from the biface edge removing the edge of the biface with the flake (Flenniken 1987; Raymond 1986, 1989).

Multiple Secondary Flakes (Figure 5a) exhibit "direct superposition of positive and negative bulbs of percussion on the interior and exterior flake surfaces respectively" (Jelinek et al. 1971:98). These flakes were produced either by striking the same platform area of the parent material twice, or by a single blow removing a pair of superimposed flakes. Flat and convex striking platforms were frequently associated with this flake type (Jelinek et al. 1971).

Assemblage Patterns. A single bulb removal flake was recovered from site 35DS34. This flake type is diagnostic of the reduction of flake blanks, although very few other flakes indicative of flake blank reduction, were recovered at 35DS34. Alternate flakes, which are indicative of the removal of square edges from flake blanks were more prevalent at the other sites. The presence of alternate flakes at 35DS485 in conjunction with the recovery of large edge modified flakes indicates that the "initial edging" of flake blanks removed during core reduction was undertaken at flow edge sites, as well as sites associated with the earlier stages of biface reduction, such as 35DS219 and 35DS220.

Biface edge removal flakes were not recovered in large numbers at any of the sites, but the majority (all but one) were found at sites where the evidence indicates biface reduction (35DS34, 35DS219, 35DS220, 35DS486) and not core reduction (35DS485). These flakes are undeniable indicators of biface production.

The category of multiple secondary flakes was added to the flake type class after an initial examination of the debitage indicated their presence in substantial numbers at all of the sites except 35DS34 (Table 2). Almost all of the multiple secondary flakes exhibited unfaceted platforms and the majority were wider than they were long, with the striking platform the widest part of the flake. The majority of these flakes are associated with sites where flake blank and core reduction have been indicated, and the presence of a flake type that removes a long (and sometimes wide) unfaceted platform from a square edge suggests that this flake type may be diagnostic of flake blank and core reduction. In other words, like alternate flakes, this flake type was the result of a technique utilized to remove a square edge, but in a technologically different manner. Replicative experiments may be able to address this question.

REDUCTION PRODUCTS:
A CONSIDERATION OF OTHER ASSEMBLAGE ATTRIBUTES

Due to relatively small samples of non-debitage cultural remains recovered from the Newberry sites in the 1990 testing, the following discussion uses sites, rather than individual cultural components, as the principal analytic unit.

Biface Reduction Stages

Technological analysis of lithic reduction has focused on the manufacture of bifaces, which are represented in reduction systems from initial raw material procurement through the most finely formed lithic artifacts. Because bifaces are generally subjected to the greatest degree of modification of any class of lithic artifact, they provide lithic analysts with many opportunities to identify culturally significant reduction systems and morphological styles.

Bifacial cores are material-efficient sources of lithic material for a variety of tool types, and the naturally reinforced edges of bifaces make them far more durable than unmodified flakes. These attributes are of significant value in a mobile hunter-gatherer economy (Flenniken and Ozbun 1988:98; Kelly 1988). It has been argued (Scott 1985; Flenniken 1987; Flenniken and Ozbun 1988; Ozbun 1991; Connolly 1991) that procurement of lithic material from Newberry Crater sources includes the production of bifaces for transport away from obsidian quarries. Bifacial flaking of lithic material at the quarry margin serves a number of purposes, including testing of the material to sort out pieces with fractures, inclusions, and other undesirable flaws, and shaping of the material to a useful and transportable form.

One of the most widely cited stage reduction sequences is that proposed by Callahan (1979), which includes 1) obtaining the blank, 2) initial edging, 3) primary thinning, 4) secondary thinning, and 5) final shaping. Skinner and Ainsworth (1990, 1991), however, have documented a slightly different reduction trajectory at the Casa Diablo obsidian quarry located in east-central California. They noted that reduction was initially focused on the dorsal surface of a flake blank, sometimes proceeding to an advanced stage before flaking began on the ventral face. As a result, the dorsal surface might exhibit characteristics of a late stage biface (e.g., Stage 4 in Callahan's system) while the ventral face exhibited minimal modification (e.g., stage 1 or 2). They identify this reduction trajectory as the Unifacial-Biface Technique. They proposed a reduction sequence for this technique that includes 1) obtaining the blank, 2) initial edging, 3) primary and secondary thinning of the dorsal face, 4) primary and secondary thinning of the ventral face, and 5) final shaping or tertiary thinning of both faces.

Differing degrees of modification are evident on opposing faces of some bifacial implements in the Newberry Crater assemblage. If all bifaces were reduced systematically on both faces, or if all were reduced on one face and then the other, then either the Callahan or Skinner and Ainsworth classification systems would be suitable. However, lithic reduction trajectories can, and do, follow multiple courses. Because neither system can adequately characterize assemblages in which both reduction trajectories appear, a classification strategy was implemented which employed the attributes of the widely used and recognized Callahan system while addressing the inadequacies observed by Skinner and Ainsworth.

For descriptive purposes, each face of an implement has been classified independently according to the stage characteristics outlined by Callahan (1979). Thus, each biface generates two stage value observations. An implement classified as 3/3 exhibits Stage 3 reduction on both faces, and would fit within Callahan's traditional Stage 3. On the other hand, an implement classified as 1/3 exhibits characteristics of the Unifacial-Biface Technique. If each face is considered an independent observation, we can derive a mean stage value for each site (Table 3) based on two observations for each implement recovered. We can see (Figure 6) that quarry and near-quarry sites exhibit lower mean stage values, and stage value rises as distance from the quarry increases.

Table 3.   Average values from biface stage analysis; sites are ordered by distance to the
nearest contemporary obsidian source.

Site	Quarry Distance	Site Type	N Observations	Mean Stage Value
35DS34	>2500	General Camp	20	3.04
35DS486	850[1]	General Camp, Biface Production	4	2.75
35DS220	300	Biface Production	6	2.50
35DS219	150	Biface Production	20	2.50
35DS485	5	Obsidian Quarry	2	2.50

1. Based on distance to the Game Hut Obsidian Flow; the Big Obsidian Flow is closer,
but post-dates this site.

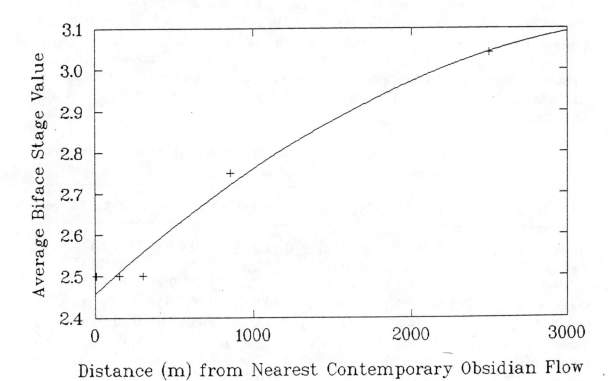

Figure 6. Average biface stage value for each site, plotted against site distance from the
nearest obsidian source; quadratic regression curve is plotted over the data
points.

Other Functional Artifact Classes

Table 4 provides a summary of artifact distributions at the investigated sites in Newberry Crater. A dendrogram derived from cluster analysis of the tool percentages shows that the five sites can be sorted into three groups (Figure 7). Group 1 is represented by the Game Hut Obsidian Quarry (35DS485). This site contained all the true cores recovered during the project. Group 2 sites (35DS219 and 35DS220) can be characterized as near-quarry lithic workshops where biface blanks were manufactured. Group 3 sites include the Paulina Campground site (35DS34) and site 35DS486. Biface production also occurred at the Group 3 sites, but these sites contain additional artifactual evidence for other camp activities, as well as cultural features. Group three sites are farthest from contemporary obsidian quarries.

In order to better understand the site clustering, a distribution analysis of artifact classes was conducted. Similarity scores for each pair of artifact classes were generated with respect to their co-occurrence within each site. A cluster analysis was then performed to isolate artifact sets that tend to co-occur. Three artifact sets were delineated (Figure 8). Group A includes cores and large edge-modified flakes, which are almost exclusive to the Game Hut Obsidian Quarry. Group B is represented by the single class, bifaces. These artifacts are predominant at 35DS219 and 35DS220, which are interpreted as biface production sites. Group C includes all other artifact classes, including projectile points and preforms, small and medium edge-modified flakes, and scrapers. Group C artifacts represent significant proportions of the assemblages from 35DS34 (the Paulina Lake site) and 35DS486, which are interpreted as sites where general camp and maintenance activities occurred.

Table 4. Recovered tool frequencies by site; sites are ordered (L to R) by decreasing distance to nearest contemporary obsidian quarry.

Artifact Class	35DS34	35DS486	35DS220	35DS219	35DS485	Total
Projectile Points	3 (11.1%)	0 (0.0%)	0 (0.0%)	0 (0.0%)	1 (8.3%)	4
Preforms[1]	2 (7.4%)	0 (0.0%)	0 (0.0%)	0 (0.0%)	0 (0.0%)	2
Bifaces[2]	13 (48.1%)	2 (50 0%)	3 (75%)	15 (78.9%)	1 (8.3%)	27
Scrapers	1 (3.7%)	0 (0.0%)	0 (0.0%)	0 (0.0%)	0 (0.0%)	1
Small EMFs[3]	4 (14.8%)	1 (25.0%)	0 (0.0%)	2 (10.5%)	0 (0.0%)	6
Medium EMFs[3]	3 (11.1%)	1 (25.0%)	1 (25.0%)	1 (5.3%)	0 (0.0%)	5
Large EMFs[3]	1 (3.7%)	0 (0.0%)	0 (0.0%)	1 (5.3%)	5 (41.7%)	7
Cores	0 (0.0%)	0 (0.0%)	0 0.0%)	0 (0.0%)	5 (41.7%)	5
Total Tools	27	4	4	19	12	57

1. Includes late stage bifaces; 2. Early stage bifaces
3. Edge-Modified Flakes; small < 15 grams, medium 20-40 grams, large > 100 grams.

EUCLIDEAN DISTANCE

0.000   50.000

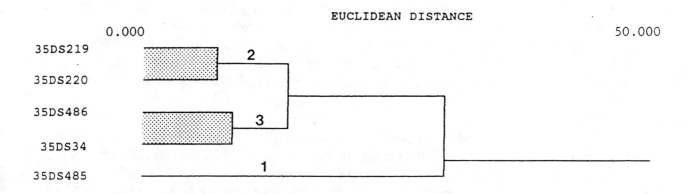

Figure 7. Average linkage cluster dendrogram based on tool occurrence percentages (see Table 4).

EUCLIDEAN DISTANCE

100.000

0.000

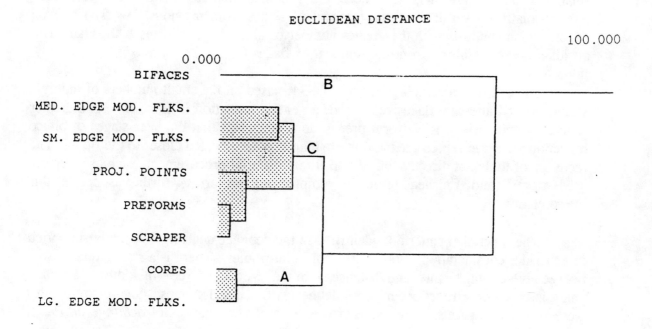

Figure 8. Average linkage cluster dendrogram, based on artifact distributions (from Table 4).

SUMMARY

The present study examined lithic artifacts (tools and debitage) from a series of quarry and near-quarry sites within Newberry Crater, central Oregon. A series of metric and non-metric attributes were systematically recorded for both lithic debitage and other artifactual remains for eleven discrete cultural components from five different archaeological sites in the crater. The analysis was structured in such a way as to allow the delineation of technological stages of biface reduction and to determine if there were differences in lithic reduction activities between the sites.

The debitage assemblage from site 35DS485 includes larger flakes than the other sites, more cortex (especially on the platform), flakes with thicker platforms, more flakes with unfaceted platforms, and the recovery of only one biface edge removal flake. The location of this site immediately adjacent to the obsidian flow, the lack of biface fragments, the presence of the only cores found during the project, and a number of large edge-modified flakes, has led to the interpretation of this site as a quarry area.

Evidence from the other investigated sites, located farther from obsidian flows, suggests that the production of blanks into either bifacial blanks or finished tools were the main lithic reduction activities undertaken. The presence of relatively smaller flakes, flakes without cortex, considerably more flakes with faceted platforms, and relatively smaller striking platforms, have been interpreted as indicators of biface reduction. Faceted platforms result from the removal of flakes from previously worked bifacial edges, which contrasts with the greater number of unfaceted platforms at the Game Hut obsidian quarry resulting from the removal of flakes from a flat core edge.

The debitage assemblage from 35DS34, based on the small numbers of multiple secondary and alternate flakes recovered, a general reduction in flake size, and greater frequency and variety of platform preparations, indicates that the later stages of biface reduction are better represented at this site than at others located closer to the flows. The recovery of tools not directly linked with lithic material procurement, such as scrapers, used flakes, and finished projectile points and preforms, further supports this interpretation.

The functional patterning identified in the debitage analysis is strongly supported in a broader consideration of other assemblage attributes. There is a strong relationship between biface stage values and distance from the obsidian source. In addition, a cluster analysis based on artifact occurrences delineates functional groups. Significantly, sites were sorted into precisely the same groups by a cluster analysis of *debitage attributes only* (platform thickness and mean flake size) by component (Figure 9). This example illustrates a potential advantage of technological analysis of debitage. While the number of tools recovered was considered inadequate to conduct a component-by-component comparison, the amount of debitage sufficient for a meaningful component-by-component functional analysis represented only a fraction of the debitage recovered.

Significantly, the metric variables recorded in the present study accurately reflect the reductive nature of the lithic technology, as expressed as a function of distance from the material source. For the debitage variables of platform thickness and mean flake size, this function takes the form of a logarithm curve, with most dramatic differences seen with close proximity to the material source (in this case, within about 1000 meters), then leveling out as distance to source increases. The implications of this relationship are important for Newberry Crater. It has been argued (Scott 1985; Flenniken 1987; Flenniken and Ozbun 1988; Connolly 1991) that the Newberry caldera functioned principally as an obsidian source. It is clear from the present analysis, however, that even with its characterization as an obsidian quarry, a considerable range of reductive behaviors are represented, and significant functional and ancillary near-quarry sites. The crater represents an important laboratory for the study of lithic reduction technology.

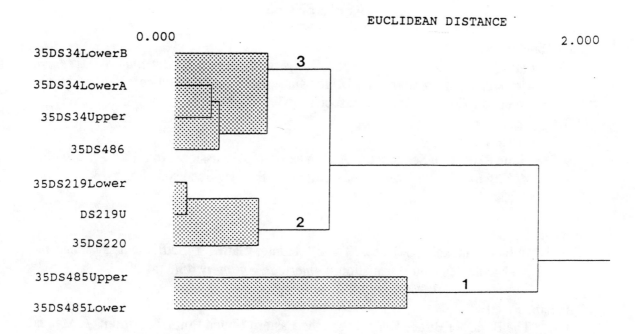

Figure 9. Average linkage cluster dendrogram, based on mean platform thickness and flake size values for all components.

The analytical classes used for the present study enabled the differentiation between core and biface reduction, based on flake type, flake size, and striking platform morphology. Differences were also delineated between early and mid to late stage biface reduction based on striking platform morphology (faceted vs. unfaceted platforms), flake size, and platform preparation. Among all attributes recorded for debitage, the two metric variables of flake size and platform thickness, and the categorical variables relating to platform type, appear to most clearly and reliably distinguish sites with respect to function in the present sample.

The analytic promise in lithic technology studies derives from the fact that it represents the products of patterned cultural behavior. The range of activities relating to lithic material procurement, tool production, and tool use, rejuvenation, and discard, is generally distributed over time and across the landscape. The distribution of these activities, and their products, forms a pattern that is a function of the user group's mobility with respect to various resource needs. All stages of lithic reduction are seldom present at a single locality; often the lithic material at a site may represent only a part of the reduction sequence. For this reason, areas such as Newberry Crater that include material representative of the entire reduction sequence take on particular importance in determining both general lithic reduction strategies and specific reduction trajectories in a context where both spatial and temporal variables are controlled.

REFERENCES

Ahler, Stanley A.
 1989 *Mass Analysis of Flaking Debris: Studying the Forest Rather than the Tree. In Alternative Approaches to Lithic Analysis.* Archaeological Papers of the American Anthropological Association 1. Washington, D.C.

Bradley, Bruce A.
 1975 Lithic Reduction Sequences: A Glossary and Discussion. In *Lithic Technology: Making and Using Stone Tools*, edited by Earl H. Swanson, pp. 5-13. Aldine, Chicago.

Binford, Lewis R.
 1980 Willow Smoke and Dog's Tails: Hunter-Gatherer Settlement Systems and Archaeological Site Formation. *American Antiquity* 45(1):4-20.

Callahan, Errett
 1979 The Basics of Biface Knapping in the Eastern Fluted Point Tradition: A Manual for Flintknappers and Lithic Analysts. *Archaeology of Eastern North America* 7(1).

 1991 Out of Theory and Into Reality: A Comment on Nami's comment. *Plains Anthropologist* 36(137):367-368.

Collins, Michael B.
 1975 Lithic Technology as a Means of Processual Inference. In *Lithic Technology: Making and Using Stone Tools*, edited by E. H. Swanson, pp. 15-34. Aldine, Chicago.

115

Connolly, Thomas J. (with contributions by Robert R. Musil and Dorothy E. Freidel)
  1991 *Archaeological Investigations Along the Paulina-East Lake Highway Within Newberry Crater, Central Oregon.* Oregon State Museum of Anthropology, University of Oregon, Report 91-6.

Cotterell, Brian and Johan Kamminga
  1987 The Formation of Flakes. *American Antiquity* 52(4):675-708.

Crabtree, Don E.
  1970 Flaking Stone with Wooden Implements. *Science* 169:146-153.

  1972 *An Introduction to Flintworking.* Occasional Papers of the Idaho State University Museum 28. Pocatello.

  1974 The Cone Fracture Principle and the Manufacture of Lithic Materials. *Tebiwa* 15:29-42.

Fish, Paul R.
  1981 Beyond Tools: Middle Paleolithic Debitage Analysis and Cultural Inference. *Journal of Anthropological Research* 37:374-386.

Flenniken, J. Jeffrey
  1987 The Lithic Technology of the East Lake Site, Newberry Crater. Report on file, Fort Rock Ranger District, Deschutes National Forest. Bend, Oregon.

Flenniken, J. Jeffrey, and Terry L. Ozbun
  1988 Archeological Investigations in Newberry Crater, Deschutes National Forest, Central Oregon. Report on file, Fort Rock Ranger District, Deschutes National Forest. Bend, Oregon.

Frison, George C. and Bruce A. Bradley
  1980 *Folsom tools and Technology at the Hanson Site, Wyoming.* University of New Mexico Press.

Henry, Don O., C. Vance Haynes, and Bruce Bradley
  1975 Quantitative Variations in Flaked Stone Debitage. *Plains Anthropologist* 21:57-61.

Jelinek, Arthur J., Bruce Bradley, and Bruce Huckell
  1971 The Production of Secondary Multiple Flakes. *American Antiquity* 36(2):198-200.

Jones, George T. and Charlotte Beck
  1990 Biface Reduction and Assemblage Variability in Late Pleistocene/Early Holocene Assemblages from Eastern Nevada. Paper presented at the 22nd Great Basin Anthropological Conference, Reno, Nevada.

Kelly, Robert L.
  1988 The Three Sides of a Biface. *American Antiquity* 53(4):717-734.

MacLeod, Norman S. and David R. Sherrod
  1988 Geologic Evidence for a Magma Chamber Beneath Newberry Volcano, Oregon. *Journal of Geophysical Research* 93(B9):10067-10079.

MacLeod, Norman S., David R. Sherrod, and Lawrence A. Chitwood
  1982 *Geologic Map of Newberry Volcano, Deschutes, Klamath, and Lake Counties, Oregon.* U.S. Geological Survey Open-File Report 82-847.

Muto, Guy R.
  1971 A Stage Analysis of the Manufacture of Stone Tools. In *Great Basin Anthropological Conference 1970: Selected Papers*, edited by C. M. Aikens, pp. 109-118. University of Oregon Anthropological Papers 1. Eugene.

Neumann, Thomas W. and Elden Johnson
  1979 Patrow Site Lithic Analysis. *Mid-Continental Journal of Archaeology* 4(1):79-111.

Ozbun, Terry L.
  1991 Boulders to Bifaces: Initial Reduction of Obsidian at Newberry Crater, Oregon. *Journal of California and Great Basin Anthropology* 13(2):147-159.

Newcomer, M. H.
  1971 Some Quantitative Experiments in Hand-Axe Manufacture. *World Archaeology* 3:85-94.

Patterson, Leland W.
  1983 Criteria for Determining the Attributes of Man-Made Lithics. *Journal of Field Archaeology* 10:297-307.

  1990 Characteristics of Bifacial-Reduction Flake-Size Distribution. *American Antiquity* 55(3)550-558.

Patterson, L. W. and J. B. Sollberger
  1978 Replication and Classification of Small Size Lithic Debitage. *Plains Anthropologist* 23:103-111.

Raymond, Anan W.
1986   Flaked Stone Technology at the East Bug-a-Boo Site (35LIN260), Linn County, Oregon.   Report submitted to the U.S. Forest Service, Willamette National Forest, Eugene.

1989   *Flaked Stone Technology at the East Bug-a-Boo Site Linn County, Oregon. In Contributions to the Archaeology of Oregon 1987-1988*, edited by Rick Minor, pp. 77-111. Association of Oregon Archaeologists Occasional Papers 4.

Schneider, Fred
1972   An Analysis of Waste Flakes from Sites in the Upper Knife-Heart Region, North Dakota. *Plains Anthropologist* 17(56):91-100.

Scott, Sara A.
1985   *An Analysis of Archaeological Materials Recovered During Test Excavations of Six Prehistoric Sites on the Deschutes National Forest in Central Oregon.* USDA Forest Service, Pacific Northwest, Deschutes National Forest Cultural Resource Report 2.

Skinner, Elizabeth, and Peter Ainsworth
1990   Problems at the Casa Diablo Quarry: Challenging the Biface Reduction Paradigm.   Paper presented at the 22nd Great Basin Anthropological Conference, Reno, Nevada.

1991   Unifacial Bifaces: More than one way to thin a biface. *Journal of California and Great Basin Anthropology* 13(2):160-171.

Speth, John D.
1972   Mechanical Basis for Percussion Flaking. *American Antiquity* 37:34-60.

Stahle, David W. and James E. Dunn
1982   An Analysis and Application of the Size Distribution of Waste Flakes from the Manufacture of Bifacial Stone Tools. *World Archaeology* 14(1):84-97.

Sullivan, Allan P. III, and Kenneth C. Rozen
1985   Debitage Analysis and Archaeological Interpretation. *American Antiquity* 50(4):755-779.

THE DYNAMICS OF ARCHAEOLOGICAL SIGNIFICANCE: A CASE STUDY FROM THE DALLES AREA OF THE PACIFIC NORTHWEST

Rick Minor
Heritage Research Associates, Inc.

ABSTRACT

Evaluation of the significance of prehistoric archaeological sites is a dynamic process, one that must take into account contemporary research concerns in regional prehistory as well as the current status of the prehistoric data base. This paper illustrates the dynamics of the significance evaluation process, using as an example prehistoric site 35WS14 on the Middle Columbia River near The Dalles, previously tested and evaluated in 1972. Reevaluation in terms of contemporary standards of archaeological signficance indicates that 35WS14, once considered unworthy of further investigation, is one of the more important prehistoric sites still remaining in The Dalles area of the Pacific Northwest.

With the emergence of cultural resource management in the 1970s, evaluating the significance of prehistoric sites has become a basic objective of much, if not most, of the archaeological field research carried out in the United States. While the quality of significance can theoretically be assessed in terms of a variety of categories (Raab and Klinger 1977), the significance of archaeological properties is most commonly measured in terms of potential eligibility to the National Register of Historic Places, generally in regard to Criterion d of 36 CFR 60.6, the extent to which a site has "yielded, or may be likely to yield, information important in prehistory or history." Using this approach, a prehistoric site is either significant, and worthy of preservation or mitigation, or not significant and no longer protected by federal legislation.

In contradistinction to the relatively static way in which archaeological significance is generally interpreted, Lynott (1980) has pointed out that the evaluation of significance must be a dynamic process, one that takes into account the evolution of regional research issues and the deterioration of the prehistoric data base. With the exception of Lynott's (1980) example of the revised evaluation of a rockshelter in central Texas, however, few case studies illustrating this important point have appeared in the archaeological literature. Building upon Lynott's previous discussion, this paper serves as a further illustration of the dynamics of the significance process, using as an example the reevaluation of prehistoric site 35WS14 near The Dalles of the Columbia River in the Pacific Northwest (Minor 1992).

TEST EXCAVATIONS AT 35WS14

The prehistory of The Dalles area is known primarily from work carried out in connection with construction of The Dalles Dam during the 1950s. On the Oregon shore, excavations in the Roadcut section of the Five Mile Rapids Site produced evidence of an early riverine-oriented culture radiocarbon dated to 7835 B.C. The later strata at Five Mile Rapids, and nearby at Wakemap Mound on the Washington shore, contained evidence of continued occupation of The Dalles area into early historic times (Cressman et al. 1960; Caldwell 1956; Butler 1960). The data collected during the reservoir salvage stage of archaeological investigations provided evidence of a late prehistoric cultural florescence that is sometimes referred to as "The Dalles Culture." This culture is radiocarbon dated as early as A.D. 860 at Wakemap Mound, but it was clearly already well developed by that time. The Dalles Culture is widely known for its elaborate carved bone, antler, and stone artifacts and rock art, much of which were executed in a distinctive art style.

Site 35WS14 is located near Columbia River Mile 187, approximately 10 km downstream from The Dalles Dam at the upper end of Lake Bonneville, the reservoir behind Bonneville Dam. The site was recorded in 1971 during a survey carried out in anticipation of the raising of the reservoir pool (Cole and Southard 1971). It was referred to as the "Bad Place Site" because it was thought to correspond to the location of the "verry Bad place" where the Lewis and Clark expedition camped during a heavy wind and rain storm on October 28, 1805 (Moulton 1988[5]:347). Subsequent interpretations have placed the location of this campsite farther downstream in the Crates Point vicinity (Minor and Beckham 1991:v, 9).

Situated on the shore just upstream from Rocky Island and a little over a kilometer downstream from the mouth of Chenoweth Creek, 35WS14 was initially described as a "midden on or around a series of rocky points" that had been "extensively pothunted" (Cole and Southard 1971:12-13). During the survey scrapers, a pestle fragment, a sinker, and cobble tools were recovered from the relic collectors' backdirt. It was "recommended that attempts be made to salvage some part of this site" (Cole and Southard 1971:13).

Test excavations were conducted at 35WS14 from August 23-27, 1972 under the direction of David L. Cole, under a contract between the Museum of Natural History, University of Oregon, and the National Park Service (Cole 1974). Testing began with

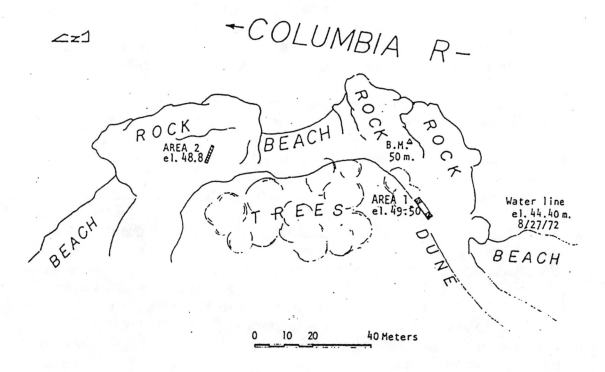

Figure 1. Sketch map of site 35WS14 (from Cole 1974:26)

excavation of an unspecified number of auger holes in an "area of approximately 200 meters." (The locations of these auger holes were not indicated on the site map for that project.) The augering results indicated that "the site was restricted to an area upon rock outcroppings, adjacent to the Columbia River. No occupation areas were found that had not been discovered previously by pothunters" (Cole 1974:25-26). Test pit excavations were then carried out in two areas of the site (Figure 1).

Area 1

Area 1 was situated in the southern (upstream) portion of the site. Two units located four meters apart were placed at the edge of the eroded river bank. These units were situated so that each began as a 1 x 2 m unit and was then expanded to 2 x 2 m at the beach level. Both were excavated to bedrock, with one unit (10-12x/12-14y) reaching 2.74 m in depth and the other (10-12x/18-20y) 3.31 m in depth (Cole 1974:26). In all, approximately 16 cubic meters were excavated in Area 1 (Cole 1974:28).

Although more subtle distinctions were recorded on the unit wall profiles (Figures 2 and 3), the sediments were interpreted to represent two basic strata. Stratum A was dune sand, within which two substrata were recognized. The upper portion (Field Stratum 1) was "a loose, white, dune sand that supported sod." The lower portion (Field Stratum 2) was "a more consolidated, light grey, dune sand that contained an occasional rock and some cultural debris." In Area 1 Stratum A was "approximately two meters" deep, with the two substrata "about equal in thickness" (Cole 1974:28).

Stratum B (Field Stratum 3) was described as "a light, reddish-brown, sandy-silt that contained many chunks of basalt from boulder to pebble size." This deposit included "several clay layers, ash lenses and lenses or layers of small gravels within the deposit." Stratum B rested on bedrock and was "as much as 1.48 m deep" (Cole 1974:28).

According to Cole (1974:28), a disconformity was observed at the contact between Strata A and B. This disconformity consisted of an angular rock layer whose presence was thought to reflect deflation of the surrounding sediments "such that it is suspected that the surface of Stratum B was subjected to flooding" (Cole 1974:28). In Unit 10-12x/18-20y the angular rock layer began at an approximate arbitrary elevation of 48.00 m (Winfield Henn, fieldnotes, 23-26 August 1972; Joanne M. Mack, fieldnotes, 23-26 August 1972). In Unit 10-12x/12-14y the angular rock layer began at an elevation of 47.60 m in the west half, sloping to an elevation of 47.50 m in the east half of the unit (John L. Fagan, fieldnotes, 24 August 1972). In both units the angular rock layer continued more or less to bedrock.

The single cultural feature recorded consisted of a "depression or pit that contained a concentration of rocks, artifacts and elk (*Cervus*) bones" encountered in the northwest corner of unit 10-12x/12-14y. First noted at an approximate elevation of 47.20 m, the pit rim was difficult to distinguish; the pit apparently bottomed out at an elevation of approximately 47.00 m (John L. Fagan, fieldnotes, 25-26 August 1972). The pit was described on the feature form as a "small circular dish-shaped pit which contains bone, large basalt slab, fire cracked angular basalt, flakes, large chert core, and charcoal." Associated artifacts included a complete maul, two maul-like pounders, a single-notched cobble netsinker, and chert and basalt flakes (Cole 1974:54, Table 6).

Area 2

Area 2 was situated "on the rocky prominence overlooking the slough that passes between Rocky Island and the mainland." Sand dune deposits overlying bedrock were described as occurring "in a triangular shaped area, about twelve to fifteen meters on each side." A similar stratigraphic sequence was encountered, with sterile white dune sand (Field Stratum 1) underlain by finer-grained yellow-brown sand containing numerous small river pebbles and abundant angular basalt (Field Stratum 2) (Winfield Henn, fieldnotes, 27 August 1972; Joanne M. Mack, fieldnotes, 27 August 1972). The excavations apparently did not extend deep enough to reach Stratum B. All fill removed in Area 2 was from the dune sand referred to as Stratum A (Cole 1974:28).

123

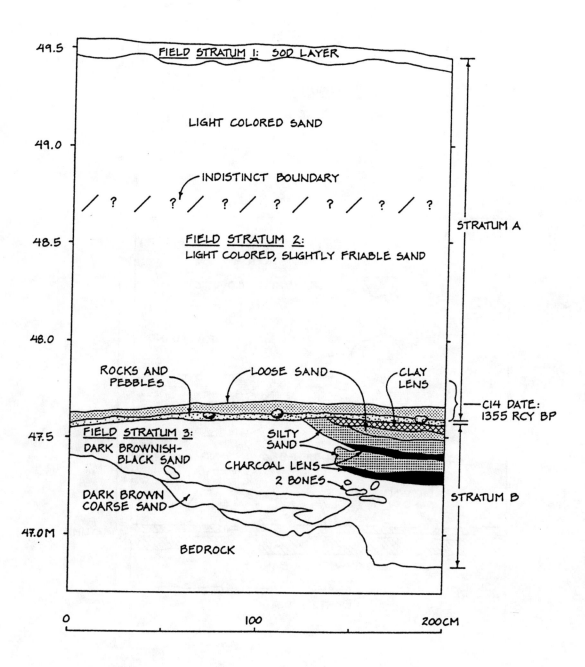

Figure 2. West wall profile from unit 10-12x/12-14y.

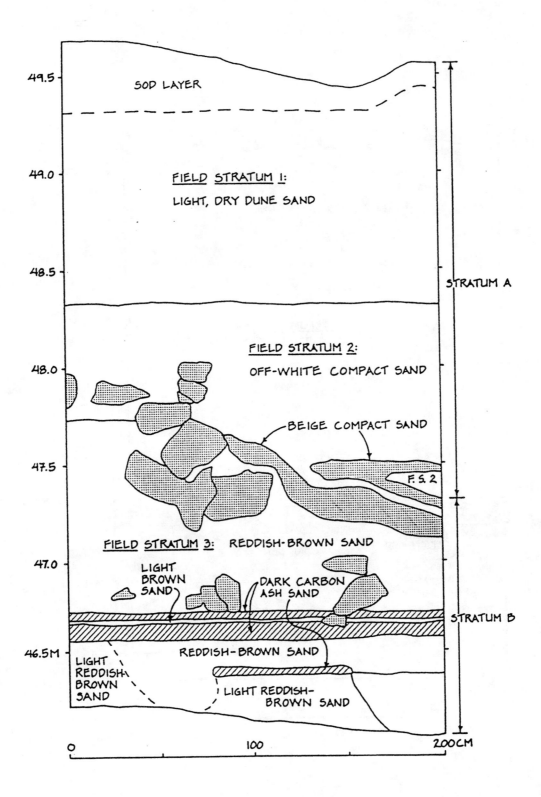

Figure 3. West wall profile from unit 10-12x/18-20y.

It is stated in the report that a 1 x 6 m trench was excavated in Area 2, but fieldnotes are available only for a 1 x 2 m unit (14-16x, 10-11y) (Winfield Henn, fieldnotes, 27 August 1972; Joanne M. Mack, fieldnotes, 27 August 1972). It is also stated in the report that this trench was excavated to a depth of 70 cm, at which point work was "halted because of time and paucity of information" (Cole 1974:26). However, transit measurements contained in the fieldnotes seem to indicate that the excavations were extended to depths ranging from 0.84 m to 1.04 m, to an elevation of 48.00 m (Winfield Henn, fieldnotes, 27 August 1972; Joanne M. Mack, fieldnotes, 27 August 1972). In all, approximately four cubic meters were excavated in Area 2 (Cole 1974:28).

These fieldnotes are consistent with the statement elsewhere in the report that "at 0.85 m below the surface, in lower Stratum A," a 2-3 cm-thick band of dark clay was encountered "just under a deflated layer of angular basalts and fire-cracked rock" (Cole 1974:30). The clay band was situated at an elevation of 48.15 m (Winfield Henn, fieldnotes, 27 August 1972). Several artifacts were associated with this "possible occupation layer," including a small projectile point, a biface fragment, a flake scraper fragment, a graver, and a long bone splinter polished from use on a naturally beveled end. Associated animal bones included bear and an artiodactyl (probably deer or mountain sheep) (Cole 1974:67). The amount of angular rock, as well as the frequency of cultural material, declined sharply in the following level (48.20-48.00 m), where the white sand of Field Stratum 2 was again encountered (Winfield Henn, fieldnotes, 27 August 1972; Joanne M. Mack, fieldnotes, 27 August 1972).

ARTIFACTS FROM 35WS14

The artifact collection recovered during the 1972 test excavations at 35WS14 consists overwhelmingly of implements made of stone. Six bone/antler artifacts were also recovered. For this reevaluation all of the artifact collection was reexamined, with the exception of "waste stone"; frequency data for the waste stone is taken from the testing report (Cole 1974). The artifact collection is summarized in terms of the same major provenience units presented in the testing report in Table 1.

Chipped Stone Tools

A total of 136 chipped stone artifacts were recovered. This sub-assemblage includes representatives of ten tool classes: projectile points, knives, drills, bifaces, scrapers, flake knives, gravers, punches, spokeshaves, and used flakes. With the exception of three projectile points of obsidian, all of the chipped stone tools were manufactured from various grades of chert. This raw material is locally available in river gravels and onshore outcrops. In contrast, the obsidian artifacts were most likely made

Table 1. Artifacts recovered from 35WS14.

Artifact Class	Area 1 Stratum A Surf.-47.60	Area 1 Stratum B 47.60-47.20	Area 1 Stratum B 47.20-bedrock	Area 2 Stratum A	General Surface	Totals
Chipped Stone						
Projectile Points:						
CS1		3	1			4
CS2		3	2			5
ES1	2	6	6		1	15
ES3		1				1
PS		1	1	1		3
Small Bipoint			1			1
Unclassifiable	2	4	10	1		17
Mule Ear Knife		1				1
Drills		2	4			6
Biface Fragments	2	4	15	1		22
Scrapers	1	2	3	1		7
Flake Knives		2	5			7
Gravers	3	4	6	1		14
Punches	2	3				5
Spokeshaves		2				2
Used Flakes		9	15	2		26
Cobble Tools						
Maul (Complete)			1			1
Maul Fragments		1	2			3
Bowl Fragment			1			1
Milling Stone Fragment		1				1
Hammers	1	6	13	1	3	24
Pounders	1	3	4			8
Flaked Cobbles:						
Unifacial	1	1	1			3
Bifacial	1	3	1		1	6
Notched Cobbles:						
Single	1	5	9			15
Double			5		1	6
Fragments		2	1		1	4
Angular Basalt Tools						
Pounder			1			1
Flaked Pieces	2		3	1		6
Used Pieces	2	4	1			7
Cores and Debitage						
Cores		3		1		4
Waste Stone:*						
Chert	273	789	586	218		1866
Basalt	73	259	65	34		431
Obsidian	1	9	17	1		28
Petrified Wood			3			3
Other	18	59	39	18		134
Miscellaneous Artifacts						
Stone Spool			1			1
Pipe Fragments	1	1				2
Bone Awl				1		1
Worked Bone		2	1	1		4
Antler Wedge			1			1

* Waste stone material frequencies from Cole (1974:68, Table 8)

from material obtained from one or more of the many sources to the south in central Oregon.

The projectile points from 35WS14 include 29 classifiable specimens and 17 fragments (Figure 4). For descriptive purposes, the classifiable specimens were measured according to four dimensions: neck width, basal width, maximum width, and thickness (Table 2). The collection consists overwhelmingly of narrow-necked specimens; the neckwidth peak is between 3.6-4.4 mm (Figure 5a). A single specimen with a neck-width of 10.2 mm was recovered, but it is too fragmentary to permit classification (Figure 4r). One other specimen is a small bipoint which lacks a neck for measurement (Figure 4q). The narrow-necked points reflect a contracting/expanding continuum, as 11 have contracting stems and 17 have expanding stems (Figure 5b). For the most part these points do not correspond to any named types, with the exception of three small specimens (Figure 4l-n) referred to as "dagger points" by relic collectors (Strong 1959:155-156, Figure 59). Seven broken points can only be classified as narrow-necked specimens.

For comparative purposes, the specimens from 35WS14 were classified in terms of both the typology previously developed for projectile points at the Wildcat Canyon site upstream (Dumond and Minor 1983) and the Portland Basin downstream from The Dalles (Pettigrew 1981). The 29 classifiable points from 35WS14 can be assigned to five types in the Wildcat Canyon site typology, with 16 points falling into two expanding stem types (ES1, ES3), nine points correlating with two contracting stem types (CS1, CS2), and three points representing the small pin stem series (Table 2). The small bipoint (Figure 4q) does not correspond to any type in the Wildcat Canyon typology. In terms of the Portland Basin typology, the points from 35WS14 can be assigned to seven types, including three diverging stem and three non-diverging stem types. The small bipoint from 35WS14 corresponds to Type 6b in the Portland Basin typology. (This classification of the 35WS14 points differs slightly from that by Pettigrew [1981:130, Table 45], but with no significant change in interpretation.) The implications of these classification systems for typological cross-dating of the projectile points from 35WS14 are discussed in a later section of this paper.

The single knife in the 35WS14 collection is a triangular specimen with an indented base; this form is often referred to as a "Mule Ear" knife (Figure 6a). It measures 3.62 cm in length, 2.59 cm in width, 0.54 cm in thickness and weighs 4.64 g. One nearly complete and five fragmentary drills (three tips and two bases) are represented in the collection. The two base fragments appear to have been modified for hafting (Figure 6b-c). Twenty-two biface fragments represent bifacially modified pieces broken during the manufacturing process.

Five of the seven scrapers in the collection are fragmentary. Of these, three specimens exhibit snap fractures suggesting that they originally might have been hafted (Figure 6d-e). Two of these scraper fragments also exhibit spalls from exposure to heat. Seven flake knives exhibit low-angled unifacial retouch along one edge indicating use as

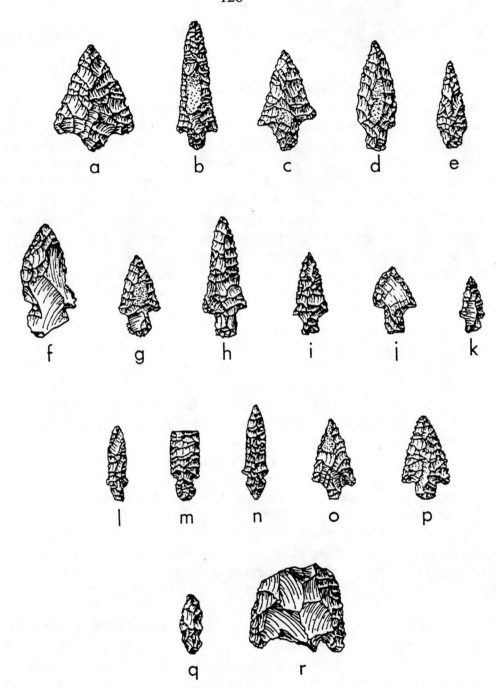

Figure 4.   Projectile points from 35WS14: a-c, Type CS1; d-e, Type CS2; f, Type ES3; g-k, Type ES1; l-n, Type ES1 "dagger" style; o-p, Pin Stem type; q, small bipoint; r, unclassifiable broad-necked point (shown actual size).

a. A4-4/3-25   d. A4-9/3-56   g. A4-2/2-1   j. A1-7/3-5   m. A4-6/3-10   p. A4-6/3-9
b. A1-7/3-9   e. A4-8/3-4   h. S-1   k. A1-6/3-20   n. A4-4/3-26   q. A4-6/3-2
c. A4-4/3-21   f. A4-8/3-5   i. A1-8/3-6   l. A1-8/3-5   o. D-2/3-1   r. A1-5/2-1

Table 2. Projectile point dimensions.

Artifact No.	Type WC	Ptld	Length (mm)	Width (mm)	Thickness (mm)	NW (mm)	BW (mm)	BW-NW	Weight (grams)	Mat.	Comments
S-1	ES1	8	31.3	11.4	4.8	4.5	5.3	0.8	1.30	C	Complete
A1-1/pf-1	ES1	8	14.0	6.9	3.5	3.0	3.8	0.8	0.30	C	Complete
A1-6/3-20	ES1	8	13.8	6.1	2.8	3.1	3.8	0.7	0.20	O	Complete
A1-6/3-22	ES1	7	18.5	11.3	3.7	4.1	5.4	1.3	0.48	C	Complete; on flake
A1-7/3-5	ES1	8	16.9	10.8	2.2	3.9	4.2	0.3	0.41	C	Complete; on flake
A1-7/3-8	ES1	7	13.8*	11.8	2.8	4.0	5.5	1.5	0.35	C	Tip broken
A1-8/3-6	ES1	8	21.0	8.7	3.1	3.3	4.1	0.8	0.46	C	Complete
A4-2/2-1	ES1	7	20.8	11.1	2.6	4.7	6.2	1.5	0.41	C	Complete; on flake
A4-5/3-11	ES1	8	18.3	10.8	2.3	3.9	4.9	1.0	0.34	C	Complete; on flake
A4-7/3-12	ES1	8	21.1	9.1	3.4	3.6	4.0	0.4	0.57	C	Complete
A4-9/3-2	ES1	7	17.7	12.9	3.2	4.1	4.3	0.2	0.51	C	Complete
A4-9/3-3	ES1	7	18.2	12.7	2.6	5.2	6.8	1.6	0.52	C	Complete
A1-8/3-5	ES1(d)	8	19.2	5.6	2.4	2.7	2.4	-0.3	0.20	C	Nicked stem
A4-4/3-26	ES1(d)	8	23.9	6.9	2.8	3.6	4.8	1.2	0.36	C	Complete
A4-6/3-10	ES1(d)	7	17.8*	7.7	2.7	3.0	5.0	2.0	0.46	C	Tip missing
A4-8/3-5	ES3	1	29.6	13.9	2.9	8.7	10.9	2.2	1.13	C	Crude; on flake
A1-7/3-9	CS1	9	33.5	11.1	3.2	3.9	0.8	-3.1	0.83	C	Complete
A4-4/3-21	CS1	10	25.9	15.1	4.0	6.2	4.1	-2.1	1.04	C	Complete
A4-4/3-25	CS1	4	27.1	21.6	4.1	7.6	1.6	-6.0	1.40	C	Complete
A4-6/3-11	CS1	9	17.0*	14.7	4.7	3.9	2.9	-1.0	0.87	C	Broken Tip
A1-6/3-19	CS2	10	17.2	9.3	2.1	4.2	3.8	-0.4	0.36	C	Complete; on flake
A1-6/3-21	CS2	10	18.1	9.7	2.3	4.2	2.9	-1.3	0.32	O	Complete; on flake
A4-4/3-22	CS2	9	16.0*	19.3	4.5	6.7	4.9	-1.8	1.31	C	Broken tip
A4-8/3-4	CS2	10	22.5	7.6	3.9	-	3.5	-.-	0.48	C	Stemless
A4-9/3-56	CS2	10	28.6	10.1	4.0	4.8	4.5	-0.3	1.09	C	Complete
A4-4/3-28	PS?	10	15.3	8.8	2.5	2.5	1.6	-0.9	0.23	C	Crude; on flake
A4-6/3-9	PS	9	21.6	12.4	3.2	4.5	4.5	0	0.70	C	Complete
D-2/3-1 (14/2)	PS	9	20.8	10.8	3.7	2.9	2.1	-0.8	0.58	C	Complete
A4-6/3-2	SL	6b	5.7	3.8	-.-	1.5	-.-	-.-	0.28	O	Complete
A1-5/2-1	--	2?	22.8*	25.3	4.9	10.2	-.-	-.-	2.79	C	Stem, tip broken
A1-7/3-1	--	--	18.2*	13.4*	3.6	3.9	-.-	-.-	0.56	C	Broken stem, barb
A1-7/3-7	--	--	18.2*	9.7	2.7	3.1	-.-	-.-	0.46	C	Stem broken
A4-2/2-3	--	--	18.2+	15.5	4.0	4.8	-.-	-.-	0.90	C	Stem broken
A4-7/3-10	--	--	22.1*	9.7	2.1	3.6	-.-	-.-	0.56	C	Broken stem
A4-7/3-11	--	--	17.8*	11.3	3.1	3.7	-.-	-.-	0.42	C	Stem broken
A4-9/3-4	--	--	13.9*	12.4	2.8	4.3	-.-	-.-	0.39	C	Stem Broken
A4-10/4-3	--	--	15.1*	8.4	3.4	3.8	-.-	-.-	0.36	C	Stem broken

WC = Wildcat Canyon   Ptld = Portland Basin   NW = Neck Width   BW = Base Width   * = measurement of broken specimen
(d) = dagger   SL = stemless   O = obsidian   C = chert

simple cutting tools (Figure 6f-g). Twelve of the 14 gravers have simple graving tips exhibiting little enhancement, but on the other two gravers the projections exhibit careful preparation through bifacial retouch (Figure 6h-i).   Five punches are all long, thin flakes that have been retouched on the distal ends to form sharp points suitable for piercing or perforating (Figure 6j-k). Two spokeshaves feature a unifacially retouched concavity creating an edge suitable for shaving or scraping convex surfaces (Figure 6-l). Twenty-six used flakes, waste stone exhibiting evidence of use as simple cutting or scraping tools, are also in the collection.

Cobble Tools

The 35WS14 collection includes 72 implements made of or directly derived from cobbles. Included are implements made by means of flaked stone technology as well as tools characterized by simple battering, abrasion, or use wear. These cobble tools are made from a variety of rocks, most commonly basalt and quartzite that are locally available in the river gravels.

The one complete maul is of the familiar heavy-flanged type (Figure 7a). It measures 19.7 cm in length, has a maximum basal width of 9.0 cm, a maximum basal thickness of 7.1 cm, and weighs 1.6 kg. This type of maul was characteristic of the Late Period (post A.D. 1000) in The Dalles vicinity (Butler 1964). Three other maul fragments, none diagnostic as to type, were also recovered. A rim/side fragment from a small basin-shaped stone bowl (Figure 7b) was recovered. Based on this fragment, the bowl is estimated to have been approximately 13 cm in diameter, 5.7 cm high, with a basin 2.9 cm deep (Cole 1974:65). The flat face of a piece of tabular basalt exhibits evidence of use as a surface for milling or grinding, probably during the processing of vegetal foods. Twenty-four cobbles and pebbles exhibit evidence of battering indicating use as hammerstones. These include twelve cobbles and one pebble that are oval to circular in form with battering wear along the rims. Eleven cobbles and one pebble are elongate in form. Most of the elongate hammerstones exhibit battering on both ends. Eight other cobbles exhibit wear indicative of somewhat heavier-duty use as pounders. All are elongate in shape and exhibit wear on both ends (Figure 7c-d). The broader ends on these specimens are flat to semi-convex and exhibit heavy grinding and crushing wear similar to that present on mauls. It seems likely, then, that these specimens had a similar use, and in effect represent "unmodified" mauls.

Nine flaked cobbles in the collection represent simple cutting or chopping tools. Included are six with bifacial and three with unifacial flake removals (Figure 8a). The unifacial specimens include one flaked around its entire periphery and two with flaking along only a portion of the periphery (Figure 8b). These unifacially-modified "peripherally flaked cobbles" were a common artifact type along the Columbia River (Valley 1979). Another 25 flat cobbles with notches are presumed to have been used as net weights (Figure 8c-d). Six have double notches, 15 have single notches, and four are fragments. Metric data for the complete specimens is presented in Table 3.

Angular Basalt Tools

Fourteen implements made of angular basalt available in cliffs and outcrops along the Columbia River are in the 35WS14 collection. This material often occurs in flat pieces with naturally sharp edges that require little, if any, modification to make them into usable cutting tools. Also included are implements characterized by simple battering and abrasion.

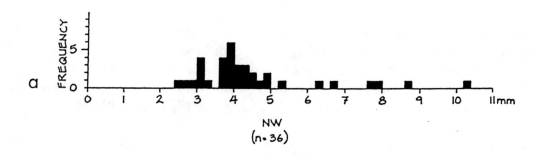

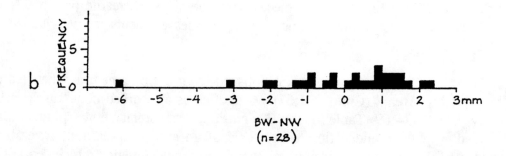

Figure 5. Distribution of projectile point neck widths (a) and stem configurations (b).

A long slender piece of angular basalt was employed in a manner similar to that of the pounders described above. The wider, presumably distal, end exhibits the battered, slightly rounded, shape indicative of use as a maul. Although some effort was made to shape the upper portion through abrasion, the natural triangular cross-section of this piece is largely unmodified. Six pieces of angular basalt exhibit edges modified by flaking and reflect use as heavy-duty cutting and scraping tools. Three specimens, one bifacial and the other two primarily unifacial, appear to have been used as choppers. Another specimen exhibits a unifacial notch suitable for use as a large spokeshave. The remaining two specimens exhibit unifacial flake removals that created edges suitable for heavy-duty cutting or sawing activities.

Seven pieces of angular basalt appear to have been employed as tools without purposeful modification. One specimen with a narrow bit may have been used as a wedge. The other six specimens have naturally sharp edges and appear to have been used as simple cutting implements. Two of these are relatively heavy pieces; the remaining four are thin tabular slabs.

Cores and Debitage

The collection from 35WS14 includes four chert cores (Figure 6m) (cf. Cole 1974). The debitage, and possibly some additional cores, were not available for reanalysis, but according to the testing report some 2462 pieces of "waste stone" were recovered, including 1866 chert (75.8%), 431 basalt (17.5%), 28 obsidian (1.1%), three petrified wood (0.1%), and 134 other (5.4%) (Cole 1974:68, Table 8).

Miscellaneous Artifacts

A small piece of basalt has been modified into a stone spool measuring 1.38 cm in length and 2.27 cm in width. Several flanges have been broken from the exterior, making its original form difficult to reconstruct (Figure 6n). The smooth interior measures 1.2 cm in diameter. Two pieces from the sides of steatite pipe bowls were recovered in Area 1. Unfortunately, no meaningful measurements can be obtained from these small fragments.

"A splinter of long bone that was polished from use on a naturally beveled end" was recovered in Area 2 (Cole 1974:67). Classified as a "worked bone" in the artifact inventory (Cole 1974:69, Table 9), this 3.6 cm-long fragmentary bone splinter exhibits a smoothed, slightly rounded tip characteristic of an awl. In addition, several other pieces of modified bone were identified among the faunal remains. Included are four short burned and abraded sections of unidentified mammal bone classified here as worked bone, and the tip of an elk antler that was used as a wedge. The latter specimen was recovered with the elk bones found "under the clay layer" in the pit designated Feature 1 in Area 1.

Table 3. Metric data for notched cobble netsinkers (cm and grams).

Specimen No.	Type	Length	Max. Width	Notch Width	Thickness	Weight
S-3	Double	6.67	5.33	4.67	1.73	86.5
A4-7/3-1	Double	6.65	5.31	4.73	1.83	98.5
A4-7/3-2	Double*	9.08	6.80	6.02	1.88	181.7
A4-7/3-3	Double*	8.93	6.78	6.30	2.37	245.9
A4-8/3-46	Double	7.48	6.12	5.40	1.63	129.7
A4-8/3-54	Double	8.47	6.03	5.40	1.62	127.7
A4-8/3-56	Double*	7.52	5.99	5.78	1.46	120.4
Test Hole	Single	9.02	5.84	4.82	2.16	163.86
A1-6/3-4	Single	7.01	5.66	5.13	1.36	88.8
A1-8/3-18	Single	8.22	6.87	5.54	2.08	150.6
A4-4/3-2	Single	6.13	5.20	4.75	1.42	72.2
A4-4/3-3	Single	7.43	6.14	5.75	1.75	125.3
A4-4/3-4	Single	8.87	7.16	6.55	2.18	225.0
A4-4/3-5	Single	7.95	6.96	6.10	2.15	171.4
A4-8/3-43	Single	7.78	5.59	5.34	2.20	149.6
A4-8/3-44	Single	8.07	6.24	5.94	1.42	130.9
A4-8/3-45	Single	7.36	5.77	5.35	1.62	109.6
A4-8/3-47	Single	9.29	7.57	6.93	1.85	222.6
A4-8/3-55	Single	8.89	6.00	5.51	2.00	185.1
A4-9/3-51	Single	6.67	5.20	5.08	1.59	91.8
A4-9/3-52	Single	8.34	7.17	6.45	2.20	210.7

* One full notch and one "incipient" notch created by crushing of the edge rather than through flake removal.

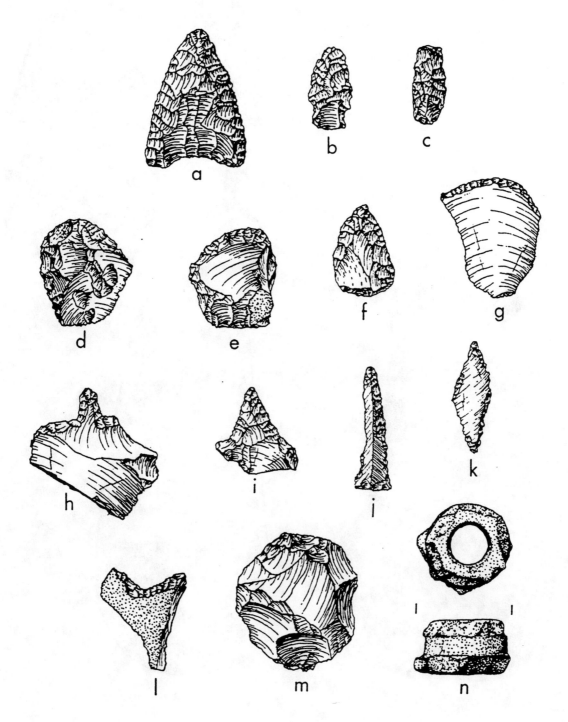

Figure 6. Miscellaneous artifacts from 35WS14:
    a, Mule Ear knife   f-g, flake knives   l,   spokeshave
    b-c, drill base fragments   h-i, gravers   m, core
    d-e, scrapers   j-k, punches   n, stone spool
                                                   (n, shown actual size).

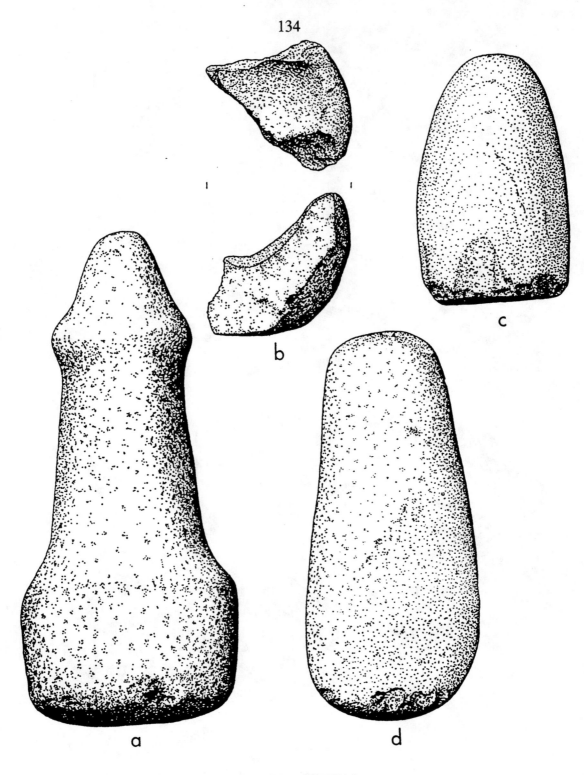

Figure 7. Miscellaneous cobble tools from 35WS14:
a, A1-8/3-21, maul b, A4-8/3-50, bowl fragment;
c, (A4-8/3-38) d, (A1-8/3-19) maul-like hammerstones
(c-d shown approximately 65% actual size).

Faunal Remains

The testing report states that animal bones were found "throughout the site," but mostly in "small pieces, either charred or decayed." Although not analyzed at that time, the faunal assemblage was said to include fish (present "throughout Stratum B"), artiodactyl, bobcat, dog (probably coyote) and elk (Cole 1974:67). In conjunction with this reevaluation of 35WS14, the faunal assemblage recovered during the 1972 test excavations was identified, with the results summarized in Table 4.

The elk remains reflect an interesting refuse pattern. The identifiable elements recovered represent four left metatarsals, a left metacarpal, and two antler fragments that may represent parts of a single antler. All of the elk remains were recovered from the pit feature recorded in Area 1 (Cole 1974:67).

In addition to vertebrate remains, a few fragments of freshwater mussel, tentatively identified as *Margaritifera falcata*, were recovered from Stratum A in Area 2. The only other subsistence remains recovered were a few charred hazelnut fragments recovered from Stratum B in Area 1 (Cole 1974:67).

FUNCTION AND CHRONOLOGY

Because of the limited extent of the test excavations, it is difficult to draw a firm conclusion about the type of settlement represented at 35WS14. No evidence of houses was encountered, but such features may have been present in areas other than those sampled during the testing project. The artifact assemblage includes many tool classes commonly found at prehistoric sites along the Columbia River. Activities represented include hunting, fishing, and perhaps the processing of vegetal foods. Overall, the density of cultural materials suggests that, if not necessarily a permanent village, this site was at least a base camp where a considerable range of activities was carried out. The location of 35WS14 suggests that it probably served as a seasonal fishing station of the kind documented in The Dalles vicinity in historic times (Suphan 1974:29-30).

Recovery of artifacts from the lower part of Stratum A led to the inference that prehistoric occupation at 35WS14 occurred during an early stage of dune formation. The dune sand was underlain by the sandy silt of Stratum B, which was interpreted as an alluvial deposit. Angular rock layers in Stratum B were believed to reflect scoured or deflated areas. On this basis, it was "assumed that there had been a flood preceeding the duning period," and that "this hypothesized pre-dune flood is held responsible for disconformities between lower Stratum A and Stratum B" (Cole 1974:70).

It was further suggested that "layers of ponding deposits near the bottom of Stratum B are attributed to slack water, which could have been created by the landslide

Table 4. Inventory of vertebrate faunal remains from 35WS14.

| | Area 1 | | | Area 2 | | |
| | Stratum A | Stratum B | | Stratum A | | |
Faunal Class	Surf.-47.60	47.60-47.20	47.20-bedrock		General Surface	Totals
Large cat (cougar?)			1			1
Canis sp. (coyote or dog size)		2				2
Deer				4		4
Elk		10			10	
Bear				1		1
Artiodactyl		1				1
Medium mammal		2				2
Medium mammal/bird			1			1
Medium/large mammal	6	38	6		50	
Large mammal	11	58	2	2		73
Unidentifiable mammal	1	8			9	
Oncorhynchus sp.	17	8	1			26
Sturgeon	3	29	3	2		37
Sucker	1	3				4
Unidentifiable fish	6					6
Unidentifiable	5	45	4			54

near Cascade Locks. If this is the case, then the dates from most of Stratum B would be after A.D. 1500" (Cole 1974:70). No radiocarbon assays were obtained in conjunction with the testing project at 35WS14, but in support of this scenario it was asserted that "the narrow stemmed projectile points found throughout Stratum B of this site are typical of projectile points from the post A.D. 1400 period" (Cole 1974:70).

The landslide at Cascade Locks referred to here is known as the Cascade or Bonneville Landslide. Occurring at Columbia River Mile 149, this landslide blocked the Columbia River, creating a temporary earthen dam that impounded a lake behind it. The impounded waters drowned a narrow fringe of forest along the banks of the river for 60 km upstream; it has been suggested that the lake behind the landslide dam "extended beyond the eastern portal of the gorge far into the treeless region of the Columbia Basin" (Lawrence and Lawrence 1958:36). The river subsequently cut a passage through the landslide debris and the release of the impounded water resulted in a catastrophic flood downstream (Lawrence and Lawrence 1958).

Tree stumps comprising the "submerged forest" upstream from the landslide were observed as early as 1805-1806 by Lewis and Clark (Moulton 1988[5]:356; 1991[7]:118, 120, 122fn). The drowned trees continued to elicit comments from travelers through the Columbia Gorge up to the 1930s when the river banks were again inundated and the trees were covered as a result of the raising of the Bonneville Dam reservoir pool (Lawrence 1936, 1937). The tree stumps were remarkably well preserved, contributing to the idea that their submergence occurred within the last 500 to 1000 years (Hodge 1932:56; 1938:916).

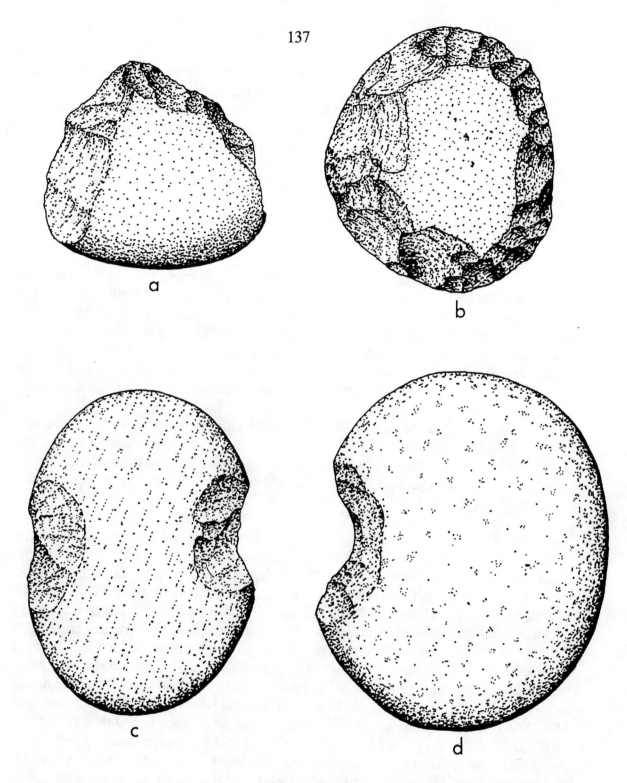

Figure 8.   Flaked and notched cobbles from 35WS14: a-b, unifacially flaked cobbles; c, double-notched netsinker; d, single-notched netsinker (shown actual size). a. A1-6/3-5 b. A4-9/3-50 c. A4-8/3-54 d. A4-8/3-47

Shortly after the development of radiocarbon dating in the 1950s, wood samples from two of these stumps were submitted for dating to the University of Michigan Radiocarbon Laboratory (Lawrence and Lawrence 1958:41; Crane and Griffin 1959:175-176). The results of the radiocarbon dating substantiated the age estimates based on geological grounds. The first sample, obtained from a large Douglas fir stump near Wyeth, Oregon, produced an uncorrected date of 670 ± 300 RCYBP: A.D. 1280 (M-722). The second sample, obtained from a Garry oak stump near Bingen, Washington, produced an uncorrected date of 700 ± 200 RCYBP: A.D. 1250 (M-761). These two tree stumps were located approximately 11 km and 34 km upstream from the landslide area, respectively.

A more recent attempt to determine the age of the Bonneville Landslide involved radiocarbon dating wood recovered in 1978 during geological investigations for the Second Powerhouse at Bonneville Dam (Minor 1984). A section from a large fir tree buried by the landslide produced an uncorrected date of 830 ± 60 RCYBP: A.D. 1120 (Beta-9960). Since it was obtained from the landslide itself, this date appears to more reliably represent the age of the Bonneville Landslide. It is also highly consistent with archaeological evidence from the surrounding area (Minor, Toepel, and Beckham 1989).

In order to test the suggestion that the disconformity between Stratum A and Stratum B at 35WS14 was related to a flood caused by waters impounded behind the Bonneville Landslide, samples of animal bones (available charcoal was insufficient) from closely associated contexts were submitted for radiocarbon dating in conjunction with the present reevaluation of 35WS14.

The first sample was obtained from Area 1, specifically from Level 5, elevation 47.80-47.60 m, in Unit 10-12X 12-14Y. This sample was taken from just above the disconformity between Stratum A and B, which fieldnotes indicate was situated at an elevation of 47.60 m in the west half of this unit, and at approximately 47.50 m in the east side of this unit (John L. Fagan, fieldnotes, 24 August 1972). The animal bones comprising the sample were identified as follows: Salmonidae: 10 vertebrae fragments, 2 unidentifiable fragments; Catostomidae: 1 operculum fragment; unidentified fish: 4 fragments; unidentified large mammal: 7 fragments; and unidentified vertebrate fauna: 4 fragments. Because the total sample weight of 9 grams was too small for conventional radiocarbon dating, it was sent by Beta Analytic, Inc. to Switzerland for Accelerator Mass Spectrometry (AMS) dating. The sample yielded an uncorrected date of 1355 ± 65 RCYBP: A.D. 595 (Beta-25155, ETH-3900). This date is more than 500 years older than the landslide, and it is thus apparent that the disconformity between Strata A and B in Area 1 at 35WS14 is not related to this major geologic event.

The second sample was taken from Area 1, "west of Unit 10-12x/12-14y, Field Stratum 2 under clay layer." It consisted of a left elk metatarsal fragment recovered from the pit designated Feature 1 encountered in this area. This bone produced an uncorrected date of 560 ± 70 RCYBP: A.D. 1390 (Beta-52523). This feature was situated at an approximate elevation of 47.20-47.00 m (John L. Fagan, fieldnotes, 25-26 August 1972). In terms of elevation, then, this sample was situated 30-40 cm or more below the level at which the previous radiocarbon date of 1355 $\pm$ 65 RCYBP was obtained. This inversion is not surprising, however, as the sample that produced the date of 560 $\pm$ 70 RCYBP was recovered from a pit apparently dug down into older sediments.

The third sample was from Area 2, Unit 14-16x/10-11y, elevation 48.20-48.00 m, Field Stratum 2. This sample was situated just below "a deflated layer of angular basalts and fire-cracked rock" (Cole 1974:30). It was suggested that "another later flood [postdating the Cascade or Bonneville Landslide] was responsible for the deflated levels of Area 2 of Site 35WS14, because dune sand occurred below that deposit" (Cole 1974:70). Consisting of an artiodactyl (deer-sized) scapula fragment and a bear tibia fragment, this sample produced a date of 800 $\pm$ 100 RCYBP: A.D. 1150 (Beta-52524). This date is statistically identical to that of 830 $\pm$ 60 RCYBP thought to most accurately indicate the age of the Bonneville Landslide (Minor 1984). This situation suggests, then, that the "deflated layer" in Area 2 may in fact have been caused by the release of waters backed up behind the Bonneville Landslide.

In addition to radiocarbon analysis, the age of the occupation at 35WS14 can be estimated by typological cross-dating of the temporally-diagnostic projectile points recovered through comparison with the Wildcat Canyon and Portland Basin typologies. In terms of the Wildcat Canyon typology, the predominance of narrow-necked Expanding Stem points (ES=16) as well as the paucity of small Pin Stem points (PS=3) indicates occupation during the late subphase of the Wildcat Phase, estimated to date from A.D. 500-1000. Other artifact classes characteristic of (but not limited to) this phase that are also represented at 35WS14 include punches, notched netsinkers, mauls, and milling stones (Dumond and Minor 1983:158-162).

In terms of the Portland Basin typology, the predominance of narrow-necked points indicates occupation during the Multnomah Phase. More specifically, the slight predominance of Type 7 (barbed, diverging stem) over Type 9 (barbed, non-diverging stem) points is considered indicative of the Multnomah 1 subphase, estimated to date from A.D. 200-1250. Other artifact classes considered characteristic of this subphase include notched netsinkers, peripherally flaked cobbles, and stone spools (Pettigrew 1981:130).

The results of projectile point cross-dating thus suggest that the assertion that "narrow stemmed projectile points found throughout Stratum B of this site are typical of projectile points from the post A.D. 1400 period" (Cole 1974:70) is also in error. In fact, this assertion would seem to be contradicted by the comparison of the projectile point assemblage from 35WS14 with those from nearby 35WS1 and 35WS4 presented in the testing report (Cole 1974:64, Table 7). This comparison indicated that "in total, the projectile points from 35WS14 are the more common varieties found in Sites 35WS1 and 35WS4" (Cole 1974:65). Sites 35WS1 and 35WS4 are both relatively old sites with long occupation spans; the latest of 10 radiocarbon dates available from these two localities is 1630 ± 90 RCYBP (unpublished records on file at OSMA). Given this information (which was also available to Cole), there would seem to be little basis for asserting that the projectile points from 35WS14 were typical of the period after A.D. 1400.

To summarize the available chronological information, instead of an occupation postdating A.D. 1400 or 1500 as originally suggested (Cole 1974:70), radiocarbon assays of A.D. 1150 and A.D. 1390 indicate occupation several hundred years earlier. These radiocarbon dates are supported by the results of projectile point cross-dating using two different typologies that yielded similar age estimates, as comparison with the Wildcat Canyon typology suggests occupation from A.D. 500-1000, while comparison with the Portland Basin typology suggests occupation from A.D. 200-1250.

The latest radiocarbon date of 560 ± 70 RCYBP: A.D. 1390 obtained from the pit feature in Area 1 is either an error or relates to much later occupation at 35WS14. As the earliest radiocarbon date of 1355 RCYBP: A.D. 525 was obtained from the bottom of Stratum A and above Stratum B in which the bulk of the artifacts were recovered, it is apparent that occupation at 35WS14 must have begun sometime before that. In view of the thickness of Stratum B, as much as 1.48 m (Cole 1974:28), it seems reasonable to suggest that occupation may have begun at 35WS14 as much as 500 or more years earlier.

The chronological information available for 35WS14 suggests, then, that occupation began toward the end of the Late Middle Period (ca. 1500 B.C.-A.D. 500) and continued into the Late Period (A.D. 500-1750) in Dalles area prehistory (Butler 1959, 1964, 1965). These periods encompassed a time of cultural florescence, during which the population occupied sedentary pithouse villages with discrete cemeteries. Elaboration in material culture in the form of wealth items, mortuary goods, and portable and rock art suggests a level of cultural complexity higher than that in any other area of the Columbia Plateau, perhaps rivaling the Formative cultures of the Northwest Coast (Minor 1988:76).

DISCUSSION

The test excavations carried out at 35WS14 in 1972 were undertaken "to discover something about the sites remaining in the Bonneville pool area and how they would be affected by raising the elevation of the water" (Cole 1974:72). Site 35WS14 was observed to be one of "three sites [that] are being affected by high waters during the contemporary period and they will continue to be affected with higher water" (Cole 1974:72). It was further observed that "the lower deposits of Site 35WS14 would be inundated by fluctuations in the pool level if the mean elevation is increased" (Cole 1974:72). In spite of these observations, Cole concluded that "it is my feeling that this site has been adequately sampled and that problems about the site, such as origins of rock deposits, are not important enough to explore further" (1974:72).

Cole's assessment of 35WS14 was based on his experience in conducting archaeological research along the Middle Columbia River. His M.S. Thesis reported the results of excavations in 1952 and 1953 at Big Eddy (35WS1) and Fivemile Rapids (35WS4) near The Dalles (Cole 1954), and he was a contributor to the important publication on the University of Oregon's work in this area from 1952 to 1956 (Cressman et al. 1960). Cole subsequently directed the University's program of survey and excavations at archaeological sites in the John Day Reservoir Area from 1958 to 1968. He was thus highly familiar with the nature and complexity of prehistoric remains along the Middle Columbia River during the period before the completion of The Dalles and John Day dams. Cole's experience in the 1950s and 1960s, then, established his frame of reference for his assessment in 1974 of the importance of 35WS14.

However, construction of The Dalles and John Day dams and raising of the reservoir pools behind them resulted in the inundation of virtually all the major prehistoric settlements along this section of the Columbia River. Important sites like Big Eddy, Fivemile Rapids, and Wakemap Mound in The Dalles reservoir and Wildcat Canyon in the John Day Reservoir are mostly, and in some cases, entirely below the waters of the reservoir pools. As a result, since the dams were constructed very little archaeological research has been undertaken in The Dalles and John Day Reservoir areas. The few projects that have been carried out were mostly survey-oriented, designed to inventory sites along the reservoir shorelines (for a brief summary of the history of archaeological research in this area, see Minor 1988:31-39).

The prehistoric sites situated above the reservoir pools and still available for archaeological investigation thus represent only a remnant of the archaeological record formerly existing in the region. While a few sites that appear on the basis of surface evidence to represent villages have been recorded, most of the known sites are smaller, shallower, and in most cases appear to represent less intensively occupied base camps, task-specific, and special purpose sites. Virtually all of these localities have been negatively affected by shoreline erosion, historic development, or relic collector vandalism. In short, the nature and completeness of the archaeological record has changed remarkably since the years of the large-scale salvage projects in the 1950s and 1960s.

At the same time, since the early 1970s when the testing and original evaluation of 35WS14 took place, research issues in regional archaeology have evolved considerably. Research during the reservoir salvage stage of investigations was primarily directed toward establishing the time depth and broader affiliations of the prehistoric cultures in the region (e.g., Cole 1954:1; Cressman et al. 1960:7-9). While these questions are still important, current research issues are focused more on the evolution of prehistoric societies in this region over time, as reflected in settlement patterns, subsistence strategies, and trade networks. These issues require the recovery of a much broader range of archaeological data (e.g., environmental, artifactual, faunal) from a range of settlement types (including smaller task-specific sites) than was the case during earlier phases in the history of regional archaeology.

When evaluated against the currently existing archaeological record and in terms of contemporary archaeological standards, 35WS14 becomes highly significant as one of the more important prehistoric sites identified in The Dalles vicinity. The test excavations at 35WS14 have already yielded "information important in prehistory," and further investigations of the cultural remains at this site can clearly contribute to a variety of research issues in regional archaeology. In addition, it appears that further study and radiocarbon dating at 35WS14 may contribute to establishing the extent of the Bonneville Landslide, which is generally assumed to have been a major catastrophic event in Lower Columbia Valley prehistory (Pettigrew 1981:121-122; Minor 1984).

CONCLUSION

In contrast to the original assessment that no further work is necessary, reevaluation of 35WS14 leads to the conclusion that this site is significant and eligible for inclusion in the National Register of Historic Places. That 35WS14 is now considered significant should not be totally surprising, and in fact perhaps should be expected, as the significance of archaeological properties may change as research issues and strategies in any given region evolve over time (Lynott 1980). The concept of archaeological significance is not static, but must continually be reevaluated in response to changes in research orientations and the condition of the archaeological resource base (Lynott 1980:120).

It seems likely that, like 35WS14, many prehistoric sites evaluated long ago are now in need of reassessment. In the Pacific Northwest, for example, there is a generation gap between archaeologists who remember the "good old days" before the dams and the present cohort of archaeologists who have known only the reservoirs. It is almost certain that a number of prehistoric sites judged unimportant during earlier stages in the history of archaeological research would now be considered significant and worthy of investigation. Clearly, prehistoric sites evaluated during earlier times should be reevaluated to insure that sites significant in terms of contemporary archaeological issues are not overlooked and inadvertently destroyed.

ACKNOWLEDGEMENTS

Reevaluation of prehistoric site 35WS14 was carried out under the terms of a contract between the Wasco County Planning and Economic Development Office and Heritage Research Associates, Inc. (HRA) of Eugene, Oregon. Faunal remains were identified by Dr. Ruth L. Greenspan. Maps and artifact illustrations were prepared by Kevin C. McCornack. Funds for radiocarbon dating were provided by HRA and by the

Portland District, U.S. Army Corps of Engineers. The fieldnotes and artifact collection resulting from the 1972 test excavations at 35WS14 are curated at the Oregon State Museum of Anthropology (OSMA), University of Oregon, under Accession No. 470. The cooperation of Dr. Don E. Dumond, OSMA Director, as well as Pamela E. Endzweig, OSMA Collections Manager, in making these materials available for examination and analysis is gratefully acknowledged.

REFERENCES

Butler, B. Robert

1959   Lower Columbia Valley Archaeology: A Survey and Appraisal of Some Major Archaeological Resources. *Tebiwa* 2(2):6-24.

1960   *The Physical Stratigraphy of Wakemap Mound: A New Interpretation.* Master's thesis, Department of Anthropology, University of Washington. Seattle.

1964   A Tentative History of Self-Handled Mauls at The Dalles of the Lower Columbia. *Tebiwa* 7(2):37-41).

1965   Perspectives on the Prehistory of the Lower Columbia Valley. *Tebiwa* 8(1):1-16.

Caldwell, Warren W.

1956   *The Archaeology of Wakemap Mound: A Stratified Site Near The Dalles on the Columbia River.* Ph.D. dissertation, Department of Anthropology, University of Washington. Seattle.

Cole, David L.

1954   *A Contribution to the Archaeology of The Dalles Region, Oregon.* Master's thesis, Department of Anthropology, University of Oregon. Eugene.

1974   *Archaeological Research in the Bonneville Dam Pool Area.* Museum of Natural History, University of Oregon. Submitted to the National Park Service.

Cole, David L. and Michael D. Southard

1971   *Archaeological Survey of the Bonneville Dam Reservoir--1971.* Museum of Anthropology, University of Oregon. Submitted to the Stanford Research Institute. San Francisco, California.

Crane, H.R. and James B. Griffin
  1959   University of Michigan Radiocarbon Dates.   *Radiocarbon Supplement,
         American Journal of Science* 1:173-198.

Cressman, Luther S., in collaboration with David L. Cole, Wilbur A. Davis, Thomas M.
Newman, and Daniel J. Scheans
  1960   Cultural Sequences at The Dalles, Oregon: A Contribution to Pacific
         Northwest Prehistory.   *Transactions of the American Philosophical Society*
         50(10).

Dumond, Don E. and Rick Minor
  1983   *Archaeology in the John Day Reservoir: The Wildcat Canyon Site, 35-GM-9.*
         University of Oregon Anthropological Papers 30.   Eugene.

Hodge, Edwin T.
  1932   *Report of Dam Sites on Lower Columbia River.*   Submitted to the Pacific
         Division, U.S. Army Corps of Engineers, San Francisco, California.

  1938   Geology of the Lower Columbia River.   *Geological Society of America Bulletin*
         49:831-930.

Lawrence, Donald B.
  1936   The Submerged Forest of the Columbia River Gorge.   *Geographical Review*
         26:581-592.

  1937   Drowned Forest of the Columbia River Gorge.   *Geological Society of the
         Oregon Country Newsletter* 3:78-83.

Lawrence, Donald B. and Elizabeth Lawrence
  1958   Bridge of the Gods Legend, Its Origin, History and Dating.   *Mazama*
         40(13):33-41.

Lynott, Mark J.
  1980   The Dynamics of Significance: An Example from Central Texas.   *American
         Antiquity* 45(1):117-120.

Minor, Rick
  1984   *Dating the Bonneville Landslide in the Columbia River Gorge.*   Heritage
         Research Associates Report 31.   Eugene, Oregon.

  1988   Prehistory.   In *Prehistory and History of the Columbia River Gorge National
         Scenic Area, Oregon and Washington*, by Stephen Dow Beckham, Rick Minor,
         Kathryn Anne Toepel, and Jo Reese.   Heritage Research Associates Report 75.
         Eugene, Oregon.

1992   *Reevaluation of Prehistoric Site 35WS14 For the Taylor Lake Trail Project, Wasco Coutny, Oregon.* Heritage Research Associates Report 114. Eugene, Oregon.

Minor, Rick and Stephen Dow Beckham
1991   *Cultural Resource Evaluation of the Crates Point Interpretive Center Site, Columbia Gorge National Scenic Area, Wasco County, Oregon.* Heritage Research Associates Report 104. Eugene, Oregon.

Minor, Rick, Kathryn Anne Toepel, and Stephen Dow Beckham
1989   *An Overview of Investigations at 45SA11: Archaeology in the Columbia River Gorge.* Heritage Research Associates Report 83. Eugene, Oregon.

Moulton, Gary E. (editor)
1988   *The Journals of the Lewis & Clark Expedition: Volume 5, July 28-November 1, 1805.* University of Nebraska Press, Lincoln.

1991   *The Journals of the Lewis & Clark Expedition: Volume 7, March 23-June 9, 1806.* University of Nebraska Press, Lincoln.

Pettigrew, Richard M.
1981   *A Prehistoric Culture Sequence in the Portland Basin of the Lower Columbia Valley.* University of Oregon Anthropological Papers 22. Eugene.

Raab, L. Mark and Timothy C. Klinger
1977   A Critical Appraisal of "Significance" in Contract Archaeology. *American Antiquity* 42(4):629-634.

Strong, Emory
1959   *Stone Age on the Columbia River.* Binfords and Mort, Portland.

Suphan, Robert J.
1974   *Ethnological Report on the Wasco and Tenino Indians.* Garland Publishing, New York.

Valley, Derek R.
1979   An Analysis of a Tool Type: Peripherally Flaked Cobbles. *Northwest Anthropological Research Notes* 13(1):51-90.

TUALATIN KALAPUYAN VILLAGES:
THE ETHNOGRAPHIC RECORD

Henry Zenk

ABSTRACT

A single source, Albert S. Gatschet's Tualatin fieldnotes of 1877, contains virtually all that we know ethnographically of Tualatin Kalapuyan villages. Relevant portions of the fieldnotes are ethnographic texts, scattered incidental notes, and word-lists identifying culturally relevant items. Using these materials, a sketch of early-historical Tualatin village life, including named sites and speculated site locations, is developed. Finally, some demurrers are raised as to the reliability and completeness of data supporting the sketch.

THE TUALATIN KALAPUYANS

The Ethnographic Record.

The name Tualatin (synonyms: Atfalati, Twalaty, Faladin, plus other less-frequently encountered spelling variations) refers to those speakers of Northern (or Tualatin-Yamhill) Kalapuyan who at the time of earliest Euro-American contact occupied most of the Tualatin River drainage, together with the Chehalem Creek and (less certainly) the North Yamhill River drainages to the south.

The modern local name is based upon Tualatin (a)tfálat'i[1] (heard as twálat'i in Central Kalapuyan and other neighboring languages), one of a number of western-Oregon indigenous names referring to groupings more inclusive than the local or village group. The ethnographic characterization of these groupings is largely conjectural; in historical as well as loose popular usage, they are generally referred to as "tribes."

In some recent discussions of theoretical and methodological issues in Willamette Valley archeology (notably Pettigrew 1980:74, Connolly 1983), the ethnographic record on the Tualatins has been referred to as the best available for any early-contact-period Kalapuyan group. The basis of this evaluation should be clarified. Except for one critical document, the record on the Tualatins is about as that preserved for other Kalapuyan groups: some scattered passing historical mentions; the usual fleeting references in treaty documents and reservation records; and linguistic and ethnographic data gleaned during the first three decades of the present century (for the Tualatins, consisting of Frachtenberg 1915, DeAngulo and Freeland 1929, Jacobs 1936a, 1936b, 1936c). The latter, which is by far the richest of these categories of data, unfortunately derives from just a few Native informants (for the Tualatins, just one), all of whom had lived all or most of their lives at Grand Ronde Reservation, the tribally and linguistically mixed community to which most surviving Kalapuyans were removed in 1856. The resulting very spotty record of pre-reservation lifeways reflects the drastic declines suffered by Kalapuyan populations during the early-historical period, the result primarily of introduced diseases.

The critical document alluded to consists of 450-plus pages of fieldnotes, taken down by the pioneer linguist A. S. Gatschet during a visit to Grand Ronde Reservation in 1877 (Gatschet 1877a, 1877b; hereafter usually referred to simply as Gatschet). Gatschet worked intensively with two of the prominent Tualatin men of that time, Peter Kenoyer (Tualatin name: k'ínai) and Dave Yatchkawa (yécgawa; known also as "Wapato Dave" or "Blind Dave," the latter owing to blindness suffered in later life), both of whom had fully experienced Tualatin life under pre-reservation conditions. The unique value of this document for Kalapuyan ethnography resides primarily in the latter circumstance. Quite simply, these two men were in a much better position to provide a record of the culture than any of the informants available to later investigators.[2]

Unfortunately for the ethnographer, however, Gatschet is a record primarily of the Tualatin language, and apart from some Tualatin ethnographic texts (edited and published by Jacobs, 1945:156-198) includes no systematic ethnographic description. In spite of this limitation, however, it does preserve a fair amount of ethnographic detail: in the foregoing texts; in additional scattered incidental notes; and in word-lists containing identifications of culturally-relevant items. The following sketch draws upon all three of these categories of data.

The Tualatin Village Unit.

The basic political unit of Tualatin society was the autonomous winter village group, or collection of one or more patrilocal extended families co-residing during the winter months. This was equally a basic social unit: persons born into one ordinarily considered themselves related, and customarily sought their spouses from different such groups. The term gáwakil, which Jacobs translates 'tribe, nation' (implying "the community of Tualatin villages," according to Jacobs 1945:185), appears in Gatschet with generalized reference to one's kin or "people," but also specifically as a term for the village group (as in ca-mámbit ni-gáwakil, that is, ca-mámbit village; table 1, fig. 1: no. 13).[3] As the primary unit of group affiliation, the village was evidently basic also to the individual's sense of personal identity: at least six of the Tualatins mentioned in Gatschet are explicitly identified with named village groups (a list of these individuals appears in Assessing the Evidence, below).

Each village, or at any rate each village of any importance, is supposed to have had a village "chief" (acámbak 'chief, wealthy one'), distinguished from fellow villagers by his greater wealth. With their immediate families, chiefs stood at one extreme of Tualatin social evaluation. At the other extreme stood slaves, who, while their actual living conditions may not have set them so sharply apart from ordinary Tualatins, were considered nothing more than chattels of their wealthy owners. The social space in between these two extremes was occupied by the majority of Tualatin villagers. Some degree of ranking based on wealth, suggesting the social ranking system of the Tualatins' fishing-dependent Chinookan neighbors, probably characterized this middle range, but specific description is lacking.

Local Organization and Seasonal Cycle

Kalapuyans in general exploited a wide range of resources, many of which were characterized by spatially and temporally limited distributions. A good deal of seasonal movement, involving a variety of local habitat types, was therefore required in the course of the yearly cycle (Zenk 1976:37-45).

The spatial dimension of resource availability was reflected in territorial relations involving neighboring village groups. All the Tualatin villages shared access to more-or-less definite hunting territories: according to a text dictated (presumably) by Peter Kenoyer (and published in Jacobs 1945:187-188), Tualatins hunted westward up to 'half the mountain(s)' separating them from Tillamook country; southward, they hunted to the Yamhill River, beyond which lay Yamhill tribal territory; and to the north, they went as far as 'half the mountain(s)' separating ca-pánaxdin village (fig. 1, no. 4) from the neighboring Clatskanie tribe. Inter-village cooperation is also evident for the annual wapato (*Sagittaria latifolia*) harvest at Wapato Lake (a marshy lake that formerly extended for several miles southeast of Gaston, Oregon), since it is indicated that "the whole tribe" assembled there, taking an entire month for the purpose.[4] By contrast, the prairies where tarweed (*Madia spp.*) grew were reportedly divided up between villages, with individual ownership obtaining within these divisions.

The temporal dimension of resource availability was reflected in the dual nature of the Kalapuyan year. According again to Gatschet, Tualatins lived about half the year in substantial houses located at winter-village sites. During the remainder of the year, they camped out of doors. During the half of the year spent indoors, stored provisions provided the main sustenance (supplemented year-round by hunted and trapped game), and attention was devoted to myth recitation and spirit-dance ceremonialism. By early spring, when the first shoots of camas began appearing, some Tualatins were beginning to move out of the winter houses. Camas was harvested at this early stage, as well as on through the summer and into the fall: indeed, camas appears to have been the single most important subsistence resource for Kalapuyans generally. Other vegetable resources were quite important also: berries and hazelnuts--available by midsummer in the hills; berries (and large game) in the mountains--late summer; tarweed and other seeds, harvested from prairies burned over for the purpose--late summer or early fall; and wapato, gotten especially at Wapato Lake--around October. Seasonal variation was also to be reckoned with in the availability of anadromous fish, although we have little basis for gauging the importance of this resource in Tualatin subsistence (evidently, there were no spring or fall salmon runs in the Tualatin River system itself).[5]

Finally, both seasonal and local variations in resource availability were evened out, at least to a degree, within regional networks of intergroup relations that involved frequent exchanges of both food and prestige goods (Hajda 1984:123-132, 222-245).

Living Sites

Gatschet provides only a fragmentary record of living sites (winter villages and seasonal or use-specific sites), with their associated structures, artifacts, and technological complexes. Most of the relevant data are confined to word lists, which I have collated below. Supplementary data occurring elsewhere in the manuscript are summarized in the explanations accompanying particular terms.[6]

Structures. hámmei 'fire', 'house'. acáf hámmei: "plank house of Tual[atins] before coming to Reserve." wadúginfist hámmei: houses joined end-to-end (house row, up to 100 yards long). ákainakw dúmmai 'the council's house': village council-house, "a big hall." ap'yuuséeld: multi-family winter house, housing 2-5 nuclear families (from -p'yuus 'winter'; also referred to as "mud house": referring to dirt banking outside?).

agúucim 'door': about 3' high, 2-3 in one house. atábiuk: wall on long side of house (40'-50'); awálhiyu: wall on short side of house. dilúpgifun, hámmei dilúpg: house roof ('cover', 'house's cover'). mánip: rafter ('pole'). aklámmat: smoke-hole. dimhéi: partition (separating families in house). atúłnackaan: sitting planks (placed around the centrally-excavated house-floor in which the fire was located; leg room provided by the sides of the excavation). asúlxəmit: bed (3' high); acác asúlxəmit: bed-guard; atúnkl asúlxəmit: planks holding beds ("painted with fancy ornaments"; nets might be stretched inside as mattresses). amhúucim 'ash-bark': sun-dried in June and used to make houses; amáll(i) 'cedar bark': used to make houses (both cedar and ash bark were also used to plug chinks in houses).[7]

améekwinfun: temporary summer shelter made of branches (from méekw 'summer'). agúudip: sweat-house.

Household Articles. háisai: mat used as mattress ('tule, *Scirpus spp.*'). agébba: (1) mat, (2) a kind of burden basket ('cattail, *Typha latifolia*').

-tíksnaaf (v.): to twist strands (of cordage) together. aláal: string. ámc'al: rope ('rawhide'). mánc'up: sinew.

aťínnana: round-bottomed water or berry basket, made of split cedar root, with step-pattern design. atúffaba: open-work basket, "carried on shoulder." akállampga: water-jug, sometimes made of hazel (-pga 'water'). afúbcei, amhúllu, aluffáms, aťwálťwi: burden baskets, not described.

aťíwwat: bucket (awádik 'wood' or adúnc(i) 'bone'). akwád: serving dish or pan (made of 'wood' or 'bone', including whale bone). akwítan: oval bowl. acúnwił: wooden bowl with handles, artistically carved. ac'ílkw: dipper-spoon (made of 'wood' or 'bone'). ałúpin: bone soup-spoon sized spoon. a'úsgan: cup (introduced or Native; probably a Chinook Jargon word).

atkwíkwal: piss-pot. acíkəl ánd 'catch-stone': forked stick for handling hot stones.

dúndek: cradle board. atúllala: head-board (for inducing frontal-occipital flattening). atáad: head-board pad, filled with cattail fluff.

Tools and weapons. anáddu: (1) flint, (2) glass, bottle (introduced). afúpi: wood fire-drill. aléedik afúpi: wood plate on which fire was produced (léedik a type of cottonwood or willow). askímmat: antler wedge for splitting wood, removing bark. aná: stone mortar. angúi': stone pestle. axótxilhid: scraper. k'ésdan: axe (probably, introduced).

agímisda 'knife'; anáddu agímisda 'flint knife' (with wood handle); wadúginfist(i) agímisda: double-ended knife; agúiyuk agímisda: (1) saw-edged flint war-knife, (2) iron war knife, held by hole in middle (iron obtained in early historical period from wrecked ships); awátwilhidi agímisda: long crooked knife. atímkat: big stone butchering knife, with antler handle (possibly identical to awátwilhidi agímisda).

abósk(i) 'bow'. anúug: (1) arrow, (2) bullet. adé'wus: boys' play arrow. a'úiyamił: war-axe with stone head. abáxsk: stone war-axe. axiwíxiwi: (1) flint lance-head, (2) a blue stick which, when dreamed of, conferred power. akálktat: full cuirass of elk neck-hide over bound seasoned sticks ("Tualatins made the best").

hámbbu 'canoe'.

Subsistence Technology. -máyampin (v.): to gather, dig (roots). -húngat (v.), -déheidin (v.): to dig camas. -gáu(yi)n- (v.): to gather (hazelnuts, berries, etc.). -débinfału (v.): to dislodge wapato tubers (done by women using their toes in shallow water). -máatin (v.): to beat tarweed seeds (from standing burnt plants).

-fúuflaat (v.): to boil (food). -múfmin (v.): to roast (over fire on coals). -yúufne̦i (v.): to dry (in sun or over fire). -múhid (v.): to dry food on a scaffold over fire. -gwit (v.): to pit-oven (cook in a ground oven). -p'úip'yaat (v.): to mash, grind, pulverize. -k'wíhin (v.): to grind tarweed seeds (in a mortar). -héipin (v.): to parch (e.g., tarweed seeds). -hiłwinin (v.): to mix (e.g., ground tarweed seeds with cooked camas). -k'ílmat (v.): to stir (e.g., mush made of pulverized acorns and deer's blood).

amúhu: scaffold for drying meat over fire. abáiblhid: roasting-spit. akúd: ground oven. amékwii: camas digging-stick; mantk: cross-handle of camas digging-stick. ałéki: wide stick with bent end, used to scoop floating wapato tubers from water. agúu: rawhide bucket into which tarweed seeds were beaten; abúb: paddle for hitting tarweed seeds into bucket; amhéip: ash-board parching tray for tarweed seeds.

-lúuwin (v.): to keep, put away (provisions). ámptank: blue clay in which acorn flesh was buried to preserve it. abúllum: 4'-5' deep storage pits for wapato tubers. amál: scaffold in house or in trees to keep provisions.

agúufilhid: fishing line. adúnc(i): fish-hook ('bone'). amúknifalhid: bait. acík'wilhid 'spearer': fish-spear. dóobid: light for night fishing (from dóob 'moon'?). awései: stationary brush fish-trap basket. atáflhid: net (any kind). amélblhid: dip-net for salmon.

ak'éinuł 'tobacco' (grown by Kalapuyans). adúmp'i ánd: pipe ('stone stem'); acápakas: pipe-stem.

Death and Burial. akwíł('')yu(u): grave. alám: wood palings around grave. ak'únd 'cover': funeral dress of corpse. -kúulhid (v.): to hang containers on sticks about the grave. (Apparently, graveyards were located near villages. The information on ca-wayéed village (fig. 1, no. 8) includes the following item attributed to Peter Kenoyer: "big graveyard there . . . --often visited by the Ind[ian]s here [i.e., Grand Ronde] & fixed again.")

Wealth items. I append a list also of durables valued as wealth items, since these often served as grave goods (see, e.g., Laughlin 1943): agáucan: (1) property, (2) valued durables (dentalium shells, beads, jewelry), (3) round beads; dúmilb agáucan: most highly valued property (dúmilb 'butt, stump'). alúfit: oblong lidded "money box" of shell, antler (lúf- v. 'fill').

acípin: largest, most valued dentalia (Chinook Jargon háikwa). atxáltxifcan: small dentalia (Chinook Jargon kúpkup). adáktifun: dentalia (another kind?).

ayúkal: beads; wacálikcicei, watúliluust, watúnktxuun, wapáac ayúkal: truncated, reddish-round, green, long beads (different types of beads). adáyu: small round ("coral") beads. adúnc'(i) 'bone': bone beads. ámpgw(i) 'hazelnuts', amúikwax: yellow round beads.

-yémhid, -yémmin (v.): to bead. -yúupin: necklace. asupsamhú: breast ornament (pendant); dúnc' (i), abíklust watúllu, wapáac watúllu, wapáac watúnktkast, atk' ínwaimax, axálxal: bone disk ('bone'), round cylinder, long cylinder, long green (bead?), brass button, Chinese coin (parts incorporated in a particular asupsamhú).

IDENTIFYING THE VILLAGES

The long list of supposed "Atfalati band" names appearing in the left-hand column of Table 1 appeared originally in the first Handbook of North American Indians (Hodge 1907-10). Column 2 gives the corresponding names as recorded in Gatschet, the source upon which Livingston Farrand, one of the Handbook compilers, based this list. Jacobs (1945:186-187) has since published, with revisions affecting phonetic transcription only, a segment of the same original source: a Tualatin- language text in which the informant-- almost certainly Peter Kenoyer--identified 13 winter-village groups.

The Hodge compilation of Tualatin "band" names has been so widely republished and cited, both from Hodge itself as well as from secondary sources (especially Swanton 1952:451-478, which for the Tualatins only recapitulates Hodge), that it has acquired the status virtually of a primary source. It is worth emphasizing, therefore, that the Hodge compilation goes back in its entirety to one source, Gatschet. Only one of the Hodge "band" identifications, Chahelim, is supported in Hodge by a citation from any other source; the spelling however follows Gatschet. Moreover, aside from a very few cursory mentions in other sources, it is safe to say that the Hodge-Gatschet compilation comprises the sum total of our ethnographic knowledge of Tualatin local groups. Unfortunately, the provisos previously cited regarding the value of Gatschet as an ethnographic record apply in full to this list. What we have, basically, are a list of names accompanied in some cases, in other cases not, by brief informant identifications; supplemented in some cases, in other cases not, by occasional references elsewhere in the manuscript.

Indeed, Hodge provides no indications of what an "Atfalati band" was, beyond the mere fact that it had a name. When we trace the Hodge band names in Gatschet, what actually results is a rather mixed bag, consisting of: (a) two names given explicitly as place-names, not as village names; (b) four not positively identified, except as names with local reference; and (c) 16 clearly given by one or both informants as winter-village names.

(a) The two Hodge names that clearly do not refer to villages in Gatschet are Chachanim (ca-cánnim) and Chachif (ca-cíif). ca-cánnim is identified as "a piece of land, no chief." ca-cíif was an important site, if not a village. This was the place at the northern end of Wapato Lake where "the whole tribe" assembled during the fall, for the annual wapato root harvest. The same name was used also as a name of Wapato Lake.

(b) Chachambitmanchal (ca-cámbit máncal), Chagindueftei (ca-góondweftei),

Chatakuin (ca-takwín), and Chatamnei (ca-támnei) are all applied in Gatschet to localities. ca-cámbit máncal is noted to have been "inhabited," ca-támnei to have been "formerly inhabited" ("tribe extinct"). In spite of the latter indications, as well as the circumstance that all four names occur in sections devoted primarily to villages, the evidently well-defined character of the winter village unit in Native conception should make us suspicious of the lack of positive identification. In fact, other local names from the same sections did not make it into the Hodge list, making it rather puzzling as to why these four did.

(c) All of the names recorded with the nominal prefix a- in column 2, table 1, appear in the winter-village text published in Jacobs (1945:186-187). That is, the informant dictating the text (assumed here to be Peter Kenoyer) gave these specifically as proper names of Tualatin winter-village groups. The text itself leaves little doubt as to the type of unit the informant had in mind. For example, the reference to ca-hée 'lim village (Table 1, fig. 1: no. 15) reads (in Jacobs 1945:186):

The hé 'lim [a-hée 'lim] went back home when it was wintertime to their winter dwelling[s] [-p'yúuseeld], their place was there at hé 'lim [ca-hée 'lim]. The name of the chief [-cámbak] they had there was wáwinxpa.

Besides wáwinxpa, the text has the names of four additional chiefs: k(w)alícadax (ca-tágił village, no. 14), baxawát'as (ca-pánaxdin, no. 4), xíuba (ca-géip'i, no. 1), and cakílxida (ca-púngatpi, no. 9).

Occasionally, informants qualify their information, or disagree with one another. Note that the following demurrers concerning chiefs in particular, while they complicate matters somewhat, may also shed some light on the nature of the village unit in Native conception.

The chief of ca-cimmahíyuk (no. 2) is stated to have been "probably same as [of] ca-géip'i" (no. 1); ca-cúkwił (no. 6) was (virtually?) "the same place" as ca-cmée 'wa (no. 5), but "had a chief or subchief" (unnamed); Peter Kenoyer and Dave Yatchkawa disagreed as to whether a man named láwicxin (of ca-pékli, no. 7) was a chief, or only a hunter; they evidently also disagreed about k(w)alícadax (of ca-tágił, no. 14), since a marginal note to the village text (information from Yatchkawa?) states that "he was only headman" (that is, something less than a chief?); and finally, Peter Kenoyer "believes" ca-wayéed (no. 8) "had a chief." It is clearly implied here that the status of 'chief' was a rather special one: prominence within one's village evidently did not automatically entitle one to be called acámbak. Also, it appears that more substantial or significant villages were expected to have chiefs, while a less significant group might not have one, or might come under the chief of a neighboring group.

Adding the villages identified elsewhere in the manuscript to the 13 named in the village text, we have a grand total of 16 names used unambiguously by one or both informants to refer to winter village groups (Table 1). Figure 1 presents one interpretation of their locations (as discussed in detail in Zenk 1976:142-155, Benson 1976). Note that since the degree of precision required for mapping exceeds the limitations of the data, the results should be taken only as a guide to general locations-- most fairly unambiguous in Gatschet--rather than as a key for accurately pegging sites.

Taking the indicated general locations at face value, the villages turn out to exhibit an interesting distribution. Specifically, the locations of villages nos. 7, 8, 9, 10, 11, 12, and possibly of 13 and 14 as well (altogether, half of all the villages named), suggest one village complex, rather than a scatter of separate centers.

A number of factors are of likely relevance for understanding this distribution. One is early-historical demographic decline, with consequent consolidation of remnant village populations. Ecological and social factors could also be relevant. With respect to the former, it is notable that Wapato Valley offers a sheltered location[8]; that it evidently provided ready access to camas prairies (according to the 1851 un-ratified treaty, excerpted in Mackey 1974:105, "Great Quantities" [sic] both of camas and wapato "grow in and about this lake"), as well as to hunting territories (note the proximity of the Coast Range and the Chehalem Mountains) and fisheries; and that it was an important source of the staple wapato tuber, which, as it just so happens, was harvested immediately before the winter houses were refurbished and re-occupied. With respect to social factors, one in particular emerges from the village data already offered: where one chief presided over more than one village (as in the case of ca-géip'i and ca-cimmahíyuk, and possibly also of ca-cméewa and ca-cúkwił), it may be implied that the chief's village of residence was the more important. Perhaps, other such (implied) center/satellite relationships help to explain the concentration of sites about Wapato Lake.

ASSESSING THE EVIDENCE

In order to further clarify the nature and extent of evidence supporting the village list, the names at (c) above may be ranked to reflect roughly how well attested each is in Gatschet, judging by frequency of mention and type of mentioned associations. This provides some basis for singling out those groups for which internal evidence in Gatschet seems most definite. At the same time, it should be pointed out that paucity of mention or mentioned association does not prove anything by itself: less well-attested names could have referred to groups that were no less historically real.

The best attested villages, by these criteria, are:

ca-púngatpi (fig. 1, no. 9). Total mentions: 10. Associations: i) informant's natal village; ii) chiefs: three named; iii) given as "tribe" name (four instances). iv) given as place-name: proper name (twice); reference point for locating other places (twice).

TABLE 1: Tualatin or "Atfalati" Kalapuyan Villages mentioned by Gatschet and Hodge (speculatively located in Figure 1.)

Hodge (1907, 1910)	Gatschet (1877a)[1]	Locations
Chachambitmanchal	ca-cámbit máncal	
Chachanim	ca-cánnim	
Chachemewa	(a-)ca-cméewa	5
Chachimewa[2]		
Chachif	ca-cíif 'crawfish place'	
Chachimahiyuk	ca-cimmahíyuk	2
Chachokwith	(a-)ca-cúkwił	6
Chagindueftei	ca-góondweftei	
Chahelim	a-hée 'lim, ca-hée 'lim	15
	(-hée 'lim 'out, outside')	
Chakeipi	(a-)ca-géipi 'beaver place'	1
Chakutpaliu	(a-)ca-gútpalyu	3
Chalal	ca-láal 'thread-grass place'	11
Chalawai	(a-)ca-lá 'wai	12
Chamampit	(a-)ca-mámbit 'creek place'	13
Chapanaghtin	a-pánaxtin, ca-pánaxtin	4
Chapokele	ca-pékli~-pókali	7
Chapungathpi	(a-)ca-púngatpi	9
Chatagithl	a-tágił, (a-)ca-tágił	14
	(-tágił 'fir-bark')	
Chatagihl[3]		
Chatagshish	(a-)ca-tágsis	10
Chatakuin	ca-takwín	
Chatamnei	ca-támnei	
Chatilkuei	a-tílkwei, ca-tílkwei	16
Chawayed	(a-)ca-wayéed	8

1 All names appear transliterated into the phonemic orthography explained in text note 1. Dashes set off the nominal prefix a- and the place-name prefix ca-; parentheses appear where different recordings of the same name show presence/absence of the parenthesized prefix.

2 Hodge's Chachemewa and Chachimewa evidently are spurious spelling variants of the same Tualatin form, ca-cméewa.

3 Chatagihl is either the same site as Chatagithl, or a separate place (not group) with the same name ('fir-bark place').

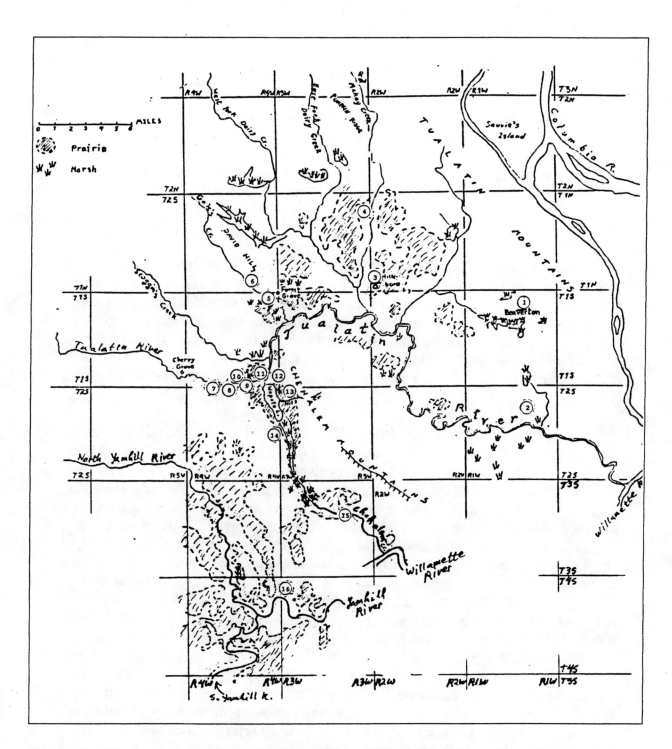

Figure 1. Conjectured locations of Winter villages (See Table 1).

ca-géip'i (fig. 1, no. 1). Mentions: four. Associations: i) chief: one named; ii) informant's father's natal village; woman alive at Grand Ronde was "1/4 breed."

ca-hée 'lim (fig. 1, no. 15). Mentions: four. Associations: i) chiefs: two named; ii) natal village of man living at Grand Ronde.

ca-pánaxdin (fig. 1, no. 4). Mentions: four. Associations: i) chief: one named; ii) mentioned in connection with Clatskanie-Tualatin boundary.

ca-gútpalyu (fig. 1, no. 3). Mentions: five. Associations: i) natal village of man living at Grand Ronde; ii) place-name (Tualatin name of Hillsboro).

Since aboriginal Tualatin winter villages were but a fading memory by 1877, it is furthermore important to establish, insofar as possible, to what degree the information about them derives from the informants' first-hand (or even second-hand, e.g. parents') experience, as opposed to what might be considered more tenuously based. By the tests applied above, it is evident that some sites, including ca-lá 'wai (no. 13: said by Peter Kenoyer to be "extinct" in his own time) and ca-tílkwei (no. 16: Kenoyer's identification contradicted by Yatchgawa) would have to be assigned to the latter category.

The list of village chiefs occurring with the winter village text permits us to gauge the informant's own historical distance from his subject matter. Recall that the text names five chiefs: baxawáť as (ca-pánaxdin village, no. 4), cakílxida (ca-púngatpi, no. 9), k(w)alícadax (ca-tágił, no. 14), wáwinxpa (ca-hée 'lim, no. 15), and xíuba (ca-géip'i, no. 1). Fortunately, we have sufficient information to determine Peter Kenoyer's generational distance from most of the mentioned chiefs (Figure 2). Kenoyer's father, k'ámmac, was chief of ca-púngatpi village. cakílxida, which the text has as chief, is noted to have been k'ámmac's father, but elsewhere, his 'older brother'. At any rate, cakílxida was chief of ca-púngatpi before k'ámmac.[9] Kenoyer's father's brother, k'áyak'ac, was chief of ca-hée 'lim, but the text has wáwinxpa (cf. "Wow-na-pa," noted in Lyman 1900:323 to have been a chief of "Chehalem village"), who is elsewhere noted (evidently by Kenoyer, again) to have been an "old man" during the treaty negotiations with General Palmer (probably, 1854 or 1855). xíuba, chief of ca-géip'i, is elsewhere noted in connection with a speech he gave about "33 years ago" (i.e., mid-1840s) (he is referred to there as "the old xíuba," which may or may not be significant). Of all the chiefs mentioned, only the one remaining seems somewhat anomalously placed in this generational schema. k(w)alícadax was one of the three principal men (the others being k'áyak'ac and informant Dave Yatchkawa himself) who represented Tualatin survivors during the Palmer treaty negotiations. Evidently, he was therefore a contemporary of k'áyak'ac.

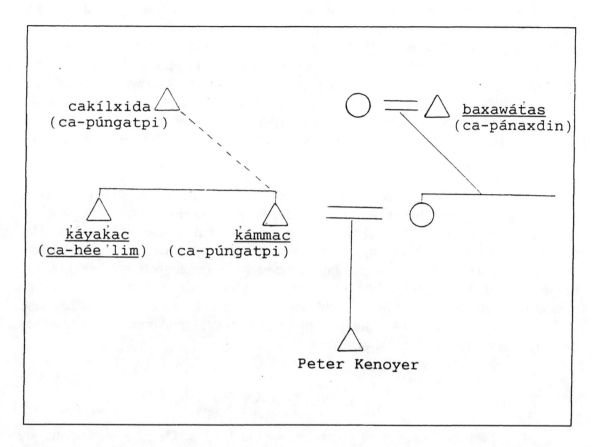

Figure 2. Partial genealology of Peter Kenoyer.

Elsewhere in the manuscript, other individuals, including a number of additional chiefs, are associated with villages:

Peter Kenoyer himself 'is a ca-púngatpi' (k'ínai mi-ca-púngatpi); mánista was chief at ca-tágsis (no. 10); according to Peter Kenoyer, láwicxin was chief at ca-pékli (no. 7), but according to Dave Yatchkawa, that individual was not a chief, but a hunter; sláwin was chief at ca-láal (no. 11); céxyan, alive at Grand Ronde in 1877, 'is a hée 'lim' (céxyan mi-hée 'lim; no. 15); yéllukti lived at ca-mámbit (no. 13), where the chief was the father of a woman named kánatamax; according to Peter Kenoyer, the father of sámxaxa (alive at Grand Ronde in 1877) was chief at ca-tílkwei (no. 16), but Dave Yatchkawa denied that there was even a village at the place; kúyapei, a warrior, was from ca-cméewa (no. 5); "Lame Jim" sílik'wa, alive at Grand Ronde in 1877, 'is a ca-gútpalyu' (mi-ca-gútpalyu; no. 3); Dave Yatchkawa, whose father was from ca-géip'i (no. 1), was himself (therefore?) "one of them," while ákemkit (Peter Kenoyer's father's brother's daughter) was "1/4 breed of them"; Dave Yatchkawa 'is [also?] a cimmahíyuk' (yécgawa mi-cimmahíyuk; no. 2), as also (apparently) was "Old Kidnu," alive at Grand Ronde in 1877.

Considering the evidence cited, it seems unlikely that all the villages named in the winter-village text could have been in existence much later than, if any later than the generation of Peter Kenoyer's grandparents. If a substantial number of them had survived into a later period, we would expect to find more mentions of younger chiefs. The paucity of such mentions strongly suggests that Kenoyer was presenting a picture of conditions as he supposed them to have been approximately during the lifetimes of the chiefs actually named. Indeed, ḵ'ámmac, by the foregoing generational criteria a "young" chief, died according to Kenoyer himself "about 45 years ago"--that is, in about 1832.[10]

The known historical demography of northwestern Oregon is entirely consistent with this genealogically-based picture.[11] By the time of the earliest treaty negotiations (un-ratified Champoeg treaty of 1851, proceedings excerpted in Mackey 1974:103-111), there were only about 65 Tualatins left. If the most drastic single decline occurred during the "fever and ague" (malaria) visitations of the early 1830s, as there is every reason to suspect (Boyd 1975, 1990:139-146), then it follows that a picture of anything approaching "aboriginal" conditions would have to apply to the early 1830s, at the latest. While such considerations have little bearing upon the text's ethnographic accuracy, they do at least attest to its historical plausibility.

CONCLUSIONS

As a "window" upon a long-vanished way of life, the Gatschet manuscripts are irreplaceable. My concern here has been twofold: to delineate a portion of the view available through that window; and to assess the sharpness and clarity of the result--that is, the degree to which it appears convincing. On the latter point, we must acknowledge that this was in all likelihood a rather faded and distant view, even for those providing its supporting documentation--Peter Kenoyer and Dave Yatchkawa. This necessary qualification only underscores the early and particularly thorough disruption of indigenous lifeways in the northwestern Oregon region.

Notwithstanding such reservations, my hope is that the ethnographic detail presented here may prove useful: as a basis of comparison for characterizing less well-documented local indigenous groups; as well as for framing hypotheses about aboriginal settlement patterns and population distributions in the region.

It remains to be seen whether independent sources of evidence will reinforce, contradict, or complicate the picture of Tualatin villages presented. It may be noted that at the present time, there exists no significant independent body of evidence against which to test this picture. Our best hope for generating such evidence in the future lies with continuing archeological exploration and analysis.

· END NOTES

1. Tualatin linguistic forms are spelled according to Berman (personal communications, 1989; Berman 1990:39), who posits the following segmental phonemes for Tualatin Northern Kalapuyan: p, b, p', t, d, t', c, c', k, g, k', kw, gw, k'w, _, f, s, ł, x, h, m, n, w, y, l, a, aa, e, ee, i, ii, o, oo, u, uu, ai, ei, ui, au, eu, iu. Consonant lengthening, symbolized by doubling the affected consonant, is usually but not always predictable; the original spellings therefore have been preserved. Stress is also phonemic.

    Phonemically reliable respellings of terms recorded by Gatschet (1877a, 1877b), Frachtenberg (1915), and DeAngulo and Freeland (1929) are possible where Jacobs (1936a, 1936b) provides a basis for reconstruction: such terms, together with a number cited directly from Jacobs, appear underlined. The earlier transcriptions, Gatschet's especially, are inconsistent or incomplete with respect to the full range of feature distinctions represented above. Forms cited from those transcriptions, although respelled in accordance with phonemic principles, must therefore be accepted tentatively; they appear here minus underlining. By the same token, single quotation marks enclosing glosses are reserved for fully verified translations; others must be accepted somewhat tentatively.

2. Jacobs (1945:155) calls attention to indications that Peter Kenoyer and Dave Yatchkawa were not the only Tualatins contributing to Gatschet: "Notations in the manuscript indicate . . . that other Tualatin informants also worked with Dr. Gatschet; they were Emmy, Enimdi, Kemkid, and possibly others." My own examination of the manuscript leads me to conclude that only one other contributor is clearly identifiable: ákemkit or Kemkid, known also as "Emmy" (she was Peter Kenoyer's father's brother's daughter; note error in Jacobs, 1945:172, where she is identified as his father's brother's wife), who dictated two or three folk-belief texts (see Jacobs 1945:156-160, 179). The form "Enimdi" traces to Frachtenberg, who apparently misread (then mis-elicited) Gatschet's (none-too-clearly handwritten) notations: to my eye, the (two) original notations at issue read "Emmie."

    The only informant consulted by later investigators was Louis Kenoyer, son of Peter Kenoyer. Louis Kenoyer also bore the inherited family name baxawát'as (see, e.g., fig. 2).

3. With respect to the apparently conflicting readings of the term gáwakil, it may be relevant that Jacobs's sole informant was Louis Kenoyer, a native and long-time resident of Grand Ronde Reservation. The Tualatin "tribe" ("nation") into which Louis Kenoyer was born consisted of no more than 65 individuals. Characterized by members' close propinquity and perceived (putative or actual) blood kinship, this unit was probably more like an

aboriginal village than an aboriginal tribe.

4.   mámpdu, the Tualatin word for wapato (*Sagittaria latifolia*), is mistranslated as 'camas' in Jacobs (1945:190; paragraph 6, sections (4), (5)), rendering the translated text at that point completely misleading. The informant describes the digging of storage pits (abúllum) to preserve wapato tubers for wintertime use, not (as the translation has it) the making of "a ground oven hole" for steaming camas; and the women 'step in the water' to get wapato, not (as the translation has it) camas.

5.   The late Mrs. Ruth Roe of Gaston, Oregon, citing local pioneer tradition, informed me that Tualatins set out from the lake during the fall to harvest fish from the Trask River system in the Coast Range (Zenk 1976:70).

6.   In the interests of methodological clarity, I have excluded terms that (a) refer explicitly to recently introduced items; or (b) are very vaguely identified. An example of a vaguely identified term is the word atátal, which appears in Gatschet (1877b) opposite the printed prompt lodge. Lacking any indications as to just what, in Tualatin terms, a "lodge" might have been, I chose the safer course and simply ignored the entry.

7.   Ethnographic data obtained by L. J. Frachtenberg and Philip Drucker for the Northern Molalas, a northwestern Oregon indigenous group that had close contacts both with Upper Chinookans and Northern Kalapuyans, suggest that the Northern Molala winter house resembled the Tualatin in certain respects:

> "Northern Molalas built rectangular, semi-excavated winter houses like those described for other interior western Oregon peoples. Plank-like slabs of hemlock and cedar bark, peeled at full thickness during the spring and then weighted down to dry flat, comprised the basic building material. A single log ridgepole, positioned in the nocks presented by two upright forked center posts, supported a gabled framework of poles, to which overlapping bark slabs were lashed vertically as walls and roof. Inside, mats and hides covered walls and floor, and there was a central square pit holding one to several hearths. Smoke-holes with moveable bark covers were located on either side of the roof peak. Dirt was banked around the walls outside. Doors were of mat or bark; according to Frachtenberg, each house had two, leading into the moderately excavated interior via dirt ramps." (Zenk and Rigsby n.d.)

It is notable that the Northern Molala term for the central excavation in which the hearth(s) lay, ťúułnæckæn, corresponds to the Tualatin term -túłnackaan, cited here. The term is transparently a loan from Chinookans, to whom it probably meant 'fire-plank' (Robert E. Moore personal communication, 1993).

8.   Wapato Lake itself constituted a natural flood-control system: it is explicitly noted in Gatschet that water flowed out of both ends of the lake. Beginning in the late-nineteenth century, the lake was extensively ditched and drained for agricultural purposes.

9.   It is possible that Tualatin kinship terminology is relevant to the conflicting relationships indicated for cakílxida and k'ámmac: the Tualatin term meaning one's 'older brother' can also mean any older male in one's paternal line (Yvonne Hajda personal communication, 1993).

    Other information, perhaps from Dave Yatchkawa, has it that k'ámmac's predecessor as chief of ca-púngatpi was a man named tókwai.

10.   According to the official register of St. Michael the Archangel Parish, Grand Ronde, Oregon, Peter Kenoyer ("Peter Conaia") himself died on Sept. 4, 1886, "at the age of about 40 years" (Munnick and Beckham 1987). The U. S. Indian census of 1885, which lists a 59 year-old "Peter Conoyer," suggests that the priest was however not a particularly good estimator of age.

11.   Village populations are not even commented upon in Gatschet. In a section probably to be attributed to Dave Yatchkawa, the following Native point of view on Tualatin historical demography is expressed: "About 100 years [ago]" (i.e., circa 1775) the Tualatins numbered "over 10,000." Reasons for the drastic decline of that population: change of diet; "bad White doctors"; small-pox (introduced through Fort Vancouver and the Hudson Bay Company, which gave infected blankets, etc., to Indians; Tualatin mortality: "10-20 a day"); "ague" ("through Whites also"; "3 times [ague?] sickness in 1823" [mistake for 1832?]). Elsewhere: small-pox, ague, and measles are mentioned as diseases that "killed lots of them."

REFERENCES

Benson, Robert L.
    1976   The Tualatin or Atfalati Indians [part 3]. *Hillsboro Argus* 2 November: 4D. Hillsboro, Oregon.

Berman, Howard
    1990   An Outline of Kalapuya Historical Phonology. *International Journal of American Linguistics* 56(1):27-59.

Boyd, Robert T.
    1975   Another Look at the "Fever and Ague" of Western Oregon. *Ethnohistory* 22(2):135-154.

    1990   Demographic History, 1774-1874. In *Northwest Coast,* edited by Wayne Suttles, pp. 135-148. *Handbook of North American Indians, Vol. 7,* W. C. Sturtevant, general editor. Smithsonian Institution, Washington, D.C.

Connolly, Thomas J.
    1983   Modeling Prehistoric Cultural Systems in the Willamette Valley: a Demonstration of Regional Diversity. In *Contributions to the Archeology of Oregon, 1981-82.,* edited by D. Dumond.   Association of Oregon Archaeologists Occasional Papers 2.

DeAngulo, Jaime, and Lucy S. Freeland
    1929   The Tfalati dialect of Kalapuya. Unpublished grammatical sketch and texts in Melville Jacobs Collection, University of Washington Archives, Seattle.

Frachtenberg, Leo J.
    1915   Linguistic Re-elicitations and Ethnographic Extracts of Gatschet (1877a). Red-ink annotations in original Gatschet manuscript, with notes; Manuscript No. 4620 in National Anthropological Archives, Smithsonian Institution, Washington; and manuscripts in Melville Jacobs Collection, University of Washington, Seattle.

Gatschet, Albert S.
    1877a   Texts, Sentences and Vocables of the Atfalati Dialect of the Kalapuya Language of Willámet [sic] Valley, North-Western Oregon. Manuscript No. 472-a in National Anthropological Archives, Smithsonian Institution, Washington, D.C.

    1877b   Tualatin Kalapuyan Vocabulary. In *Introduction to the Study of Indian Languages,* by J. W. Powell's. Manuscript No. 472-d in National Anthropological Archives, Smithsonian Institution, Washington, D.C.

Hajda, Yvonne P.
    1984   *Regional Social Organization in the Greater Lower Columbia, 1792-1830.* Ph.D. dissertation in Anthropology, University of Washington, Seattle.

Hodge, F. W.
    1907-10 *Handbook of American Indians North of Mexico. 2 vols.* Bureau of American Ethnology Bulletin 30. Washington, D.C.

Jacobs, Melville

    1936a   Linguistic Re-elicitations of DeAngulo and Freeland (1929). (Annotations in carbon copy of original DeAngulo and Freeland manuscript). Melville Jacobs Collection, University of Washington, Seattle.

    1936b   A Tualatin Kalapuya Autobiographic Fragment with Some Other Tualatin texts. Manuscript in Melville Jacobs Collection, University of Washington Archives, Seattle.

    1936c   Kalapuya Element List; Typed Copy of Original Received by A. L. Kroeber in 1936. Manuscript in Melville Jacobs Collection, University of Washington Archives, Seattle.

    1945   *Kalapuya Texts*. University of Washington Publications in Anthropology 11. Seattle.

Laughlin, W. S.

    1943   Notes on the Archeology of the Yamhill River, Willamette Valley, Oregon. *American Antiquity* 9(2):220-229.

Lyman, H. S.

    1900   Indian Names. *The Quarterly of the Oregon Historical Society* 1(3):316-26.

Mackey, Harold

    1974   *The Kalapuyans: A Sourcebook on the Indians of the Willamette Valley.* Salem: Mission Mill Museum.

Munnick, Harriet Duncan, and Stephen Dow Beckham

    1987   *Catholic Church Records of the Pacific Northwest: Grand Ronde Register I (1860-1885); Grand Ronde Register II (1886-1898); St. Michael the Archangel Parish, Grand Ronde Indian Reservation, Grand Ronde, Oregon.* Binford and Mort Publishing, Portland.

Pettigrew, Rick

    1980   *Archeological Investigations at Hager's Grove, Salem, Oregon.* University of Oregon Anthropological Publications 19. Eugene.

Swanton, John R.

    1952   The Indian Tribes of North America. *Bureau of American Ethnology Bulletin* 145. Washington, D.C.

Zenk, Henry

1976   *Contributions to Tualatin Ethnography: Subsistence and Ethnobiology.*
Master's thesis in Anthropology, Portland State University, Oregon.

Zenk, Henry and Bruce Rigsby

n.d.   Molala. In *Handbook of North American Indians, Vol. 12: Plateau.* Deward
Walker, ed.   William C. Sturtevant, gen. ed.   Washington: Smithsonian
Institution.   In Press.

PREHISTORIC OCCUPATION ON THE LUCKIAMUTE RIVER

Paul W. Baxter
Department of Anthropology,
Western Oregon State College

Robin L. Smith
Department of Anthropology,
Western Oregon State College

ABSTRACT

In the summer of 1990 Western Oregon State College conducted limited excavations at two lithic scatters located adjacent to the present Luckiamute River. Analysis showed these sites, selected for excavation based on their apparent differences, were virtually identical. This article summarizes the excavations and analyses of those sites and attempts to place the sites into perspective.

The 1990 Western Oregon State College archaeological field school was conducted in the Luckiamute River basin, a sub-basin of the Willamette River (Figure 1). The field crew consisted of 15 students under the direction of Paul W. Baxter. Robin L. Smith directed the laboratory work. The project was funded jointly by a grant from the State Historic Preservation Office and Western Oregon State College.

This initial field season represents the first stage of what is hoped will be a long-term commitment on the part of anthropologists and scholars in allied fields at Western to study the scope and variability of human occupation in the mid-Willamette Valley. This project addresses the prehistoric period, but in the future we expect to investigate more recent occupations through historic archaeological, ethnohistoric, ethnographic and oral history fieldwork.

THE CONTEXT OF HUMAN OCCUPATION

The 58 mile long Luckiamute River is one of 11 hydrologic sub-basins which make up the Willamette River system (Figure 2). It heads in the Coast Range and drains an area ranging in elevation from 3,246 feet at Monmouth Peak to 160 feet at the confluence of the Luckiamute and Willamette rivers near Albany, Oregon. The 309 square mile sub-basin sees its lowest water in September/October and only two months later in December discharges as much as 32,900 cfs (Moser and Farnell 1981:11).

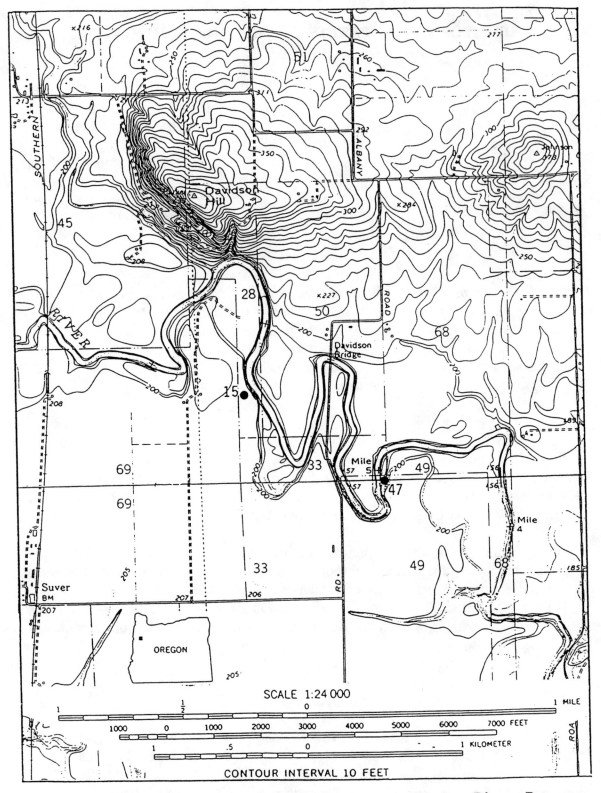

Figure 1. The locations of 35PO15 and 35PO47 on the Luckiamute River. Base map from portions of USGS Monmouth and Lewisburg 7.5 minute quadrangles.

The two sites test excavated during this project are directly adjacent to the Luckiamute River at an elevation of about 200 feet on the edges of modern grass-seed fields. They have been heavily disturbed by agricultural leveling and plowing activities, and by constant artifact collection. The 200 feet elevation was, prior to flood control systems, the natural high water mark of normal winter floods, forming a demarcation line dividing farm land and Riverine forest. Today intensification of farming has resulted in the clearing of low lying lands and thus the disturbance of many archaeological sites, as well as the destruction of much of the remaining natural valley environment.

The climate of the valley is temperate with average temperatures ranging from 63°. in the summer to 40° F. in the winter and mean precipitation coming as some 51.66 inches of rain. Vegetation varies with elevation, with conifer forested uplands giving way to oak woodland, open grass prairies and riparian forests. However, constant prehistoric and historic human activity through field burning, clearing, introduction of non-native plants, domestic animals, logging and other actions, have made the entire Willamette Valley "seminatural in character (Franklin and Dyrness 1973: 110)". Hills are often dominated by oak (*Quercus garryana*) on the drier southern slopes and Douglas fir (*Pseudotsuga menziesii*) on their wetter northern flanks (Albright 1991:9). Oak, Conifer and Big Leaf Maple (*Acer macrophyllum*) have been thought by some to be the natural climax vegetation (Johannessen et al. 1971; Sprague and Hansen 1946), but grasslands were common due to annual burning and Franklin and Dyrness (1973: 122) feel that soil and moisture conditions in some areas of the Willamette Valley would have made grasses the climax vegetation. Whatever the case, today agricultural fields and introduced grasses have replaced the widespread prairies and virtually all the native grasses.

Wildlife and fish of the valley included a variety of fur-bearers such as beaver (*Castor canadensis*), raccoon *(Procyon lotor), muskrat (Ondatra zibethica)*, marten (*Martex americana*), mink (*Mustela vison*) and otter *(Lutra canadensis)* which first attracted the interest of whites. Large game included Black-tailed deer *(Odocoileus hemionus columbianus)* and the now near extinct Columbia white-tailed deer *(Odocoileus virginianus leucurus)*. Anadromous fish which appeared above Willamette Falls on a yearly basis included only lamprey (*Lampetra planeri* and *L. tridentata*). No historic or archaeological evidence clearly attests to the presence of salmon or prehistoric salmon fishing above the falls, however, in flood years salmon may have ascended the falls and been taken. Salmon and steelhead were available in the nearby Coast Range and may have been part of the seasonal round. However, trout (*Salmo spp.; Salvelinus spp.*), suckers (*Catostomus macrocheilus and Pantosteus platyrhynchus*), bullhead catfish (*Ictalurus spp.*) and others were certainly locally present (Minor 1981).

The eleven sub-basins of the Willamette Valley were home to 13 independent bands all speaking languages belonging to the Kalapuya language family. The Luckiamute Valley was home to the Luckiamute band. Kalapuyan ethnographic data is

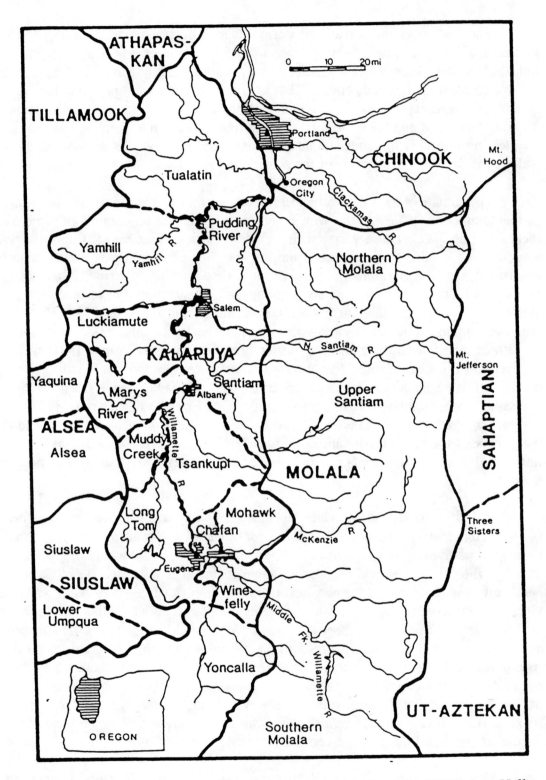

Figure 2. Distribution of the Kalapuya Bands in the sub-basins of the Willamette Valley.
Note the Luckiamute band (From Beckham 1976:7).

limited (see Zenk this volume for an appraisal), and due to historical accident, biased in favor of the Tualitin-Yamhill. This presents a problematical ethnographic model since they were the closest band to the apparently culturally more dynamic Chinook and may have exhibited traits, such as infant head flattening (Zenk 1990:548), or huge, 6 m X 12 m, rectangular, multifamily, semi-subterranean or earth banked structures, which may not have been found as frequently, or perhaps at all, among the other Kalapuya bands. (Certainly, only one pit house--a round one--has been reported archaeologically from the Valley (White 1975)).

Even so, the data suggest that the Kalapuya were exogamous, marrying into surrounding bands and tribes, and patrilocal. Zenk (1976:17-18) has suggested that the sub-basin, occupied by several related, low population winter villages, each speaking a dialect of the local language, and each exploiting a relatively large area consisting of riverine, lowland, and upland habitats may have formed a loose political unit. Zenk believes the need for a variety of limited, scattered resources may have kept the populations low and dispersed, and would have provided the otherwise politically autonomous villages within a sub-basin a reason to come together, however loosely. Thus each village represented a band and the combined villages of a sub-basin a tribe. So the Luckiamute band of the Kalapuya would more properly be called the Luckiamute tribe. While the Tualatin may have had a more complex political structure, the rest of the Kalapuya "bands" were apparently politically organized at the tribal level (Zenk 1990; 1994 personal communication). Of course by historic times, as the 44 members of the Luckiamute band present at the Champoeg treaty negotiations show, they had been reduced by contact conditions to the size of a single band.

Each village had a headman, usually the head of an extended family, and often the wealthiest man in the village, but while kinship was a factor in status, leadership was more likely to be derived from personal competence than kinship or the control of fleeting wealth. The major social distinction was between freeman and slave, although in later times, perhaps due to contact, "chiefly persons" may also have been distinguished (Zenk 1990:550, and this volume).

The Kalapuya followed a settlement-subsistence pattern which saw them in temporary open camps from about March to at least October. Since the settlement pattern was subsistence based, the open sites were often summer basecamps out from which task specific groups ranged for short periods of time to exploit various resources. The quickly constructed brush summer structures contrasted sharply with the ethnographically reported huge semi-subterranean winter structures. In March /April they began the camas harvest which continued though the summer and into fall. Large cakes were formed from pounded bulbs for winter subsistence and as trade items. Hazel nuts and berries were collected, as were acorns, wapato, lupine, cattail, skunk cabbage, bracken fern and other plants. In the fall the prairies were burned to prepare the tarweed for harvest. Hunting was undertaken throughout the year, both locally and in the Coast Range and Cascades with deer and black bear the major targets. There were some groves which were never

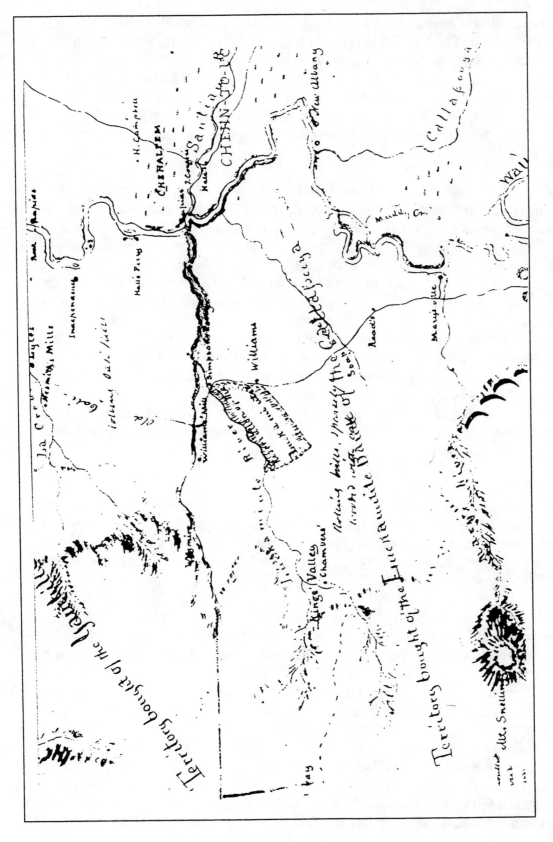

Figure 3. Portion of 1851 Gibbs-Starling treaty map showing location of Luckiamute Band territory. (Note locations of Luckiamute and Mary's Rivers.)

burned, apparently to concentrate game for easy hunting (Zenk 1976:22-25; Towle 1979). Migrating water fowl and the lamprey run were exploited as were the large populations of grasshoppers and tent caterpillars.

Interestingly, at the 1851 Champoeg treaty negotiations the Luckiamute band, consisting of 12 women 16 men and 16 children, described the boundary (Figure 3) of their land as including the basin from the confluence of the Willamette and Luckiamute rivers, to the crest of the Coast Range and from the north fork of the Luckiamute to the north bank of Mary's River (Mackey 1974:85-146). This in essence shifts the center of their territory one/half sub-basin to the south from what has been generally agreed on as the Luckiamute territory (Zenk 1990; Beckham 1976:7). The presence at the negotiations of the Yamhill band which claimed Rickreall Creek, generally included in the Luckiamute basin, and the absence of the Mary's River band may have "facilitated" a late period territorial shift, but interestingly, the map of Kalapuyan bands in "Kalapuya Texts" (Jacobs et al. 1945:154), places only the Luckiamute band north of Mary's River. It remains to archaeology to answer this intriguing question.

Archaeological work in the Luckiamute sub-basin has been minimal. In 1964 a date of 5250±270 radiocarbon years bp was obtained by two soils geologists on charcoal collected from what became known as the Luckiamute hearth (Reckendorf and Parsons 1966). This hearth, now apparently completely gone, was eroding out of the bank of the Luckiamute River, in the vicinity of Highway 99. No other archaeological data was obtained from the site. In 1972 a site was reportedly tested by Oregon College of Education, but no report or collection from that project has been found. James Bell (1981), in the process of producing a Masters Thesis on settlement patterning in the Luckiamute basin, recorded five sites and verbally reported the test excavation of a sixth site within the sub-basin. The site's owners had collected a number of musket balls, coins, beads and various stone tools. Although interpreted as a village site, no structures were located. In the 1980s Leland Gilsen began an on-going survey of the sub-basin and had located 45 sites. Four of these were tested, but remain unreported.

THE 1990 EXCAVATIONS

Site 35PO15 and 35PO47 lie on the alluvial terrace of the Luckiamute river, with 35PO47 about one mile east and downstream of 35PO15. They were test excavated using 1 m by 1 m test units and 10 cm arbitrary excavation levels. In addition, three pits were excavated in 35PO14, but that work will not be discussed here (see Smith and Baxter 1994). All fill was screened through 1/8" mesh. At each site a transect of excavation units, spaced at approximately 10 m intervals, was placed along the edge of the field adjacent to the river. At 35PO15 an additional pit was excavated to fully expose a hearth bringing the total volume excavated to 6.7 m³. At 35PO47, 7.0 m³ were excavated (Figure 4a and b). At both sites the maximum depth of materials was 1.0 m in one or two units, but the average depth of materials was between 40 and 50 cm. However, the

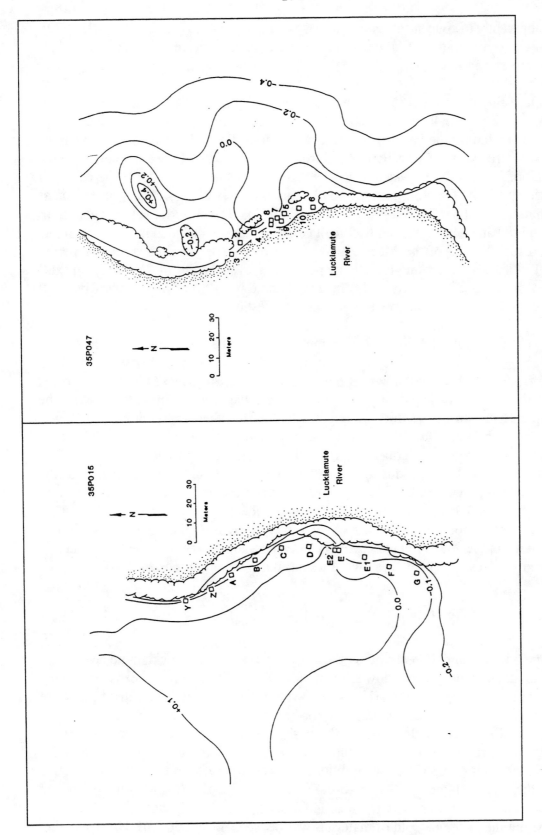

Figure 4. Topography and location of excavation units at 35PO15 and 35PO47.

geomorphological analysis of the site suggests that buried materials are the result of disturbance, not of occupational and natural deposition over time. So the occupational deposition at the sites is essentially surficial.

Unfortunately, the sites lie on the edges of producing grass seed fields which have recently been extended into the riverine forest border. The tree clearing, plowing and leveling process had severely disturbed the sites, and while the densest cultural debris at the sites as determined during survey was reported to be in the fields, we were restricted to excavating along the edge of the field. Also, during the excavation period the fields were in cultivation and we could not conduct a surface survey and collection to revise or refine surficial site boundaries.

The Luckiamute sites are located on the Champoeg geomorphic surface, which may be older than 34,000 years bp. Excavation and soils analysis (Friedel 1990) resulted in the description of two major stratigraphic units. Unit I (0-80 cm at 35PO15 and 0-75 cm at 35PO47) consists of an undisturbed clay loam in which iron and manganese nodules have formed over millennia of repeated wet/dry cycles. A plow zone exists to a depth of 26 cm in the 35PO15 profile. At both sites clay has been leached downward to form an argillic horizon, a process estimated to take a minimum of 5000 years in the Willamette Valley (Balster and Parsons 1968). Unit II is below about 80 cm and consists of a possible buried soil (Figures 5a and 5b).

A single cultural feature, a hearth, was located in Units E and E2 at 35PO15 (Figure 5a). The hearth was extremely visible, the yellow-tan clay having been heavily oxidized to a bright red-orange. Measuring 84 by 126 cm, it continued from about 30 cm to 108 cm below the surface. Given the nature of the geomorphic surface, it seems likely the upper 30 cm were destroyed by plowing. The hearth contained no stones. Two radiocarbon dates returned on charcoal from the hearth dated to 4800±80 (Beta 43248) and 4810±90 (Beta 43249). Samples subjected to flotation screening and floral analysis (Stenholm 1990) produced charcoal from Douglas fir *(Pseudotsuga menziesii)* branches, cones and bark, as well as traces of unidentifiable "edible plant tissue."

Obsidian flakes from both sites were relatively small, and so while ten were submitted from each site, only eight from 35PO15 and six from 35PO47 were large enough for Atomic absorption characterization at the Oregon State University facility (Skinner and McBirney 1990). All but three sourced to Inman Creek subgroup A. Those three, all from 35PO15, sourced to Inman Creek subgroup B. That is, all were of local origin.

CULTURAL MATERIAL

Eight ground stone tool fragments, two cobble tools, 53 chipped stone tools and 2151 pieces of debitage were recovered from 35PO15, while the 35PO47 collection

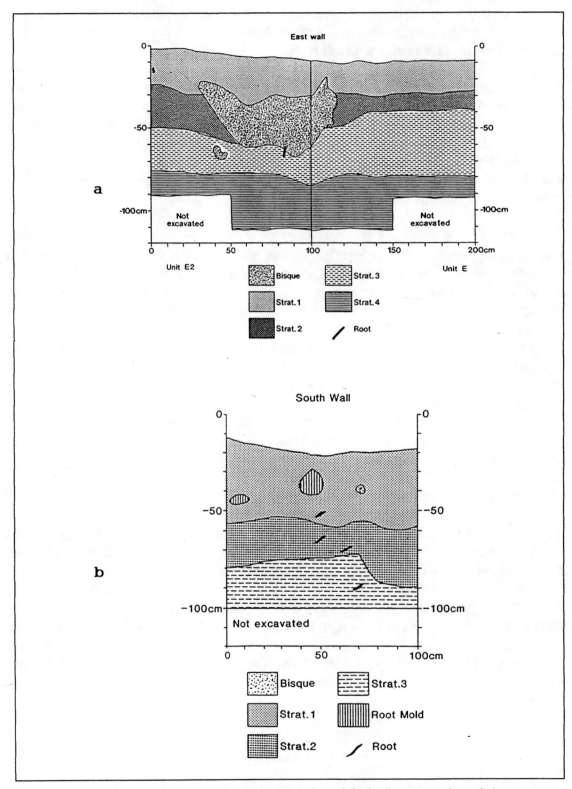

Figure 6.   a. Profile of east walls, Units E, E2 at 35PO15.   (Note hearth.)
             b. Profile of south wall, Unit 5 at 35PO47.

Table 1. Summary of artifacts from 35PO15 and 35PO47.

Artifact Class	35PO15	35PO47	Total
Chipped Stone:			
Projectile Points	1	-	1
Biface Fragments	5	2	7
Unifaces	3	3	6
Drill/Perforators	7	5	12
Utilized Flakes	31	26	57
Cores	6	3	9
Debitage	2151	1796	3947
Ground Stone:			
Mortar Rims	2	-	2
Pestle Fragments	1	1	2
Mano Fragments	1	1	2
Abraders	3	1	4
Unident. Fragments	1	-	1
Cobble Tools:			
Hammerstones	1	-	1
Anvils	1	-	1
Chopper	-	1	1

includes three ground stone fragments, one cobble tool, 39 chipped stone tools and a total of 1796 pieces of debitage (Table 1).

Chipped Stone Tools.

1. Projectile Points. Generally bifacially flaked, symmetrical artifacts with low edge angles on the blades, and sharp tips. 35PO15: A single complete round based, serrated edged, foliate, chert projectile point was recovered. The point measures 7.85 cm long, 2.65 cm wide, 1.15 cm thick and weighs 15.7 gms. This point was located at 67 cm below the surface, next to the hearth. The geomorphology of the site suggests that a buried surface within stratigraphic Unit I is unlikely, so the presence at that depth of this point and other artifacts is likely to be due to a disturbance mechanism, perhaps bioturbation. 35PO47: No whole projectile points were recovered from this site, but a number of points and other chipped stone artifacts were removed by a local collector (Gilsen 1989:145-153).

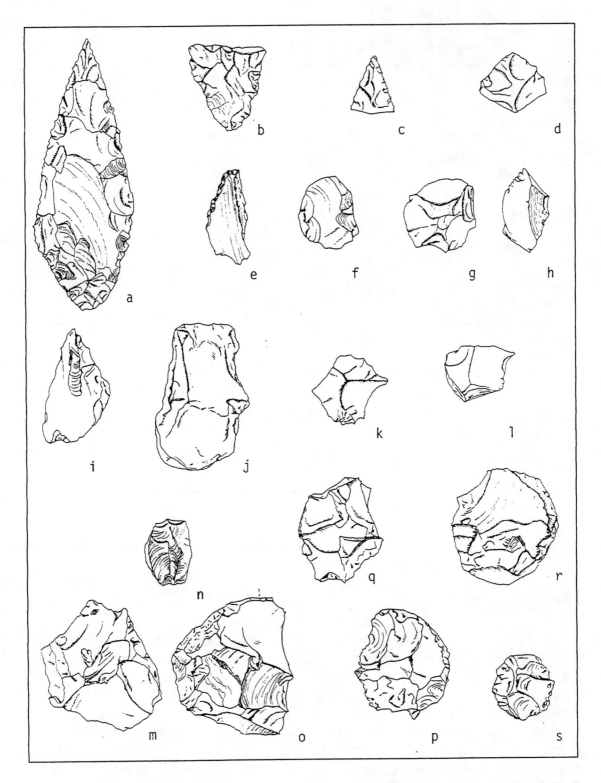

Figure 8. Chipped stone artifacts from 35PO15 and 35PO47. a, Projectile Point; b-d,
Biface fragments; e-h, scrapers; i-l, drill\perforators; m-s, cores and core
fragments (35PO15: a-c, f, g, i, j, m-p; 35PO47: d, e, h, k, l, q-s)

2. Biface Fragments. These are bifacially flaked specimens too fragmentary to categorize further. 35PO15: Four chert and one obsidian biface fragments were collected. All of these are of a size to suggest they are from projectile points. 35PO47: An obsidian and a chert biface fragment were collected. One is a tip, perhaps that of a large projectile point or knife, and one is a blank fragment.

3. Scrapers. Unifacially flaked tools with one or more generally high edge angle working edges. 35PO15: Three flakes shaped with unifacial edges and generally referred to as scrapers, one of chert and two of obsidian, were collected from the site. 35PO47: One obsidian and two chert scrapers were recovered from the site. One is denticulated.

4. Utilized Flakes. Flakes showing no modification other than that obtained through expedient use as cutting, drilling or scraping implements. 35PO15: Thirty-one flakes unaltered except by use were collected; twenty-one of chert, eight of obsidian and two of basalt. 35PO47: Twenty-six used flakes (eight obsidian, 15 chert and three basalt) were noted in the collection.

5. Drill/Perforators. Minimally, these consist of an unshaped flake with an elongated pointed bit, shaped for drilling or perforating. These can be entirely shaped. 35PO15: Seven flakes minimally shaped with drilling or perforating bits were recovered. Six are chert and one is obsidian. 35PO47: Five minimally altered chert flakes exhibited bits with use wear suggesting use as drills or perforators.

6. Cores. These consist of irregular chunks of stone, sometimes flakes, sometimes nodules with at least two flake scars. 35PO15: Six nodules with multiple flake removal scars were identified as cores or core fragments; one of obsidian, three of chert and two of basalt were collected. 35PO47: Three cores, one obsidian and two chert, were identified.

7. Debitage. Debitage consists of the waste materials from flint knapping. Analysis included material type, presence/absence of cortex, flake type (Sullivan and Rozen 1985) and flake size. 35PO15: The 2151 pieces of debitage collected included 292 (13.5%) pieces of obsidian, 1761 (82%) pieces of chert and 98 (4.5%) fragments of basalt (Table 2). 35PO47: The 1796 flakes and debris recovered included 259 (14%) pieces of obsidian, 1416 (79%) pieces of chert and 121 (7%) pieces of basalt (Table 3).

Ground Stone Tools.

1. Mortar Rims. Mortars were made from basalt cobbles and boulders by hollowing and then shaping the sides and rims. 35PO15: Two small fragments of basalt were recovered which were curved and had V-shaped edges. These were identified as fragments of mortar rims. 35PO47: None found.

Table 2. Debitage by Material, Type and Size at 35PO15.

Material/ Flake Type	Size (cm)[1]							TOTAL TYPE	%
	.5	1	2	3	4	5	>5		
Obsidian									
Complete	5	22	7	1	-	-	-	35	12
Broken	14	58	31	-	-	-	-	103	35
Fragment	16	75	36	3	1	-	-	131	45
Debris	2	15	4	2	-	-	-	23	8
Subtotal	37	185	78	6	1	-	-	292	
%	13	58	27	2	<1				
Chert									
Complete	6	26	37	13	2	1	-	85	5
Broken	19	101	74	18	1	-	-	213	12
Fragment	123	487	313	40	5	-	-	968	55
Debris	54	173	199	53	15	-	1	495	28
Subtotal	202	787	623	124	23	1	1	1761	
%	12	45	35	7	1	<1	<1		
Basalt									
Complete	-	1	2	7	3	-	-	13	13
Broken	-	1	6	5	1	-	-	13	13
Fragment	-	5	23	14	3	1	-	46	47
Debris	-	4	10	10	-	-	2	26	27
Subtotal	-	11	41	36	7	1	2	98	
%	-	11	42	37	7	1	2		
TOTAL SIZE	239	968	742	166	31	2	3	2151	
%	11	45	35	8	1	1	<1		

1 = length of longest axis

2. *Manos.* These are flat cobbles, generally 10-20 cm in length and five cm thick which were used as the moving hand stone in conjunction with a grinding slab. They exhibit one or more flat, ground or polished surfaces. 35PO15: A single fragment of a basalt cobble with a ground surface which may have been used as a hand stone for grinding was identified. 35PO47: A single mano fragment was collected from this site.

3. *Pestles.* Pestles can be made of wood or stone and are used as the grinding implement in a mortar. 35PO15: A single stone pestle handle fragment was collected. 35PO47: A cylindrical pestle handle was recovered from the surface of this site.

4. *Abraders.* Sandstone cobbles or fragments were often used as sandpaper, for the shaping of bone or wood. 35PO15: Three sandstone abrader fragments were collected from the site. 35PO47: One sandstone abrader was found.

SUMMARY AND DISCUSSION

Samples from the river-side margins of two small prehistoric sites on the lower Luckiamute River were collected and analyzed. The sites lie on the Champoeg geomorphic surface, estimated to date to at least 34,000 years ago, and the development of an argillic soil horizon attests to the millennia old integrity of the soil unit. That is, the sites were occupied essentially on the present surface and buried cultural materials are most likely the result of disturbance.

Site 35PO15 was radiocarbon dated to about 4800 bp on Douglas fir hearth charcoal. This places the site in the Middle Archaic Lingo Phase even though that phase is defined, in part, by the overwhelming presence of broad necked projectile points. However,

> Leaf-shaped projectile points are sometimes present in low frequencies in sites dating from this time. Mortars and pestles also constitute an important part of the artifact assemblages, reflecting the increased importance of vegetal resources in the subsistence practices... (Minor and Toepel 1981:167).

Thus the date, the willow leaf point and the presence of mortars and pestles correlate well with our present understanding of Willamette Valley cultural chronology.

Our test excavations at 35PO47 did not produce datable charcoal or temporally significant artifacts. However, the private collection of 44 chipped stone artifacts from the site contained a large number of narrow neck points and a few broad neck dart points, prompting Gilsen (1989:153) to suggest a Late Archaic Period, Fuller Phase date between AD 200 and AD 1750 (Minor and Toepel 1981:161-176). It is hoped that in the future

Table 3. Debitage by Material, Type, and Size at 35PO47.

Material/ Flake Type	.5	1	Size (cm)[1] 2	3	4[2]	TOTAL TYPE	%
Obsidian							
Complete	1	9	6	1	-	17	7
Broken	4	39	27	-	-	70	27
Fragment	18	104	37	-	-	159	61
Debris	2	7	4	-	-	13	5
Subtotal	25	159	74	1	-	259	
%	10	61	29	<1			
Chert							
Complete	-	30	41	8	1	80	6
Broken	7	71	93	12	-	183	13
Fragment	71	420	285	18	3	797	56
Debris	42	148	141	23	2	356	25
Subtotal	120	669	560	61	6	1416	
%	8	47	40	4	<1		
Basalt							
Complete	-	-	1	5	2	8	7
Broken	-	1	14	6	-	21	17
Fragment	2	13	42	6	2	65	54
Debris	-	6	16	5	-	27	22
Subtotal	2	20	73	22	4	121	
%	2	17	60	18	3		
TOTAL SIZE	147	848	707	84	10	1796	
%	8	47	39	5	1		

1 = length of longest axis; 2 = no flakes larger than 4 cm

Table 4. Comparison of site assemblages by percent of assemblage[1].

Site Number	Bi-face	Uni-face	Drill/ Perf.	Utilized Flake	Core	Mortar Rim	Pestle Frag.	Mano Frag.	Abrader	Unident. Frag.	Hammer Stone	Anvil	Chopper
35PO15	9.5	5	11	49	9.5	3	1.5	1.5	5	1.5	1.5	1.5	-
35PO47	5	7	12	60	7	-	2	2	2	-	-	-	2

1 = Debitage not included.

with more funding, some of the obsidian flakes may be subjected to obsidian hydration analysis. Such work might be used to test the hypothesis that 35PO15 predates 35PO47, and begin the process of developing a mid-Willamette Valley hydration data base.

The analysis of materials from these two sites proved surprising. The sites were chosen for test excavation because the survey data suggested they had served different functions. Site 35PO15 was identified as a lithic scatter and 35PO47 as a "possible village". However, analysis showed that artifact densities were very similar. At 35PO15, 371 flakes and 0.8 kg of artifacts per cubic meter were excavated, while at 35PO47, 278 flakes and 0.3 kg of artifacts per cubic meter were excavated. The disparity may simply be due to the location of a feature at 35PO15, and the placement of the test pits at 35PO47 some five meters closer to the river.

The surficial nature of the deposits made these sites particularly susceptible to constant farming disturbance and private collecting activities. However, these facts not withstanding, and taking into account the small size of the sample, the variety of tools and their frequencies showed that a remarkably similar range of stone tool using activities were undertaken at these two sites (Table 4).

Another measure of the similarity of these sites can be seen in the debitage collections. By every measure--material type, various flake size and types, and the presence of cortex, as well as the probable flake production methods--the collections are virtually identical (Table 5).

Patterson (1990) used experimental data to distinguish between core reduction debitage and biface reduction debitage. Using a logarithmic scale, he showed that core reduction debitage created a non-linear graph, while biface reduction created a linear graph. The debitage of both sites was subjected to this analysis by material type. The

Table 5. Comparison of 35PO15 and 35PO47 debitage collections by percent.

Site Number	MATERIAL			CORTEX[1]		FLAKE TYPE[2]				FLAKE SIZE[3]							DEBITAGE COUNT
	Obs.	Chert	Bas.	P	A	C	B	F	D	0.5	1	2	3	4	5	>5	
35PO15	14	82	5	8	92	6	15	53	25	11	45	35	8	1	1	<1	2151
35PO47	14	79	7	9	91	6	15	57	22	8	47	39	5	1	-	-	1796

1 = Cortex Present or Absent; 2 = Complete, Broken, Fragment, Debris; 3 = length of longest axis in centimeters

results were identical. The obsidian and chert debitage form generally linear patterns, although the presence of minor curving suggests some core reduction. The basalt graph was very non-linear. We have interpreted this to mean that most of the debitage was due to a great deal of tool manufacture and maintenance at the site.

Limited obsidian sourcing showed the obsidian to be the Inman Creek variety, which is locally available in the Willamette River, and perhaps as flood deposits in the Luckiamute River. The small size of obsidian cores and debitage (less than 1% of the obsidian debitage is more than 3 cm long) and the fact that 21% of the obsidian debitage exhibits cortex strongly suggests that small obsidian pebbles, 5-6 cm in diameter, were being found nearby, not traded in from more extensive deposits upstream to the south.

Only 5% of the chert debitage exhibits cortex and only 9% of the flakes are larger than 3 cm long. This suggests that primary reduction and perhaps initial heat treatment of chert cores was taking place elsewhere, but that nodules were being brought to the site rather than large flake cores.

The low number of basalt flakes suggests a very limited use of this material at the sites. It is likely that rather than being due to basalt core reduction some, perhaps many, of these flakes were simply spalls created from "camp rock" by accident or while using cobble tools such as hammerstones and pestles.

The analysis of excavated artifact collections have strongly suggested a similar function for these sites. Archaeologists have long linked the presence of ground stone to village or base camp site functions, where a variety of subsistence activities were undertaken. But, while location of our test pits may have missed the main areas of the sites, the density and variety of artifacts seems too thin and limited to be seen as winter village or even summer base camp debris. The density of artifacts (371 flakes/m^3 and 278 flakes/m^3) is relatively moderate when compared with other Willamette Valley sites. Two sites categorized as summer base camps in the Long Tom Basin produced 1833 and 5050 flakes/m^3 (Cheatham 1988). Two sites at Hager's Grove, near Salem, Oregon, categorized as seasonal campsites produced 111 and 201 flakes/m^3 (Pettigrew 1980), while three sites, in the Luckiamute Basin, interpreted as a village, camp and lithic scatter respectively, produced 66 flakes/m^3, 151 flakes/m^3, and 220 flakes/m^3 (Gilsen 1989).

It should be noted that outside of overwhelming numbers and varieties of artifacts, the defining characteristic for a Willamette Valley village or base camp remains the presence of structures. However, such a defining criterion of village or summer base camp presents a particularly troubling problem. It seems unlikely that we will find patterns of post holes or even shallow housepits in ground that is regularly plowed and intermittently subjected to a process called "deep soiling" which turns the sediments over to a depth of four feet. In fact, winter villages were located above flood waters, in the areas that have been farmed the longest. Thus, it seems likely that artifact collections, from heavily disturbed, frequently collected sites, may well be our most common, if not our only data. And site functions are going to be interpreted in terms of regional comparisons, not single (or double) site excavations.

In an attempt to associate sites with site functions, Gilsen (1989:165-171), like others (Minor 1983; Baxter 1986; Connolly 1986), listed 16 implied activities based on the presence of various artifact types (for instance: projectile points = hunting; ground stone = plant food processing). He used a presence-absence chart to cluster sites located during survey and identified five clusters. These include the unique Luckiamute hearth site, lithic manufacturing sites, base camps, hunting camps and small villages.

The technique is sound, although problems arise in systematic artifact classification, as well as linking those artifacts to specific behavior. It seems the development of bridging arguments linking artifacts to tool kits and tool kits with specific behavior is needed before we can be entirely comfortable in assigning functions to sites based simply on the subjective notion of a wide versus a narrow variety of artifacts.

Also, it is clear that these four site types make too meager a list and do not reflect the rich, millennia old, well adapted lifeway suggested by even the limited ethnographic data, or for that matter the present body of archaeological data. Clearly a wide variety of task specific campsites existed, as well as various permutations of the winter villages, summer base camps and so on. For example, Cheatham (1988) suggests the presence of winter villages, upland winter task sites, smaller lowland summer base camps, and lowland summer task sites.

Having thus argued that we are presently unable to comfortably assign site type designations and having noted the limited nature of the testing at these sites, some things can be said about 35PO15 and 35PO47.

The collections are essentially identical suggesting a similar function for both sites, and if the tentative Middle and Late Archaic period dates are correct, that function was part of a settlement-subsistence adaptation which was valuable for a considerable length of time. However, while the site collections show a limited variety of chipped stone, ground stone and cobble tools, no trade materials, such as imported obsidian or marine shells were recovered. This suggests a limited occupation, limited task site.

In addition, both sites are located in the flood plain on the banks of the Luckiamute River, so it seems likely they were occupied during the spring and summer, and not during the winter flood season. However, only one hearth, with no clear evidence of edible plant remains was found. Indeed charcoal was not prominent at either site and a combined total of under three kilograms of fire cracked rock was collected at the sites. It seems likely that camas roasting, which produces a large amount of both charcoal and fire cracked rock was not a major pursuit at these sites.

Thus altogether the evidence points to the short duration, intermittent use of these sites for centuries or millennia. The use was probably not during the winter, and was associated with some plant food processing, but perhaps not camas to any degree. Points, bifaces, and other chipped stone tools, as well as the chopper may point to hunting, hunting preparations or perhaps some butchering. The debitage, hammerstone and anvil suggest chipped stone tool making or maintenance.

This article has reported the limited test excavations of two sites in the Luckiamute sub-basin of the Willamette Valley. This is the opening work of a long term commitment by Western Oregon State College to the understanding of human occupation in the Luckiamute which will eventually include historic archaeology, as well as oral history. The findings reported here have detailed the presence of an apparently common site type, a short duration, seasonal camp at which a specific task (or tasks) was undertaken. The exact nature of that task is as yet undetermined. Future work will help elucidate the nature of these sites and the rest of the prehistoric Luckiamute Valley settlement-subsistence pattern.

ACKNOWLEDGEMENTS

This work was accomplished with a matching grant from the Historic Preservation Fund administered by the State Historic Preservation Office and the financial assistance of Western Oregon State College. Laboratory cleanup, cataloging and curational tasks were accomplished by Michelle Kuntzelman and Alisa Parks.

REFERENCES

Albright, Donald A.
  1991 *Changing Forest Distribution in the Luckiamute Valley: 1852-1986.* Senior honors thesis, Western Oregon State College, Monmouth.

Baldwin, E.M.
  1981 *Geology of Oregon.* Kendall/Hunt Publishing Company, Dubuque, Iowa.

Balster, C.A. and Parsons, R.B.
  1968 *Geomorphology and Soils, Willamette Valley, Oregon.* Oregon State University Agriculture Experiment Station, Special Report 265. Corvallis.

Baxter, Paul W.
  1986 *Archaic Upland Adaptations in the Central Oregon Cascades.* Ph.D. dissertation, Department of Anthropology, University of Oregon. Eugene.

Beckham, Stephen Dow
  1976 Map of Indian territories in Oregon. In *Atlas of Oregon*. University of Oregon Books, Eugene.

Beckham, Stephen Dow, Rick Minor and Kathryn Anne Toepel
  1981 *Prehistory and History of BLM Lands in West-Central Oregon*, edited by C. M. Aikens. University of Oregon Anthropological Papers 25. Eugene.

Bell, James
  1981 Regional Archaeological Model of the Luckiamute Band Settlement Patterns. Master's thesis, Oregon State University, Corvallis.

Connolly, Thomas J.
  1986 Cultural stability and change in the prehistory of Southwest Oregon and Northern California. Ph.D. dissertation, University of Oregon, Eugene.

Franklin, Jerry F. and C. T. Dyrness
  1973 *Natural Vegetation of Oregon and Washington*. Pacific Northwest Forest and Range Experiment Station General Technical Report PNW-8.

Freidel, Dorothy E.
  1990 Report on the Geomorphology and Soils of 35PO15 and 35PO47. Department of Geography, University of Oregon. On file at the Department of Anthropology, Western Oregon State College, Monmouth.

Gilsen, Leland
  1989 Luckiamute Basin Survey: Phase 1 survey. Draft report on file State Historic Preservation Office, Salem, Oregon.

Jacobs, Melville, Leo J. Frachtenberg, and Albert S. Gatschet
  1945 *Kalapuya Texts*. University of Washington Publications in Anthropology 11.

Johannessen, Carl L., W. A. Davenport, Artimus Millet and S. McWilliams
  1971 The Vegetation of the Willamette Valley. *Annals of the Association of American Geographers* 61:261-302.

Mackey, Harold
  1974 *The Kalapuyans: A Sourcebook on the Indians of the Willamette Valley*. Mission Mill Museum Association, Salem, Oregon.

Minor, Rick
  1983 *Aboriginal Settlement and Subsistence at the Mouth of the Columbia River*. Ph.D. dissertation, Department of Anthropology, University of Oregon, Eugene.

1981 Environmental Overview. In *Prehistory and History of BLM Lands in West-Central Oregon*, edited by C. M. Aikens, pp. 13-40. University of Oregon Anthropological Papers 25.

Minor, Rick and Kathryn Anne Toepel
1981 Archaeological Overview. In *Prehistory and History of BLM Lands in West-Central Oregon*, edited by C. M. Aikens, pp. 117-186. University of Oregon Anthropological Papers 25.

Minor, Rick, S. D. Beckham, P. E. Lancefield-Steeve and K. A. Toepel
1980 *Cultural Resource Overview of the BLM Salem District, Northwestern Oregon*, edited by C. M. Aikens. University of Oregon Anthropological Papers 20.

Moser, Stephen A. and James E. Farnell
1981 *Luckiamute River Navigability Study*. Report to the Oregon Division of State Lands, Salem.

Musil, Robert R. and Thomas J. Connolly
1991 Debitage Analysis. In *Archaeological Investigations Along the Paulina-East Lake Highway within Newberry Crater, Central Oregon*. Oregon State Museum of Anthropology Report 91-6, University of Oregon, Eugene.

Patterson, Leland W.
1990 Characteristics of Bifacial Reduction Flake-Size Distribution. *American Antiquity* 55(3): 550-558.

Reckendorf, Frank F. and Roger B. Parsons
1966 Soil Development Over a Hearth in Willamette Valley, Oregon. *Northwest Science* 40:46-55.

Skinner, Craig and Christine McBirney
1990 Letter Report from Oregon State University Reactor Facility on the atomic absorption trace element characterization of obsidian flakes from 35PO15 and 35PO47. On file at Department of Anthropology, Western Oregon State College.

Smith, Robin L. and Paul W. Baxter
1994 *Archaeology on the Luckiamute: Report of excavations at 35PO14, 35PO15 and 35PO47, Polk County, Oregon*. Department of Anthropology, Western Oregon State College. Submitted to State Historic Preservation Office, Salem, Oregon.

Sprague, F. LeRoy and Henry P. Hansen
1946 Forest Succession in the McDonald Forest, Willamette Valley, Oregon. *Northwest Science* 20:89-98.

Stenholm, Nancy
  1990 Letter Report from Botana Labs of Seattle, on analysis of flotation samples from 35PO15 hearth. On file at Department of Anthropology, Western Oregon State College.

Sullivan, Alan P. III, and Kenneth C. Rozen
  1985 Debitage Analysis and Archaeological Interpretation. *American Antiquity* 50(4):755-779.

Toepel, Kathryn Anne and Stephen Dow Beckham
  1981 Ethnographic Overview. In *Prehistory and History of BLM Lands in West-Central Oregon*, edited by C. M. Aikens, pp. 41-116. University of Oregon Anthropological Papers 25. Eugene.

Towle, Jerry
  1979 Settlement and Subsistence in the Willamette Valley: Some Additional Considerations. *Northwest Anthropological Research Notes* 13:12-21.

White, John R.
  1975 Proposed Typology of Willamette Valley Sites. In *Archaeological Studies in the Willamette Valley, Oregon*, edited by C. M. Aikens, pp.17-140. University of Oregon Anthropological Papers 8. Eugene.

Zenk, Henry B.
  1976 Contributions to Tualatin Ethnography: Subsistence and Ethnobiology. M. A. Thesis, Department of Anthropology, Portland State University.

  1990 Kalapuyans. In *Northwest*, edited by Wayne Suttles, pp. 547-553. Handbook of North American Indians, Volume 7. General editor William C. Sturtevant, Smithsonian Institution, Washington, D.C.